Enterprising Women

Enterprising Women

Expanding Economic Opportunities in Africa

Mary Hallward-Driemeier

A copublication of the Agence Française de Développement and the World Bank

ISBN (paper): 978-0-8213-9703-9
ISBN (electronic): 978-0-8213-9809-8
DOI: 10.1596/978-0-8213-9703-9

Cover photo: Maasai women make, sell, and display their bead work in Kajiado, Kenya. 2010. © Georgina Goodwin/World Bank. *Cover design*: Debra Naylor, Naylor Design Inc.

Library of Congress Cataloging-in-Publication Data
Hallward-Driemeier, Mary, 1966–
   Enterprising women : expanding economic opportunities in Africa / Mary Hallward-Driemeier.
      p. cm.
   Includes bibliographical references and index.
   ISBN 978-0-8213-9703-9 — ISBN 978-0-8213-9809-8 (electronic)
1. Women—Africa, Sub-Saharan—Economic conditions. 2. Women—Africa, Sub-Saharan—Social conditions. 3. Businesswomen—Africa, Sub-Saharan. 4. Women—Employment—Africa, Sub-Saharan.
I. Title.
   HQ1788.H35 2013
   331.4096—dc23
                                                                                    2012049861

Africa Development Forum Series

The **Africa Development Forum series** was created in 2009 to focus on issues of significant relevance to Sub-Saharan Africa's social and economic development. Its aim is both to record the state of the art on a specific topic and to contribute to ongoing local, regional, and global policy debates. It is designed specifically to provide practitioners, scholars, and students with the most up-to-date research results while highlighting the promise, challenges, and opportunities that exist on the continent.

The series is sponsored by the Agence Française de Développement and the World Bank. The manuscripts chosen for publication represent the highest quality in each institution and have been selected for their relevance to the development agenda. Working together with a shared sense of mission and interdisciplinary purpose, the two institutions are committed to a common search for new insights and new ways of analyzing the development realities of the Sub-Saharan Africa region.

Advisory Committee Members

Agence Française de Développement
Rémi Genevey, Director of Strategy
Alain Henry, Director of Research

World Bank
Shantayanan Devarajan, Chief Economist, Africa Region
Santiago Pombo-Bejarano, Editor-in-Chief, Office of the Publisher

Sub-Saharan Africa

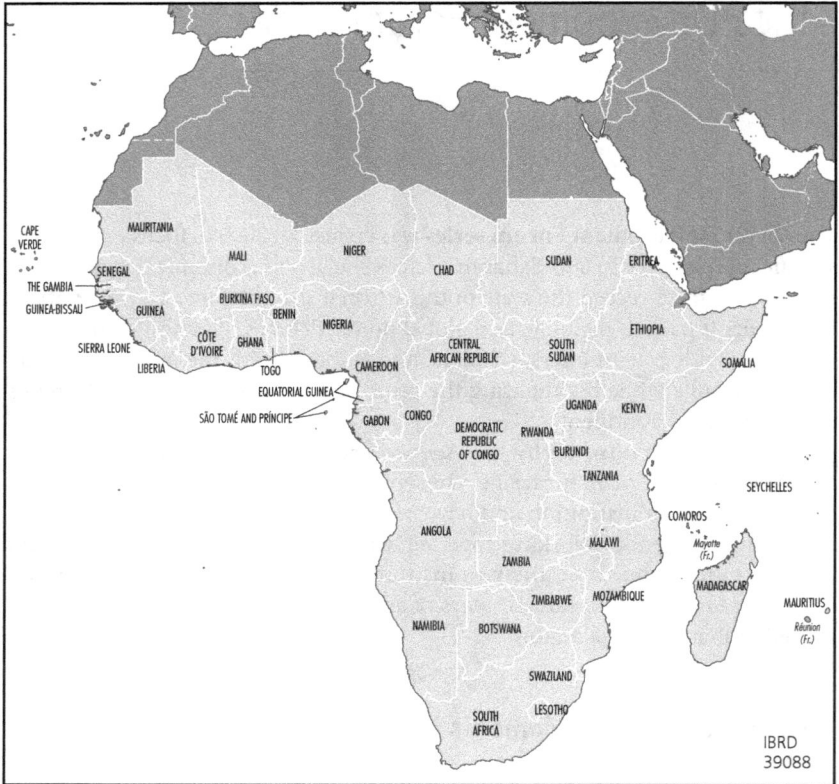

CAPE VERDE
MAURITANIA
MALI
NIGER
SENEGAL
THE GAMBIA
GUINEA-BISSAU
GUINEA
BURKINA FASO
BENIN
NIGERIA
CHAD
SUDAN
ERITREA
CÔTE D'IVOIRE
GHANA
TOGO
SIERRA LEONE
LIBERIA
CAMEROON
CENTRAL AFRICAN REPUBLIC
SOUTH SUDAN
ETHIOPIA
EQUATORIAL GUINEA
SÃO TOMÉ AND PRÍNCIPE
GABON
CONGO
DEMOCRATIC REPUBLIC OF CONGO
RWANDA
BURUNDI
UGANDA
KENYA
SOMALIA
TANZANIA
SEYCHELLES
ANGOLA
MALAWI
COMOROS
Mayotte (Fr.)
ZAMBIA
ZIMBABWE
MOZAMBIQUE
MADAGASCAR
MAURITIUS
Réunion (Fr.)
NAMIBIA
BOTSWANA
SWAZILAND
LESOTHO
SOUTH AFRICA

IBRD
39088

Titles in the Africa Development Forum Series

Free access to all titles in the Africa Development Forum series is available at
https://openknowledge.worldbank.org/handle/10986/2150

Contents

Boxes

Figures

Tables

Foreword

Women's economic empowerment is critical for development. The international community recognizes that this agenda is important—and that more needs to be done to further it. Expanding opportunities for women is of intrinsic value. It is also instrumental in fostering development; realizing the potential of all people is needed in order to ensure growth, productivity, and a vibrant society. *Enterprising Women: Expanding Economic Opportunities in Africa* analyzes new data from 41 countries in Sub-Saharan Africa to provide practical recommendations on how to help more women move into higher-return activities.

Women entrepreneurs are a significant resource in Sub-Saharan Africa. Their efforts and investments contribute to higher living standards for themselves and their families. More women are already economically active in Sub-Saharan Africa than in any other region. But these women too often operate in the informal sector, in small firms, and in traditional sectors where profits and opportunities for expansion are more limited. They are not fully able to realize their potential.

This book shows how economic empowerment for women is particularly needed in Sub-Saharan Africa. Entrepreneurship can reflect choices and the pursuit of opportunities, but it can also reflect necessity and a lack of alternative options. Sub-Saharan Africa has the world's lowest nonagricultural wage employment, often the alternative to entrepreneurship—and demonstrates the largest gender gaps of any region.

Improving the prospects of existing businesses is part of the solution. And addressing constraints in the investment climate that burden informal and smaller enterprises will disproportionately benefit women. But the larger goal is to enable more women to shift the nature of what they do. This book outlines a four-part agenda that can provide more women with the incentives and abilities to run larger enterprises in the formal sector in higher-value-added industries.

Four sources of gender gaps need to be closed. The first regards human capital; gender gaps in education in Sub-Saharan Africa still remain, and business training and access to networks are too often geared toward men.

The second involves ownership and control of assets. The companion to this volume, *Empowering Women: Legal Rights and Economic Opportunities in Africa,* demonstrates the extent of gender gaps in formal economic rights and the practical constraints to accessing justice. These first two gaps affect the third source of gender gaps: access to finance. With less control over collateral and less education and training, women are seen as less attractive borrowers, and hence are more restricted in the type of activities they can pursue. Lastly, there is a gap in voice. Women need to be included at the table when policy reforms are being designed and prioritized.

This book provides examples from countries across the region of how to achieve success. The data show the gender patterns across types of entrepreneurial activities—but they are not uniform. Variations in these patterns and analyses of reforms show how shifting conditions make a difference. More indeed can be done, and this book provides a roadmap of how to do it.

Ngozi Okonjo-Iweala
Coordinating Minister of Economy and
Minister of Finance for the Federal Republic of Nigeria

Preface

This book is about expanding nonfarm entrepreneurship opportunities for women in Sub-Saharan Africa. It examines the extent of gender differences in economic activities pursued by female and male entrepreneurs, and the returns they receive. It uses substantial new microevidence to examine where and why gender gaps appear in the size, formality, and sector of women's and men's enterprises, and the implications of these gaps for the performance of these businesses. It analyzes the factors that help explain these outcomes, so as to provide an agenda for expanding economic opportunities for women. Key themes include the need to address continued gender gaps in access to human capital and in access to and control of assets, and the need to increase the efficacy and authority of women's voices in shaping improvements in the business environment.

The book does not aim to provide a full analysis of labor markets in Africa. It puts entrepreneurship in the broader patterns of labor market participation to show the importance of entrepreneurship relative to other economic activities and to demonstrate how gender patterns across employment categories in Sub-Saharan Africa differ from those in other regions in the world. It also explores how prior work experience affects the choice of entrepreneurial activity. It does not, however, explore directly the relative benefits of wage employment versus entrepreneurship; nor does it examine individuals' transitions across employment categories.

The analysis uses many sources of microdata—household, labor force, and enterprise surveys—to examine the full spectrum of entrepreneurial activities, disaggregated by gender. Appendix A provides more details about each data source and the countries covered by each type of data. The text and figures indicate which data source is used in discussing the various results. Household and labor force surveys provide information on entrepreneurs, particularly those in the informal sector, the self-employed, and those running micro- and small enterprises. The enterprise surveys focus primarily on formal firms with employees and upper-end, market-based informal enterprises. The analysis pays particular attention to the higher end of this spectrum—that is, larger and market-based informal firms and registered firms, as these are both where opportunities are greatest and where gender gaps are largest. Explanations for the patterns documented include factors external to the enterprises, such as the legal framework and investment climate, and the background and education of the entrepreneurs themselves. The book examines entrepreneurs' household characteristics where available, but a full analysis of intrahousehold bargaining or a larger time-use analysis is beyond its scope. In compiling and analyzing new microdata and original research on 41 countries in Sub-Saharan Africa, it provides valuable new insights, and it also makes recommendations on how to expand economic opportunities for the region's women entrepreneurs.

About the Author

Mary Hallward-Driemeier is a lead economist and adviser to the Chief Economist of the World Bank. She has published articles on entrepreneurship, firm productivity, the impact of the investment climate on firm performance, the impact of financial crises, and determinants of foreign direct investment. She was the deputy director for *World Development Report 2005: A Better Investment Climate for Everyone*. Mary helped establish the World Bank's Enterprise Surveys Program, now covering more than 100,000 enterprises in 100 countries. She is also a founding member of the Microeconomics of Growth Network and is co-leading the Jobs Knowledge Platform. She received her MS in development economics from Oxford University as a Rhodes Scholar and her PhD in economics from the Massachusetts Institute of Technology.

Acknowledgments

The principal author of this book is Mary Hallward-Driemeier. The book was written with the important contributions and assistance of colleagues in the World Bank. Ousman Gajigo oversaw the new survey work conducted for this book and coauthored the background paper analyzing the results across firm sectors, sizes, and registration status. Alejandro Rasteletti coauthored the background work on household employment dynamics and household enterprises, building on the database assembled by Claudio Montenegro. Mark Blackden contributed substantially to chapter 10 on public-private dialogue as well as other chapters, and provided invaluable assistance with his introductions to key local partners, his gift for moderating workshops, and his push to enlarge the scope of the work. Tazeen Hasan, Jane Kamangu, and Emilia Lobti collected information on the formal legal economic rights of women in the region and assembled the Women's Legal and Economic Empowerment Database for Africa (Women-LEED-Africa database) discussed in chapters 3 and 7, which also serves as the basis for the companion volume, *Empowering Women: Legal Rights and Economic Opportunities in Africa*. Reyes Aterido, Thorsten Beck, and Leo Iacovone provided the background work on household and individual access to finance that contributed to chapter 8. Manju Shah used the World Bank's Enterprise Surveys to provide useful inputs on patterns across formal enterprises and microenterprises.

Insightful comments and suggestions were provided by participants in the workshops in Addis Ababa, Cape Town, Dakar, and Nairobi as well as Washington, DC, with participants from Cameroon, the Democratic Republic of Congo, Ethiopia, The Gambia, Ghana, Kenya, Malawi, Mali, Nigeria, Rwanda, Senegal, South Africa, Sudan, Tanzania, and Uganda. Particular thanks are given to Reena Badiani, Elena Bardasi, Laura Chioda, Aline Coudouel, Susan Deller Ross, Asli Demirgüç-Kunt, Shanta Devarajan, Louise Fox, Anne Goldstein, Markus Goldstein, Benjamin Herzberg, Sarah Iqbal, Sandra Joireman, Maureen Lewis, Andrew Mason, Ana Maria Munoz Boudet, Pierella Paci, Rita Ramalho, Ana Revenga, Bob Rijkers, Carolina Sanchez-Paramo, Sudhir Shetty, and

Sevi Simavi for their comments and suggestions. The text benefited from the editorial services of Bruce Ross-Larson.

Financial support from the Dutch BNPP Trust Fund, Gender Action Plan, and Africa Chief Economist Regional Studies Program is gratefully acknowledged, as is the additional support from the World Bank's Finance and Private Sector Development Chief Economist Office, Finance and Private Sector Development Africa Department, and Research Department. The study was carried out under the overall guidance of Marilou Uy, Director for Finance and Private Sector Development in Africa, and Shanta Devarajan, Chief Economist for the Africa Region.

Abbreviations

GDP   gross domestic product
IFC   International Finance Corporation
ILO   International Labour Organization
OECD   Organisation for Economic Co-operation and Development
PPD   public-private dialogue

Overview

This book brings together new household and enterprise data from 41 countries in Sub-Saharan Africa to inform policy makers and practitioners about ways to expand women entrepreneurs' economic opportunities. Women's empowerment is recognized as the third Millennium Development Goal; in 2012 the World Bank dedicated its annual flagship, the *World Development Report*, to gender equality and development (World Bank 2011); and the Nobel Prize for Peace was awarded to three pioneering women (two from Liberia) working for peace in their countries' fights for democracy and for greater opportunities for women.

This book focuses attention on Sub-Saharan Africa, and specifically on entrepreneurship in the nonagricultural sector. The issue of gender disparities in economic opportunities in the region has been studied in terms of gaps in wage income and in job sorting in wage work (Arbache, Kolev, and Filipiak 2010; Fafchamps, Söderbom, and Benhassine 2009; Kolev and Sirven 2010). Other cross-country work has looked at entrepreneurship in Sub-Saharan Africa, but rarely with much attention paid to gender (Bigsten and Söderbom 2006; Tybout 2000; World Bank 2004). But entrepreneurship is where women in Sub-Saharan Africa are most active outside of agriculture. So it is critical to look at entrepreneurship to understand the extent of gender disparities in economic opportunities, determine the underlying reasons for these gender patterns, and develop an agenda to enable more women to realize their full potential.

This book contributes new empirical analysis in four parts.

Part I analyzes gender-disaggregated patterns of entrepreneurship in Sub-Saharan Africa and compares them with patterns elsewhere. The highest share of women entrepreneurs in the world is found in Sub-Saharan Africa, but the women are disproportionately self-employed rather than employers. Relative to men, women are pursuing lower-opportunity activities, with their enterprises more likely to be smaller, informal, and in low-value-added lines of business (see, for example, Bigsten and others 2003; ILO 2002; Liedholm and Mead 1999;

McPherson 1996; Mead and Liedholm 1998; Parker 2004; Sinha and Kanbur 2012). The challenge in expanding opportunities is not helping more women become entrepreneurs, but enabling them to shift to higher-return activities.

What explains the gender sorting in the types of enterprises that women and men run—that is, why do more women operate smaller, informal, and low-value-added enterprises? Part II shows that many Sub-Saharan countries present a challenging environment for women (Bardasi, Blackden, and Guzman 2007). Two dimensions of particular importance for entrepreneurs are access to and control over assets, and the quality of human capital. Recent data from Sub-Saharan Africa show that gender gaps along both these dimensions are still common, and that they are associated with the gender patterns in being self-employed and being an employer, as discussed in part I. More-detailed investigations into the characteristics of entrepreneurs—their age, marital status, educational attainment, prior work experience, and motivation for being an entrepreneur—further explain variations in the types of business that women and men run.

Gender sorting across types of enterprises significantly shapes economic opportunities. Where women and men work helps explain much of the gender gap in average productivity. Part III demonstrates that women's productivity is lower not because of their gender but because informal, smaller firms are less productive—and more women run these types of businesses. Among similar types of enterprises, little systematic gender gap is apparent in productivity or firm growth. A similar finding holds for constraints: they vary far more by type of enterprise than by gender (with some exceptions for dealing with red tape, getting start-up capital, and suffering from harassment).

Part IV examines four key areas of the agenda for expanding women's economic opportunities in Africa: strengthening women's property rights and ability to control assets, improving their access to finance, building human capital in business skills and networks, and strengthening women's voices in business-environment reform. These areas are important both because they have wide gender gaps and because they help explain gender differences in entrepreneurial activities.

Why Seek to Improve Women's Opportunities?

There are several reasons why it is important to improve opportunities for women entrepreneurs in Sub-Saharan Africa. First, simple fairness requires letting all individuals make their own decisions in critical areas of their lives and pursue opportunities equally. Second, realizing women's contributions to economic activities has an instrumental value—it unleashes the potential of all members of society and spills over to others in the household, particularly girls. Third, action will be needed to close many of the gender gaps mentioned above; economic development alone is not enough to ensure women's access to legal and economic rights or participation in policy decisions. True, gender gaps in education tend to close with higher incomes, but gaps in women's property rights do not. Such gaps are as common in middle-income countries as low-income countries in Sub-Saharan Africa, so simply raising a country's income will not give women equal ability to control assets (Hallward-Driemeier and Hasan 2012). This finding helps explain why the share of female employers in a country is associated with equality of economic rights in the country and not with the country's income.

Why Focus on Sub-Saharan Africa?

Women in the region have fewer alternatives to entrepreneurship than do women in other regions. Self-employment is higher in Sub-Saharan Africa, and wage employment is lower, than in any other region. But these metrics also have a stark gender dimension. This is the only region where women's self-employment is more common than their wage employment (see figure O.1), and the gender gap in the share of wage employment is the highest in the world. If wage employment is less of an option for women in Sub-Saharan Africa, it is more important for entrepreneurial opportunities to be fruitful—and for women to be able to pursue them to the same degree as men.

Aggregate country data on gender equality and women's empowerment suggest that many women in Sub-Saharan Africa face a particularly challenging environment. Disparities in education and property rights remain very high—higher than in most other regions. Gaps in formal economic rights are often reinforced by the role of customary law and practice. Many countries in the region have multiple and overlapping legal systems that make women's economic rights less secure. These gender gaps weaken women's abilities and incentives to start and run the types of enterprises associated with better outcomes—that is, enterprises with higher productivity and profits.

Access to finance is systemically a larger issue for businesses in Sub-Saharan Africa (whether run by males or females) than it is in other regions. The region's businesses are 40 percent less likely than those elsewhere to have any formal financial access. Although gender patterns in access to finance among formal firms with five or more employees are not that significant, the share of female entrepreneurs running such firms is significantly lower than the overall share of female entrepreneurs. Differences in access to start-up capital could be particularly important in explaining some of the gender sorting across types of enterprises.

Part I. Mapping Women's and Men's Entrepreneurial Activities

Both men and women are active in the labor force and in entrepreneurship, but there are important differences in the types of activities they engage in (figure O.1). Women are far more likely to be in self-employment, as opposed to being employers or wage workers. Within entrepreneurship, the share of women who are employers remains fairly constant across countries sorted by income level, while the share of women in self-employment falls with income (figure O.2a). Looking within employment categories at the share of women, the share of employers who are women is similarly fairly constant even as income grows (figure O.2b). Within Sub-Saharan Africa, which dominates the right-hand side of the graphs, half of the self-employed are women, yet only a quarter of employers are women.

Female entrepreneurs are, unsurprisingly, not distributed uniformly across all industries. This uneven distribution has important ramifications because— as with whether an enterprise is formal or informal ("formality")[1]—industries differ in their size, profitability, and opportunities for growth. Women, particularly women microentrepreneurs, are more likely than men to be in services

Figure O.1 Women and Men Are Economically Active in Different Types of Employment, with Women's Labor Force Participation Highest in Sub-Saharan Africa

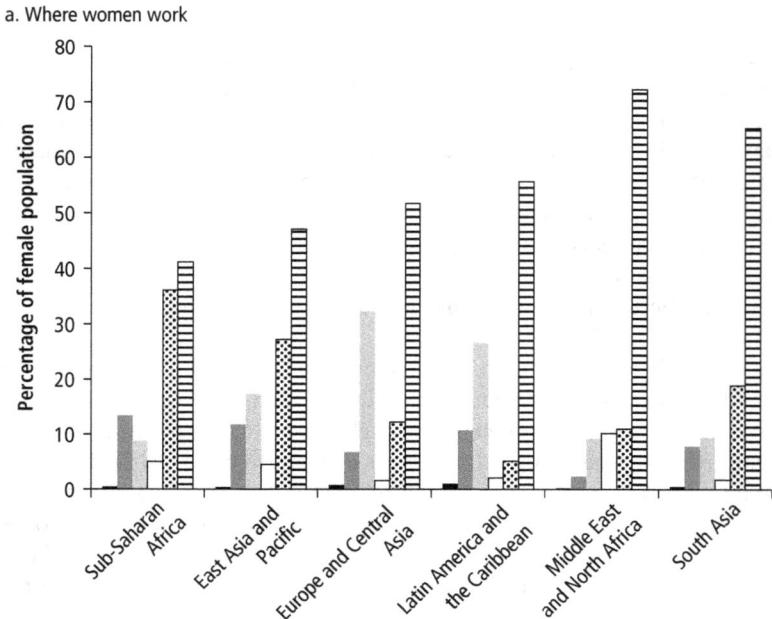

a. Where women work

Figure 0.1 *(continued)*

b. Where men work

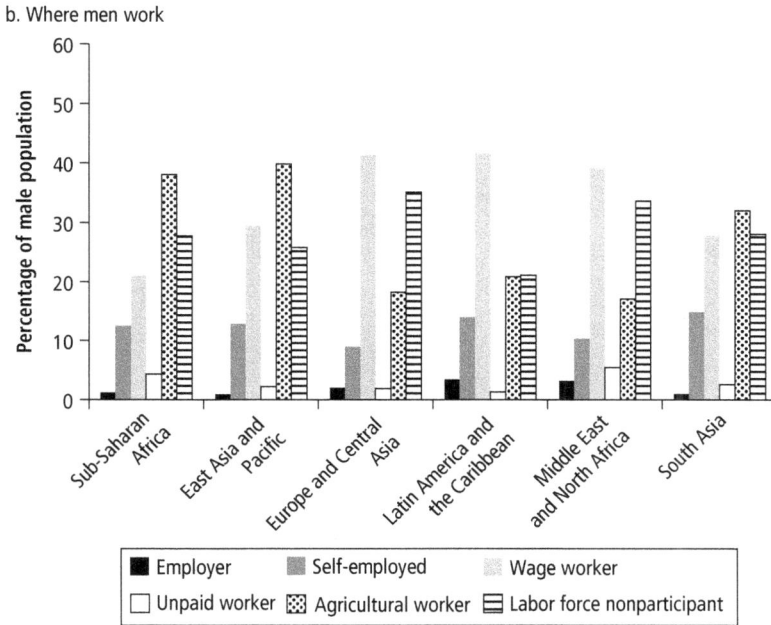

Source: National household and labor force surveys for 101 low- and middle-income countries, most recent years (2000–10).

and in traditional lower-value-added sectors such as the garment and food-processing sectors. They are also less likely to be registered. Men are more likely to be in metals and other manufacturing. So, among those who are entrepreneurs, women are more likely than men to be running small informal firms in lower-value-added sectors.

Expanding women's economic opportunities is thus not so much about expanding entrepreneurship itself; rather, it involves tackling constraints to women's abilities and incentives to expand their business and move into higher-value-added activities.

Enterprise performance is markedly affected by size, formality, and the line of business. Using value added per worker as the base measure of performance for a sample of 37 countries in Sub-Saharan Africa with available data, we find that women and men have a gender gap in labor productivity of about 6 percent. But after analysis controls for the size and line of business, and for the entrepreneur's education, these gaps shrink and, depending on formality, can disappear altogether. Particularly among registered enterprises, gender in itself does not

Figure O.2 Female Self-Employment Falls with Country Income, but the Share of Employers Is Stable

a. Where women work

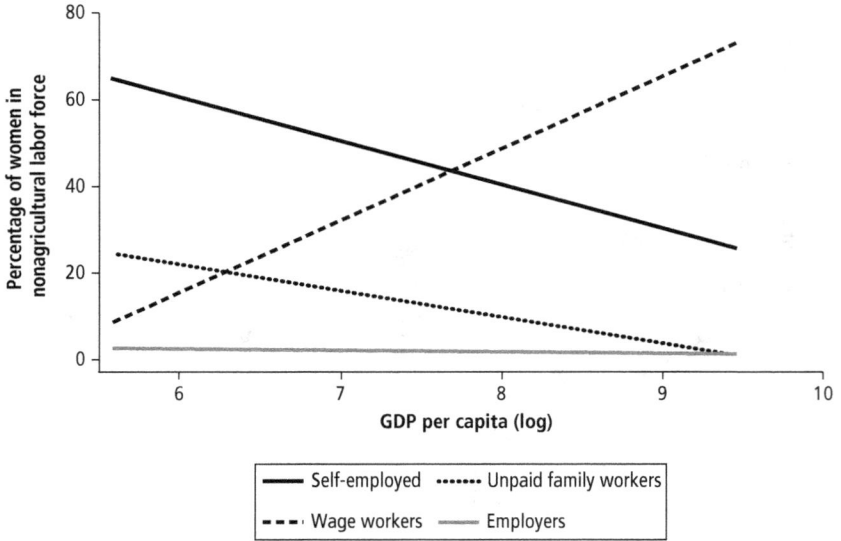

b. Female share within employment category

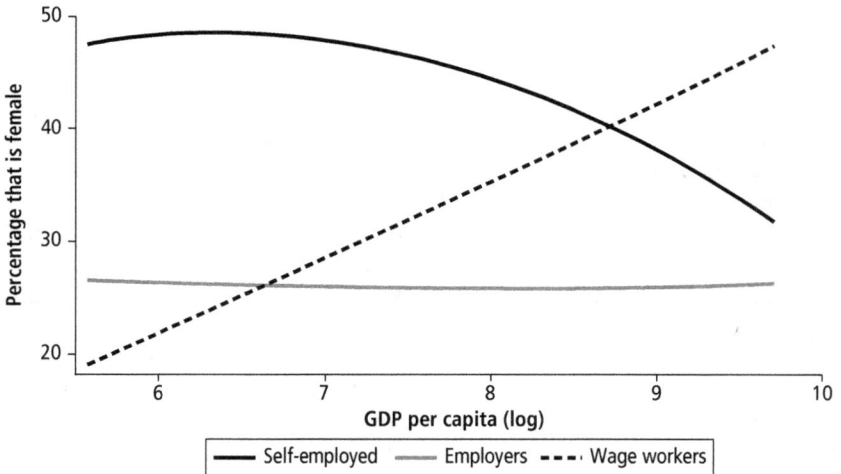

Source: National household and labor force surveys for 101 low- and middle-income countries, most recent years (2000–10).
Note: GDP = gross domestic product. Analysis excludes agriculture.

account for productivity differences. Instead, gender gaps exist because women account for such a small share of entrepreneurs in the formal sector (figure O.3).

The way "female ownership" is defined also affects results: the gender gap in performance is larger with a narrower definition that stresses who controls the business rather than who owns it (since a business may be owned by more than one person, not all of whom have the same role in making major decisions regarding the business). If enterprises with female minority owners who do not have decision-making power are classified as female owned, the data may obscure gaps between the genders. The effect is significant because in almost half of the enterprises that have multiple owners, at least one of whom is female, women are not among the decision makers. In the non-household-based informal sector, other enterprise and entrepreneur characteristics account for most of the productivity gap. The type of enterprise where gender gaps persist, even controlling for other characteristics, is informal home-based enterprises. Differences in hours of operation seem to account for much of these gaps (data are scarce, however).

After controlling for other key enterprise characteristics—ensuring that one is comparing like with like—it is encouraging to find no or few significant differences in performance for female and male entrepreneurs. The finding

Figure O.3 Controlling for Enterprise Characteristics Removes the Gender Gap in Productivity (registered firms)

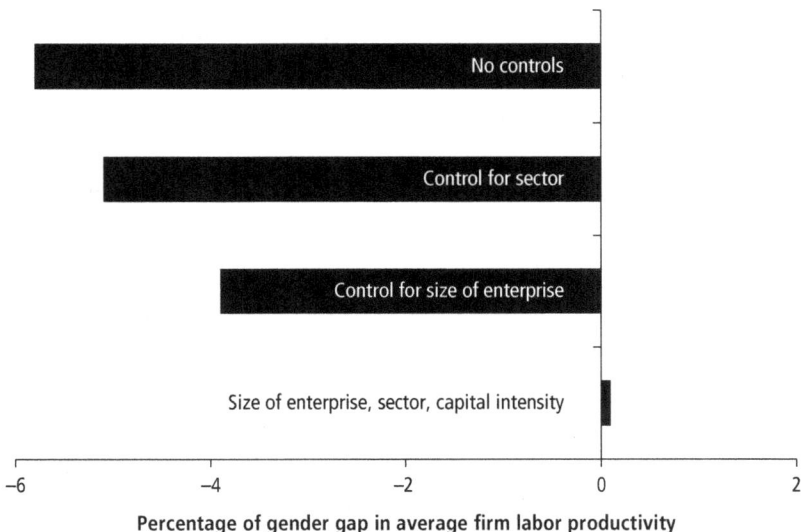

Percentage of gender gap in average firm labor productivity

Source: Hallward-Driemeier and Rasteletti 2010.
Note: Analysis is based on regressions using data from 37 Sub-Saharan African countries, with country dummies included to capture country-invariant effects. Thus the results are all based on within-country differences. A dummy is included for whether there is female participation in ownership.

confirms that Sub-Saharan Africa has considerable hidden growth potential in its women, and that tapping that potential—including improving women's choices of where to be active economically—can make a real contribution to the region's growth. This finding also underscores the need for policy makers to understand where differences exist in the obstacles that men and women face, and why the observed patterns of entrepreneurship persist.

As with performance, once the characteristics of the enterprise are controlled for, differences in obstacles faced by men's and women's businesses are not significant. That is, gender gaps are largely explained once enterprise characteristics are taken into account. Thus for businesses of similar sizes and in similar industries, women and men report similar constraints. For example, if accessing land is harder for women than for men, it is mainly because small firms report this as a greater constraint—and women are more likely to be in smaller firms.

Three caveats apply, however. First, how "female ownership" is defined affects the findings, as pointed out above. Second, data are not available to analyze properly how constraints affect the entry decision—or the size, formality, and line of business. So, although we can look at the effects of gender within firm size categories and conclude that size is more important than gender, we cannot determine to what extent gender differences explain why women are more likely to run smaller firms. Lastly, focus groups revealed that some challenges facing female entrepreneurs are different in kind (not just degree) from those facing men. For example, women found that the "gifts" sought by some suppliers, moneylenders, and officials went beyond the financial to include the sexual.

Part II. Understanding Sorting

The greater concentration of women in smaller firms, in the informal sector, and in traditional industries is important because these three dimensions are correlated with opportunity. Larger and formal enterprises in higher-value-added lines of business tend to be more productive and more profitable (Ayyagari, Beck, and Demirgüç-Kunt 2007; Tybout 2000; World Bank 2012)—although, again, the gender dimension is not examined in detail in the existing firm-level work on Sub-Saharan Africa (Bigsten and Gebreeyesus 2007; Bigsten and Söderbom 2006; Sleuwaegen and Goedhuys 2002; Söderbom 2012; Van Biesebroeck 2005). Hence it is important to look at gender gaps across these three dimensions and to examine why these gender-differentiated patterns of entrepreneurial activity exist in different countries. With gender patterns in the types of entrepreneurial activity largely driving gender differences in the returns to entrepreneurship, the relevant issues are why women and men undertake different economic activities, and whether they do so through choice or necessity (see Klapper and Parker [2010] and Minniti [2009] for reviews of the broader literature beyond just Sub-Saharan Africa).

Both country characteristics (income, measures of the business environment, human capital, and property rights) and individual characteristics (education, marital status, age, prior work experience) are examined to understand their impact on gender sorting and gender gaps in firm performance. At the country level, many gender gaps are associated with a country's income, but income alone does not explain everything. Not all gaps close with income, most importantly gender gaps in property rights, which are discussed below. And some country characteristics have an independent effect on gender gaps in firm performance, even taking income into account; these characteristics include the quality of governance, extent of corruption, political stability, and rule of law. Better governance is generally associated with better private sector outcomes, and better governance shows a mild gender effect in that the gender gap in firm performance is smaller in better-governed countries.

Other aggregate measures of women's empowerment developed by international organizations suggest that women in Africa (Sub-Saharan Africa and the Middle East and North Africa) face a particularly challenging environment. Indeed, countries with weaker institutions of gender inclusion or equality tend to have slightly wider gender gaps in performance. But because many of these aggregate measures add little information beyond what is available from country income data, this study turns to measures of gender inequality that are more relevant to entrepreneurship and that are not simply correlated with income: human capital and property rights affecting access to assets.

As a proxy for human capital, the study examines adult literacy, since this measure captures an important skill for the full working-age population better than current enrollment rates, which measure the potential of the future labor force. For a measure of property rights, the study uses the Women's Legal and Economic Empowerment Database for Africa (Women–LEED–Africa) developed in the companion volume.[2] It groups countries in the region based on the strength of key legal rights for women—rights that indicate whether women have the same legal capacity as men to make independent contractual arrangements and whether they have the same rights to own and control property. These rights are important because gender gaps persist precisely in these legal areas. They are also important because such rights affect not only the ability to open a business, secure collateral, and make contracts, but also the ability to keep the earnings of the business. Thus they affect the very incentive to be an entrepreneur.

Grouping countries on the two dimensions of gender gaps in human capital and economic rights sends an important message to policy makers. First, it shows that women's legal capacity and rights are not correlated with country income. Changes will require active political engagement. Second, it shows that gender gaps in these rights are of considerable importance for women's entrepreneurial opportunities. While larger gaps in literacy are generally associated with larger shares of women being self-employed, greater legal protection for women is associated with women having more opportunity to become employers. With higher literacy, women are more likely to partici- pate in a wider range of business lines, including higher-value-added sectors. In low-literacy countries, women's nonagricultural activities are much more highly concentrated in services than even in simple manufacturing.

From the perspective of individuals, several key (usually sequential) choices are involved in determining the type of entrepreneur one is likely to become.[3] First there is the decision to participate in the nonagricultural labor force, then to become an entrepreneur rather than a wage earner, then to operate in the formal or informal sector. Finally there is the choice of the line of business and scale of enterprise.

Both household and enterprise surveys show that education is a key deter- minant in these choices, with smaller roles played by prior work experience, marital status, age, and relevant business skills. Gender gaps in education have been closing over time, but for middle-aged women and men they are sub- stantial in many countries. Thus lower educational attainment for women, and particularly for middle-aged women, is a large reason why more women operate in smaller firms and in the informal sector. It is striking, however, that there are large differences in educational attainment between those in the informal and formal sectors, but little gender difference in education levels within each sector (figure O.4).

Prior work experience is also important. Indeed, entrepreneurship-related experience can be a bigger determinant of productivity than general formal education, even at the tertiary level. For its part, marital status (for women) determines legal standing, property rights, and the ability to engage in business.

Part III. Expanding Opportunities for Women Entrepreneurs

The analysis addresses four factors vital for expanding opportunities for women entrepreneurs in Sub-Saharan Africa. The first is women's access to and con- trol of assets and resources required for entrepreneurship, which are affected by gender differences in legal capacity and property rights, particularly where married women are concerned. The second is education and experience, which are important drivers of economic choice, opportunity, and performance. The third is limited access to finance, which is a key obstacle to business devel- opment. The fourth is women's limited opportunities for networking and exclu- sion from decision-making bodies and from policy dialogue, which (especially in the business environment) mean that business-climate reforms rarely tackle issues for women entrepreneurs.

Figure 0.4 Education Varies More by Sector Formality Than by Gender

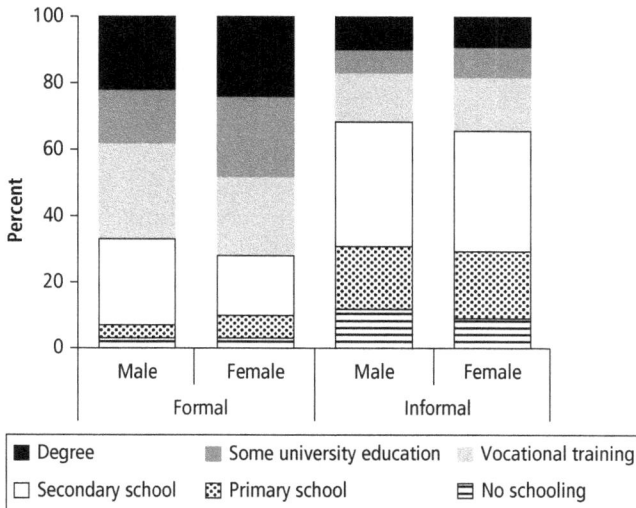

Legend:
- ■ Degree
- ▨ Some university education
- ▨ Vocational training
- ☐ Secondary school
- ▨ Primary school
- ☰ No schooling

Source: Gajigo and Hallward-Driemeier 2010.
Note: Data are for newly established enterprises in Côte d'Ivoire, Kenya, Nigeria, and Senegal.

Increasing Women's Right to Own and Control Assets

Women—especially married women—often have lower legal status and fewer property rights than men. Women–LEED–Africa shows that business regulations rarely have gender-differentiated provisions. But their impact in practice may not be gender neutral if women face greater time constraints, have more limited mobility, face cultural restrictions on the transactions they can engage in, or are perceived as softer targets for harassment. Consequently, gender-neutral or gender-blind regulations do not necessarily translate into gender equality in economic rights.

Other areas of the law beyond business regulations are critical in assessing whether women may face greater obstacles to running a business. The laws that also matter include those that frame people's economic rights, such as family law governing marriage, divorce, and inheritance, and laws governing land rights and labor markets. These laws, rather than business regulations, determine whether women and men can make economic decisions in their own name, or whether there are restrictions on their ability to enter contracts or to own, administer, transfer, or inherit assets and property. Family law, seldom addressed in programs to improve the business environment, shapes the business environment for women. Marital status, and the capacities and limitations associated with it, determine women's effective property rights and economic autonomy, so that they are often markedly different from men's.

Yet it is precisely these areas of the law that show gender differences the most. Laws in these areas are often granted formal exemption from countries' nondiscrimination provisions and are commonly subject to overlapping legal systems in Sub-Saharan Africa, with many constitutions and statutes explicitly recognizing marriage, inheritance, and property as domains where formal customary or personal law applies (figure O.5). These exemptions are important because differences in men's and women's legal rights contribute substantially to the region's gender-differentiated entrepreneurship patterns: women are more likely to sort into self-employment in countries with weaker legal rights and to become employers in countries with stronger legal rights.

Practical constraints, including distance, cost, language, and bias, further shape the ability to exercise formal economic rights, with important gender-differentiated effects. Equally, much of the population has little to do with the formal legal system—nor do people have much knowledge of the legal protections it affords. Particularly in areas with lower incomes, lower levels of education, or strong customary traditions—or areas that are more rural—people rarely see the formal system as relevant for securing economic rights. Customary law, instead, plays a significant role, both as a formal source of law and as an influence on informal practice, touching the lives of the majority of the population in much of Sub-Saharan Africa (Tamanaha, Sage, and Woolcock 2012).

Figure O.5 Gender Gaps in Legal Rights Remain in Sub-Saharan Africa—and Do Not Necessarily Close with Countries' Income

a. Head-of-household rules

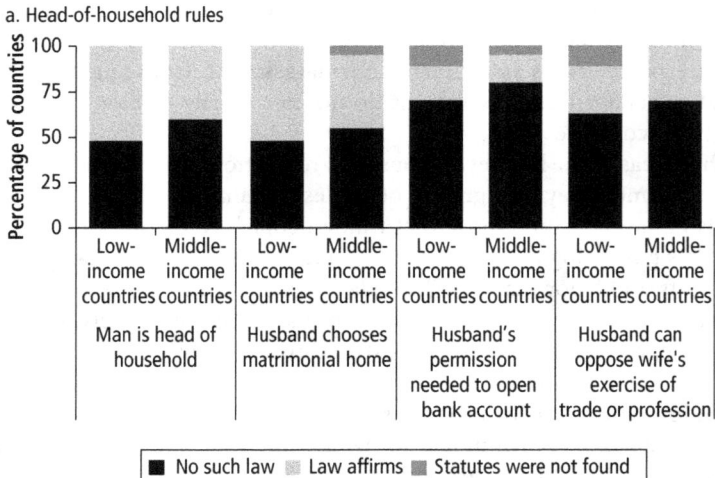

No such law   Law affirms   Statutes were not found

Figure O.5 *(continued)*

b. Constitutional recognition of customary law

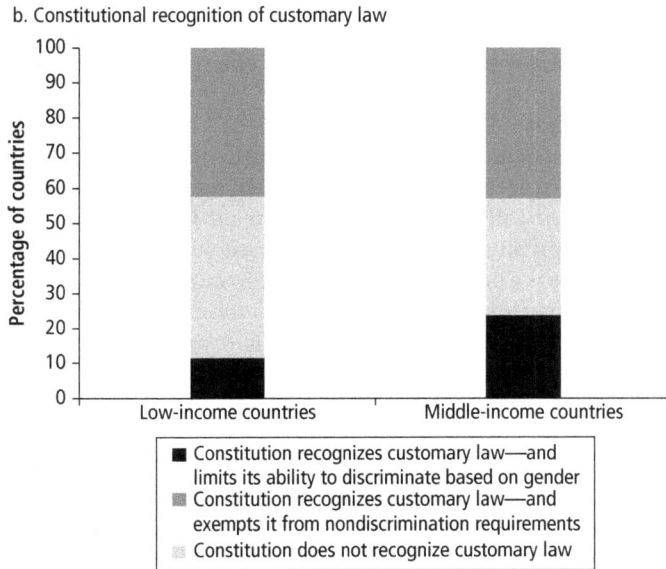

Sources: Hallward-Driemeier and Hasan 2012; M. Hallward-Driemeier, T. Hasan, M. Blackden, J. Kamangu, and E. Lobti, Women's Legal and Economic Empowerment Database.
Note: Figures are based on all 47 Sub-Saharan African countries.

As the companion volume discusses in more detail (see Hallward-Driemeier and Hasan 2012), three key messages on women's legal status emerge from the Women–LEED–Africa database. First, the principle of nondiscrimination is recognized in all countries—in constitutions or treaties they have signed (or both). But formal exceptions are widespread: despite recognizing nondiscrimination as a guiding principle of law, many countries' statutes still discriminate.

Second, many of the discriminatory provisions women face apply not to women as women, but to women as married women. From a legal standpoint, marriage changes, in some cases radically, the legal status and rights of women, often conferring legal capacities and responsibilities on husbands and removing them from wives. This change in women's legal status applies particularly to property regimes, to rights in and after marriage, and to rules affecting women's economic capacity and decision making within marriage (figure O.5b).

Third, the treatment of women's economic rights is not closely related to a country's level of income or development (see figure O.5). Simply raising national income is unlikely to improve women's legal and economic rights—more interventionist reforms will be needed. Some countries have expanded national income even with gaps in women's economic rights, while others, with strong protection against discrimination, have not. Of course, the legal frame-work is not the only determining factor. But the strength of legal protections clearly affects women's economic opportunities, particularly their ability to move out of self-employment and to run larger enterprises (see box O.1).

Expanding Women's Access to Finance

Entrepreneurs' access to financial services is crucial for three main reasons. It is key for securing access to productive resources (internal resources are rarely sufficient for growth). It can smooth cash flow. And, in the other direction, it matters for savings (particularly if other members of the household may divert resources).

Access to finance is a particularly pressing constraint in Sub-Saharan Africa: fewer than one in five households has access to formal financial services. It is a systemic issue for businesses (male or female owned), which are substan-tially less likely than their peers in other regions to have any formal financial access. Larger companies, however, still have an advantage in accessing financial services (Bigsten and others 2003).

An analysis of individual entrepreneurs strongly suggests that women's lower levels of access to formal financing are explained by gender differences in income, education, and employment status. Women are more prominent in borrowing informally and are more likely to be excluded from formal financial services (Fafchamps 2000). After controlling for individuals' education and experience, the gender gap in accessing formal finance is largely explained,

---

BOX O.1

Strengthening Women's Property Rights Affects Opportunities Pursued

Ethiopia changed its family law in 2000, raising the minimum age of marriage for women, removing the ability of the husband to deny permission for the wife to work outside the home, and requiring both spouses' consent in the administration of marital property. While this reform now applies across the country, it was initially rolled out in three of the nine regions and two chartered cities. Using two nationally representa-tive household surveys, one in 2000 just prior to the reform and one five years later, we were able to carry out a difference-in-difference estimation of the impact of the reform. Five years later, we find a significant shift in women's economic activities. In particular, women's relative participation in occupations that require work outside the home, full-time work, and higher skills rose relatively more where the reform had been enacted (controlling for time and location effects).

Source: Hallward-Driemeier and Gajigo 2011.

although results can vary by country (Aterido, Beck, and Iacovone, forthcoming; de Mel, McKenzie, and Woodruff 2009).

Beyond acting as a potential constraint to the growth of a business, how much does access to finance have a gender dimension as a barrier to entry? Certainly among newly started enterprises, women's businesses have less access to finance than men's. This gender difference is strongly associated with the respective nature of their businesses (figure O.6). The data, though inconclusive, suggest that prior to becoming entrepreneurs, women have more limited access, consistent with their starting smaller and less-capital-intensive firms, which are then less likely to get external finance once they are running.

Enterprises that are run by women who have successfully entered the formal sector do not seem more financially constrained than enterprises run by men. Access to financial resources depends more on the size and nature of the firm than on the gender of the manager. But because women have such a small proportion of large formal firms—precisely those with more access to finance—indirect gender dynamics may be at work in access to finance.

Figure O.6 Male Formal Entrepreneurs Had More Start-Up Capital Than Other Groups

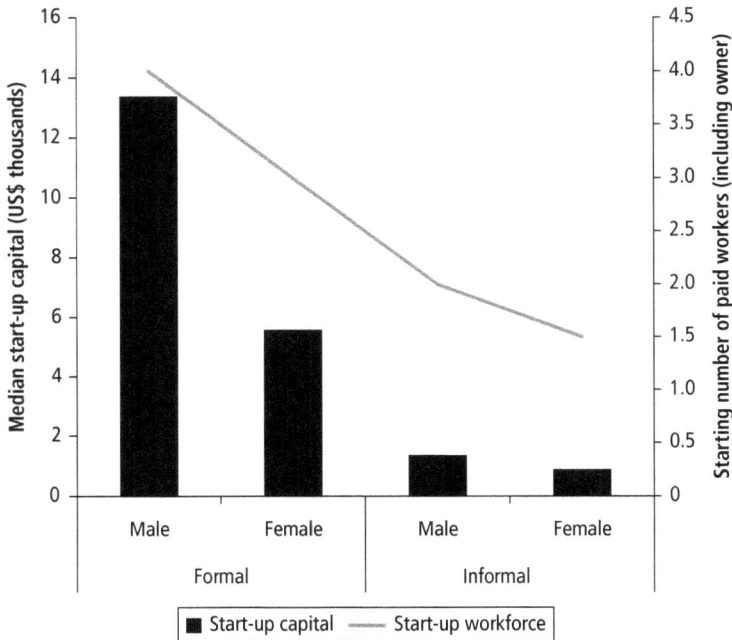

Source: Gajigo and Hallward-Driemeier 2010.
Note: Data are for newly established enterprises in Côte d'Ivoire, Kenya, Nigeria, and Senegal.

Enriching Managerial and Financial Skills

The positive effect of education on enterprise productivity, for women and men, is one of the most robust findings in the literature (Mead and Liedholm 1998; Parker 2004; World Bank 2004, 2012). This study's analysis also shows that education is a significant determinant of revenue per worker in enterprises. Education can also signal other qualities such as discipline, motivation, and versatility in dealing with new challenges (Blau 1985; Parker and van Praag 2006; Van der Sluis, van Praag, and Vijverberg 2008).

Specifically, entrepreneurs with at least secondary education and some vocational training have significantly higher revenue per worker than those with no education. Primary education has no higher productivity effect over no schooling. The differences in productivity associated with higher education are not statistically different for women and men. Although women in general may have less education, those who are educated obtain more benefit from it by running more productive firms than do their male counterparts.

Four management techniques had a significant effect on productivity among firms sampled in five countries (Bloom and Van Reenen 2007, 2010). Gender differences were not apparent for two techniques (formal objectives and monitoring of employee performance) but were apparent in the other two (process innovation and participatory decision making). Male entrepreneurs scored significantly higher than female entrepreneurs in process innovation, but the reverse was true in participatory decision making.

Education and management quality seem to have important effects, and women can benefit from them as much as men—although results can also depend on broader business environment conditions (Bruhn and Zia 2011; Bruhn, Karlan, and Schoar 2010; de Mel, McKenzie, and Woodruff 2009; Mansuri and Giné 2011). Experience—through previous employment in the formal sector, exposure to running a business, or having had a parent who was an entrepreneur—also counts (Aterido and Hallward-Driemeier 2011; Djankov and others 2007). The fact that there is a gender gap in the last area suggests that women are less exposed to the experience of business in general, and lack the role models and opportunities for networking available to their male counterparts. It also suggests that as more women become successful entrepreneurs, and as more women have the opportunity to network and to make their voices heard in the enterprise sector, a virtuous cycle may be created that will boost the human capital of the next generation of women entrepreneurs.

Strengthening Women's Voices in Business Environment Reforms

Despite the active involvement of women as entrepreneurs in Sub-Saharan Africa, women are rarely at the table when business-related policies are discussed, and the issues facing businesswomen as opposed to businessmen are rarely debated or addressed in policy-making forums. Women are largely excluded from policy making in the private sector and from the mechanisms and instruments used to promote dialogue between the public and private sectors. So although in the private sector women are important economic actors in their own right, they lack comparable representation in policy-making and decision-making institutions.

Women need to be active in business environment reform, not only because they are strongly involved as entrepreneurs, but also because the obstacles and constraints they face, and the perspectives they bring, can be and often are quite different from those of their male counterparts. As indicated earlier, women are more likely to operate in the informal sector and be engaged in smaller and lower-value-added sectors. Even where men's and women's businesses share similar characteristics, women are likely to have different experiences of legal, regulatory, and administrative barriers to business than their male counterparts.

Business associations, including those focusing on women's businesses, provide an important platform for promoting women's business interests. But women are often poorly represented in mainstream business associations. Many women's business associations are not centrally involved in mainstream dialogue and advocacy—and lack the capacity and experience to pursue their work effectively. This study identifies some useful experiences of promoting businesswomen's associations, and some important new initiatives to amplify the voices of women entrepreneurs in policy making and in investment-climate reform. The recent establishment of the Africa Businesswomen's Network is a case in point.

Women consistently raise as challenges their lack of voice in decision making, the absence of opportunities for networking, the lack of appropriate role models and mentors, and the lack of business skills. In some countries there are additional challenges to increasing women's involvement with business associations. Cultural and social imperatives can discourage women from mixing freely with men, especially those from outside their families. In such circumstances, the presence of a specialized women's business association makes sense. Such networks provide women business owners with support. They also help spread new business ideas, facilitate making business contacts, and provide avenues for larger-scale marketing and distribution.

The effectiveness of women's voices will depend in part on the extent to which there are solid gender-informed and sex-disaggregated analyses available to inform policy making. Advocacy for policy reforms needs to be grounded in solid country-specific analysis of the opportunities and constraints in the business environment—and, specifically, of the ways they differ for men and women. A gender-informed analysis of investment-climate obstacles provides the essential underpinning needed to identify, and advocate for, needed legal and regulatory reforms. In recent years, there have been several country-specific gender-focused analyses of investment-climate obstacles in Africa. Drawing on broader analysis of the legal environment and links between gender inequality and economic growth, these assessments focused on regulatory and administrative barriers to business registration, operation, and closing; business licensing and taxation; access to land and finance; access to justice; and issues of concern in particular sectors. The studies identified gender-based differences in application of business regulations, and proposed regulatory reforms to address them (see Simavi, Manuel, and Blackden 2010).

In parallel, recent studies capturing the voices of women entrepreneurs in Africa provide valuable insights into how women perceive the business environment and what obstacles and challenges they face. They reveal both the importance attached to networking and the problems women face in participating effectively in associations and networks. These problems make the task of developing new opportunities, building a customer base, and expanding markets all the more difficult. Consistent across all countries are issues associated with balancing work and family obligations, the complexity of (and the time involved in complying with) regulations, the higher probability that women will be the subject of harassment and discrimination by public servants and officials in positions of power, and the problems with access to finance already mentioned.

Any approach to bringing more women to the table, and to ensuring that issues important to women are on the agenda, needs to address the underlying questions of whether it is better for women to work through parallel structures focused on women, or to seek stronger integration into "mainstream" mechanisms of policy dialogue and business associations. That is, is it better to encourage more women's business associations, or to promote greater female participation within existing business associations? A related question is whether efforts should focus on issues specific to women in business (a gender perspective) or should expand the ways in which women participate in, and contribute to, advocacy on issues that are not gender-specific but are of importance to business more generally. The study suggests that there is no simple answer—and that in many instances a dual-track approach, involving both separate women's mechanisms and better integration into the mainstream, is required.

Investment-climate reform that enables women, as well as men, to become more effective participants in business and in stimulating economic development must address challenges faced by both men and women. This approach is more likely to be followed if women are full participants in policy discussions and reform efforts. One mechanism examined here is the process of public-private dialogue (PPD), supported by the International Finance Corporation. PPD is regarded as an important means of enlarging the "reform space" by ensuring greater inclusion of stakeholders in reform deliberations and facilitating greater local ownership of reform measures (Herzberg and Wright 2006). While early efforts did not include a focus on gender inclusion, PPD programs now promote greater gender inclusion and make space for identifying and tackling business environment issues of particular interest to women.

Policy makers, researchers, and members of the development community are paying more attention to understanding and addressing the gender dimensions of the business environment, and developing practical steps to tackle gender issues in investment climate reform. The importance of evidence-based research and analysis, as the foundation for effective lobbying for policy change, cannot be overstated, and this study aims to fill some important gaps in this area. It is still necessary to persuade policy makers and practitioners that addressing women's issues in business is important in its own right—and that doing so can have valuable payoffs for the business sector and the economy as a whole.

Part IV. Toward an Action Agenda

This book outlines policy reforms that can improve women's opportunities for entrepreneurship in Africa and enable women to engage in larger, formally registered businesses in higher-value-added areas.

Reforming the Business Environment

Reforming the business environment expands opportunities for growth, higher productivity, and employment—for all. Broader reforms, such as improving the infrastructure, tax administration, and regulations, are likely to benefit both women and men. The extent of indirect gender effects depends on the types of enterprises that benefit most from reform. For example, lifting constraints on smaller firms and encouraging formalization should help women disproportionately.

Constraints to entrepreneurship that affect women more than men—as the analysis here shows, they are strongest in areas of property rights, access to finance, and harassment—reduce half the population's potential to participate and compete equally in productive activities, thereby lowering aggregate economic growth. They have a broader effect on stunting competitive pressures, lowering innovation, and cutting aggregate productivity growth, particularly if they distort financial markets, so that capital is not allocated to the most productive activities. And they restrict higher-potential women's enterprises the most. Thus there is an intrinsic and instrumental case for removing gender-based constraints to entrepreneurship.

Increasing Women's Right to Own and Control Assets

The Women–LEED–Africa database shows in which countries and in which areas of the law reforms are still needed to close gender gaps in legal capacity and property rights. To close these gaps, governments need to ratify, "domesticate," and then enforce international treaties and conventions, including the Maputo Protocol, the Convention on the Elimination of all Forms of Discrimination against Women, and key International Labour Organization conventions. Within a coherent international framework, they need to examine their constitutions to address discriminatory provisions, enhance provisions for gender equality, review the ways the legal system recognizes customary law, and ensure that constitutional nondiscrimination provisions are applied in family law and property rights in marriage. Governments also have to make particular effort to address contradictory and inconsistent provisions in the law.

To strengthen women's legal and property rights, the following key items should be addressed:

- Giving women equal say over the administration and transfer of marital property
- Limiting or removing head-of-household laws that allow husbands to deny permission to their wives to engage in a trade or profession, or to choose the marital home
- Removing provisions requiring a husband's signature to enter into contracts or open a bank account
- Enabling married women to testify equally in court
- Recognizing women's rights to marital property upon divorce or in inheritance
- Applying constitutional provisions of nondiscrimination in areas of marriage, property, and inheritance
- Building awareness of gender bias, and measures to counteract such bias, among judges and within the broader legal community

Reforms in the administration of law and in the institutions responsible for delivering justice can really help improve women's access to justice and the capacity of the system to respond to women's concerns. Measures include facilitating physical access to justice, through more, and more appropriately focused, courts (such as for family matters and small claims); increasing the participation and representation of women throughout the justice system; and enabling those administering and dispensing justice at all levels to respond to the different constraints and priorities of men and women. Such action requires political will and the determination to address the power relations and abusive practices that can undermine the effectiveness of the legal system.

Expanding Women's Access to Finance

A repeated finding in this book is that the line of business, its size, and its formality are more important drivers than gender in access to formal finance. Of real concern is the extent to which access to finance constrains choice—not only the choice to become an entrepreneur, but the choice of business line, size, and formality. With access to collateral, education, and prior work experience as significant predictors of initial bank loans, women are at a disadvantage. This cycle can then perpetuate itself: if women are less likely to get loans, they may be more likely to enter less-remunerative lines of business, and so will be less likely to get credit and less likely to expand their business. In the longer term, breaking the cycle involves tackling underlying gaps in legal rights and in access to human capital, but some more-immediate steps can also benefit women.

Measures to improve women's access to finance include the following:

- Enriching women's human capital. This underlies the agenda of expanding women's access to finance.
- Improving property rights for women. This will strengthen women's control over assets and their capacity to provide collateral for bank loans.
- Building property registries that include movable property. This will also strengthen women's ability to use movable property as collateral.
- Setting up credit registries that capture women's credit history and repayment records in microfinance. This will benefit women disproportionately, given their greater reliance on microfinance.
- Directing financing mechanisms to women, including microfinance and mobile banking.

Enriching Managerial and Financial Skills

Formal education is important for building women's human capital, but other dimensions also matter, especially in building business-specific skills and capacity. Schooling and management training are effective in raising the productivity of both women's and men's enterprises, though the benefits of a more entrepreneurial background appear greater for men. Much work is still needed to expand even rudimentary knowledge of financial concepts to the wider population, who could benefit from them in running businesses.

Key activities to build managerial and financial skills among women include the following:

- Encouraging opportunities for sharing experiences among businesswomen
- Developing a stronger cadre of female role models in business

- Strengthening women's management training and access to consulting services
- Pairing financial literacy and business skills training with access to finance; tailoring programs to increase women's participation (for example, choice of time, location, provision of child care services)
- Promoting mentoring and other networking opportunities to facilitate the development of business contacts, marketing opportunities, and product development

Strengthening Women's Voices in Business Environment Reforms

Measures to strengthen women's voices in business-climate reform include the following:

- Animating women business owners and associations to join PPDs
- Encouraging greater participation of women in business associations
- Building the capacity of business associations to provide better services to members and to contribute more to advocacy for policy reforms
- Carrying out a systematic, gender-informed analysis of business environment obstacles to highlight issues of concern to businesswomen, and then integrating this analysis into dialogue and policy making
- Strengthening the presence of women in PPD institutions and structures, and building the capacity of women to influence the agenda of the PPD itself

Areas for Research

Gaps in the data hamper researchers' ability to undertake gender-disaggregated analyses. Two gaps are particularly relevant. The first relates to the need to know more about how constraints in the investment climate, particularly in access to finance, shape the entry decision. Data at the individual (as opposed to household) level on constraints facing those who do not decide to become entrepreneurs are scarce. One solution would be to add relevant questions to household surveys.

The second relates to transitions between entrepreneurship and wage employment. Research done on Latin America shows that there can be a fair amount of mobility between the two, for men and single women. Much less is known about these transitions in Sub-Saharan Africa. Panel surveys of individuals and their labor force decisions could significantly contribute to narrowing this gap.

Notes

1. See ILO 2002 for a broader discussion of definitions and data availability on work in the informal sector.

2. The companion volume is *Empowering Women: Legal Rights and Economic Opportunities in Africa* (Hallward-Driemeier and Hasan 2012). The database, cited in the overview below and throughout the volume, is M. Hallward-Driemeier, T. Hasan, M. Blackden, J. Kamangu, and E. Lobti, Women's Legal and Economic Empowerment Database.

3. Some of these decisions may not actually represent true "choices"; where wage employment is scarce, entrepreneurship may be the only realistic option.

References

Arbache, J. S., A. Kolev, and E. Filipiak, eds. 2010. *Gender Disparities in Africa's Labor Market*. Washington, DC: World Bank.

Aterido, R., T. Beck, and L. Iacovone. Forthcoming. "Gender and Finance in Sub-Saharan Africa: Are Women Disadvantaged?" *World Development*.

Aterido, R., and M. Hallward-Driemeier. 2011. "Whose Business Is It Anyway?" *Small Business Economics* 37 (4): 443–64.

Ayyagari, M., T. Beck, and A. Demirgüç-Kunt. 2007. "Small and Medium Enterprises across the Globe." *Small Business Economics* 29: 415–34.

Bardasi, E., M. Blackden, and J. C. Guzman. 2007. "Gender, Entrepreneurship, and Competitiveness." In *Africa Competitiveness Report 2007*, edited by World Economic Forum, African Development Bank, and World Bank, 69–86. Washington, DC: World Economic Forum, African Development Bank, and World Bank.

Bigsten, A., P. Collier, S. Dercon, M. Fafchamps, B. Gauthier, J. W. Gunning, A. Oduro, R. Oostendorp, C. Patillo, M. Söderbom, F. Teal, and A. Zeufack. 2003. "Credit Constraints in Manufacturing Enterprises in Africa." *Journal of African Economies* 12 (1): 104–25.

Bigsten, A., and M. Gebreeyesus. 2007. "The Small, the Young, and the Productive: Determinants of Manufacturing Firm Growth in Ethiopia." *Economic Development and Cultural Change* 55 (4): 813–40.

Bigsten, A., and M. Söderbom. 2006. "What Have We Learned from a Decade of Manufacturing Enterprise Surveys in Africa?" *World Bank Research Observer* 21 (2): 241–65.

Blau, D. 1985. "Self-Employment and Self-Selection in Developing Country Labor Markets." *Southern Economic Journal* 52 (2): 351–63.

Bloom, N., and J. Van Reenen. 2007. "Measuring and Explaining Management Practices Across Firms and Countries." *Quarterly Journal of Economics* 122 (4): 1351–408.

———. 2010. "Why Do Management Practices Differ across Firms and Countries?" *Journal of Economic Perspectives* 24 (1): 203–24.

Bruhn, M., D. Karlan, and A. Schoar. 2010. "What Capital Is Missing in Developing Countries?" *American Economic Review* 100 (2): 629–33.

Bruhn, M., and B. Zia. 2011. "Stimulating Managerial Capital in Emerging Markets: The Impact of Business and Financial Literacy for Young Entrepreneurs." Working Paper, World Bank, Washington, DC.

de Mel, S., D. McKenzie, and C. Woodruff. 2009. "Are Women More Credit Constrained? Experimental Evidence on Gender and Microenterprise Returns." *American Economic Journal: Applied Economics* 1 (3): 1–32.

Djankov, S., Y. Qian, G. Roland, and E. Zhuravskaya. 2007. "What Makes a Successful Entrepreneur? Evidence from Brazil." Working Paper 104, Center for Economic and Financial Research, Moscow.

Fafchamps, M. 2000. "Ethnicity and Credit in African Manufacturing." *Journal of Development Economics* 61(1): 205–35.

Fafchamps, M., M. Söderbom, and N. Benhassine. 2009. "Wage Gaps and Job Sorting in African Manufacturing." *Journal of African Economies* 18 (5): 824–68.

Gajigo, O., and M. Hallward-Driemeier. 2010. "Entrepreneurship among New Entrepreneurs." Working paper, World Bank, Washington, DC.

Hallward-Driemeier, M., and O. Gajigo. 2011. "Strengthening Economic Rights and Women's Occupational Choice: The Impact of Reforming Ethiopia's Family Law." Paper presented at Centre for the Study of African Economics annual conference, St. Catherine's College, Oxford, March 20–22.

Hallward-Driemeier, M., and T. Hasan. 2012. *Empowering Women: Legal Rights and Economic Opportunities in Africa.* Washington, DC: World Bank and Agence Française de Développement.

Hallward-Driemeier, M., and A. Rasteletti. 2010. "Women's and Men's Entrepreneurship in Africa." Working paper, World Bank, Washington, DC.

Herzberg, B., and A. Wright. 2006. *The PPD Handbook: A Toolkit for Business Environment Reformers.* Washington, DC: World Bank.

ILO (International Labour Organization). 2002. "Women and Men in the Informal Economy: A Statistical Picture." Gender and Employment Sector, ILO, Geneva.

Klapper, L., and S. Parker. 2010. "Gender and the Business Environment for New Firm Creation." *World Bank Research Observer* 26 (2): 237–57.

Kolev, A., and N. Sirven. 2010. "Gender Disparities in Africa's Labor Markets: A Cross-Country Comparison Using Standardized Survey Data." In *Gender Disparities in Africa's Labor Market*, edited by J. S. Arbache, A. Kolev, and E. Filipiak, 23–54. Washington, DC: World Bank.

Liedholm, C., and D. Mead. 1999. *Small Enterprises and Economic Development: The Dynamics of Micro and Small Enterprises.* London: Routledge.

Mansuri, G., and X. Giné. 2011. "Money or Ideas? A Field Experiment on Constraints to Entrepreneurship in Rural Pakistan." Working paper, World Bank, Washington, DC.

McPherson, M. A. 1996. "Growth of Micro and Small Enterprises in Southern Africa." *Journal of Development Economics* 48 (March): 235–77.

Mead, D. C., and C. Liedholm. 1998. "The Dynamics of Micro and Small Enterprises in Developing Countries." *World Development* 26 (1): 61–74.

Minniti, Maria. 2009. "Gender Issues in Entrepreneurship." *Foundations and Trends in Entrepreneurship* 5 (7–8): 497–621.

Parker, S. C. 2004. *The Economics of Self-Employment and Entrepreneurship.* Cambridge: Cambridge University Press.

Parker, S. C., and M. van Praag. 2006. "Schooling, Capital Constraints, and Entrepreneurial Performance." *Journal of Business and Economic Statistics* 24 (4): 416–31.

Simavi, S., C. Manuel, and M. Blackden. 2010. *Gender Dimensions of Investment Climate Reform: A Guide for Policy Makers and Practitioners.* Washington, DC: World Bank.

Sinha, A., and R. Kanbur. 2012. "Informality: Concepts, Facts, and Models." *Journal of Applied Economic Research* 6 (2): 91–102.

Sleuwaegen, L., and M. Goedhuys. 2002. "Growth of Firms in Developing Countries, Evidence from Côte d'Ivoire." *Journal of Development Economics* 68 (June): 117–35.

Söderbom, M. 2012. "Firm Size and Structural Change: A Case Study of Ethiopia." *Journal of African Economies* 21: 126–51.

Tamanaha, B., C. Sage, and M. Woolcock, eds. 2012. *Legal Pluralism and Development: Scholars and Practitioners in Dialogue.* New York: Cambridge University Press.

Tybout, J. R. 2000. "Manufacturing Firms in Developing Countries: How Well Do They Do, and Why?" *Journal of Economic Literature* 28 (March): 11–44.

Van Biesebroeck, J. 2005. "Firm Size Matters: Growth and Productivity Growth in African Manufacturing." *Economic Development and Cultural Change* 53 (3): 545–83.

Van der Sluis, J., M. van Praag, and W. Vijverberg. 2008 "Education and Entrepreneurship Selection and Performance: A Review of the Literature." *Journal of Economic Surveys* 22 (5): 795–841.

World Bank. 2004. *World Development Report 2005: A Better Investment Climate for Everyone.* New York: Oxford University Press.

———. 2011. *World Development Report 2012: Gender Equality and Development.* New York: Oxford University Press.

———. 2012. *World Development Report 2013: Jobs.* New York: Oxford University Press.

Part I

Where Women and Men Work

We start with the facts—laying out the patterns of where women and men work. The first chapters put entrepreneurship in the context of other employment categories across regions. They also examine the gender patterns across types of enterprises, showing the extent to which each gender operates in larger firms, the formal sector, and higher-value-added activities. Women are disproportionately active in the informal sector, smaller firms, and traditional sectors. But there is significant variation in these patterns across countries and across groups of women within a country. These gender patterns, and their variation, need to be explained, with an eye to enabling more women to shift into higher-value-added activities.

Chapter 1

Self-Employed, Employers, and Wage Earners in the Formal and Informal Sectors

Development is about realizing potential. Yet too often, obstacles or a lack of access to key resources makes realizing potential impossible. The problem is compounded when some groups face greater systemic hurdles than others. The group of interest in this book is women, but there are others as well.[1]

Not all women are disadvantaged. It is precisely by seeing how and where women succeed and by looking at variations in gender gaps that we can identify the conditions and policy levers to expand women's opportunities more broadly.

Women's economic empowerment is a central development goal. Women have been working to expand their ability to earn and control assets, individually and collectively, for a very long time. These efforts gained a boost from the international community in recent years. Women's empowerment is recognized as the third Millennium Development Goal; in 2012, the World Bank dedicated its annual flagship, the *World Development Report*, to gender equality and development (World Bank 2011);[2] and the Nobel Prize for Peace was awarded to three pioneering women (two from Liberia) working for peace in their countries' fights for democracy and for greater opportunities for women.

This book focuses attention on Sub-Saharan Africa, and specifically on entrepreneurship in the nonagricultural sector. The issue of gender disparities in economic opportunities in the region has been studied in terms of gaps in wage income and in job sorting in wage work (Arbache, Kolev, and Filipiak 2010; Fafchamps, Söderbom, and Benhassine 2009; Kolev and Sirven 2010). Other cross-country work has looked at entrepreneurship in Sub-Saharan Africa, but rarely with much attention paid to gender (Bigsten and Söderbom 2006; Nichter and Goldmark 2009; Tybout 2000; World Bank 2004). But entrepreneurship is where women in Sub-Saharan Africa are most active outside of agriculture. So it is critical to look at entrepreneurship to understand the extent of gender

BOX 1.1

Expanding Opportunities

Strengthening women's economic opportunities has both an inherent value—all people should have the same chance to reap the rewards of their efforts and investments and be able to pursue income-generating opportunities—and an instrumental value. Realizing the potential of all people contributes to higher standards of living and productivity, and to a vibrant society.

This book is about entrepreneurs, the self-employed as well as employers. Expanding their opportunities could mean improving the returns in their current business and helping them move into higher-return businesses, but might also mean moving out of entrepreneurship into other types of employment, namely wage employment. Transitions into and out of entrepreneurship are beyond the scope of this book, but the book does compare patterns of entrepreneurship with those of wage earners to show the likely trade-offs and ability to move from one to the other.

Some entrepreneurs seek to work independently, see opportunities in new ways of doing business, and want to be their own boss. Indeed, such entrepreneurs are an important source of innovation and productivity growth—and a source of employment for others. Providing an enabling environment for these entrepreneurs is indeed part of the agenda. However, for those who are entrepreneurs out of necessity rather than choice, the need to succeed is also great. Addressing their constraints and expanding their access to higher-return activities will also impact poverty reduction and job creation.

---

disparities in economic opportunities, determine the underlying reasons for these gender patterns, and develop an agenda to enable more women to realize their full potential (see box 1.1).

Gender Patterns in Entrepreneurship: Laying Out the Facts

To expand women's economic opportunities in Sub-Saharan Africa, we have to know where women are currently economically active. This chapter describes how many women work (box 1.2) in the region and where, comparing the patterns with men. It also compares Sub-Saharan Africa with other regions. Two broad sets of patterns are examined. The first concerns employment categories: in the labor market, unemployed, wage earner, self-employed, or employer. The focus of this book, nonagricultural entrepreneurship (self-employed plus employer), is often discussed relative to wage employment. The second set of patterns, discussed in chapter 2, concerns the types of enterprises run by entrepreneurs such as their formality, size, and industry. Mapping the gender gaps in

---

BOX 1.2

_____

Types of "Work"

The International Labour Organization has developed standardized definitions of six categories to capture people's employment status. The first distinction is whether or not someone is "in the labor force," referring to all those who are engaged in economic activities. Among those participating in the labor force, there are five key categories: the self-employed, employers, wage earners, unpaid workers, and the unemployed. "Entrepreneurs" are the self-employed and the employers.

We follow this classification, with one exception. We make a distinction between agricultural and nonagricultural employment activities, focusing on the latter. Thus we make no distinctions between those in the agriculture sector (combining those who are wage earners, unpaid workers, self-employed, and employers). The categories used in this book are shown in figure B1.2.1.

Figure B1.2.1 Typology of Employment Status Categories

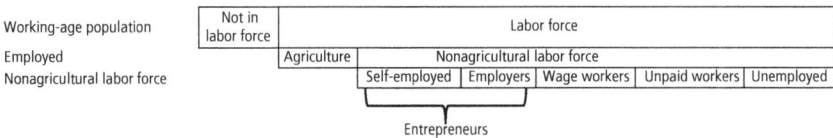

Working-age population	Not in labor force	Labor force				
Employed		Agriculture	Nonagricultural labor force			
Nonagricultural labor force			Self-employed	Employers	Wage workers	Unpaid workers	Unemployed

Entrepreneurs

---

participation rates helps identify the constraints that women face and the scope for expanding their opportunities.

The data show, overwhelmingly, that women in Sub-Saharan Africa are active in the labor force, and that their participation rates are higher than in any other region. And most women working outside of agriculture are entrepreneurs.

Is this good news? Does it signal that the private sector is dynamic or that few alternative opportunities are available? It is critical to look within entrepreneurial activities to answer these questions.[3]

Several gender-disaggregated patterns hold across almost all the region's countries: women are far more likely to be self-employed than to be either employers or wage earners (and less likely than men to be employers or wage earners). Among entrepreneurs, the share of employers remains fairly constant across countries, as does the share of women among employers. Across the Sub-Saharan African region, fully half of those who are self-employed are women, yet only a quarter of employers are women. Of entrepreneurs, women are more likely to be running small informal firms in lower-value-added activities.

These patterns strongly suggest that strengthening women's economic opportunities is not about expanding entrepreneurship. Instead it is about tackling constraints on women's abilities and incentives to expand their businesses and move into higher-value-added activities—in short, the agenda is about shifting the composition of entrepreneurial activities.

A variety of country studies finds similar patterns of women's relative concentration in smaller firms, in the informal sector, and in traditional activities (for example, Bigsten and others 2003; ILO 2002; Mammen and Paxon 2000; McPherson 1996; Mead 1991, 1994; Mead and Liedholm 1998; Parker 2004; Sinha and Kanbur 2012). This finding is important because, if one is to be self-employed or an employer, further characteristics of the enterprise are correlated with opportunity. Larger enterprises, formal enterprises, and higher-value-added industries tend to be more productive—including in developing countries and in Sub-Saharan Africa (Bigsten and Söderbom 2006; Tybout 2000; World Bank 2004, 2012). Thus it is important to look at gender gaps across these three dimensions—size, formality, and industry—and to examine why these gender-differentiated patterns of entrepreneurial activity exist. At the same time, different ways of defining and measuring women's ownership of enterprises affect the results and have different policy implications.

A central challenge in examining entrepreneurship is that entrepreneurs compose a wide spectrum of individuals in their abilities, motivations, and outside options, and that entrepreneurs are engaged in a large gamut of types of enterprises.

Some women are entrepreneurs by choice, pursuing an opportunity with a goal of expanding their business. Others are entrepreneurs by default or necessity. Faced with the need for income and the inability to find wage employment, they run their own business as an option of last resort. They may not have any particular aptitude in running a business or any motivation beyond meeting subsistence needs. The data do not make it easy, however, to distinguish "opportunity" from "necessity" entrepreneurs.[4]

To set the stage for understanding the key stylized facts about the opportunities being pursued, this chapter presents labor force participation rates by region, including agriculture, and then looks at the prevalence of the self-employed, employers, and wage earners in nonagricultural activities. Both the self-employed and employers can include necessity and opportunity entrepreneurs—and can represent successful and unsuccessful enterprises. But employers are more likely to be opportunity entrepreneurs and possess a demonstrated ability to expand a business; the self-employed are more likely to have a larger share of necessity entrepreneurs, particularly in countries at lower levels of development.

Within these two groups, further characteristics of the enterprise are correlated with opportunity. Larger enterprises, formal enterprises, and higher-value-added sectors tend to be more productive. The next chapter focuses on gender gaps by type of enterprise along three dimensions: size, formality, and industry.

This mapping exercise then sets up the rest of the book, which examines what factors, at the country or individual level, can help explain these gender-differentiated patterns of entrepreneurship.

The early chapters draw primarily on enterprise and household surveys to provide a map of women's and men's involvement as self-employed entrepreneurs, as employers, or as wage earners (box 1.3 and appendix A). Later chapters use this information to examine the factors associated with the gender patterns of entrepreneurship discussed here. One aim is to illuminate the policy levers that could shift these patterns of what women entrepreneurs do, so as to expand economic opportunities for women.

BOX 1.3

Primary Sources of Data Used in This Book

Four types of surveys of enterprises are included in this work. All were administered by the World Bank, with respondents sampled on the basis of the population of enterprises.

Enterprise Surveys.[a] The Enterprise Surveys cover stratified random samples of registered firms in key industrial centers in a country. They also cover both manufacturing and services, including information on the owner of the enterprise, enterprise performance measures, and measures of constraints facing the enterprise. There are Enterprise Survey data for 37 countries in Sub-Saharan Africa.

Enterprise Surveys—microenterprises. Very similar to the previous instrument, they cover 25 countries in Sub-Saharan Africa. The sampling differs in that it targets microfirms that are generally not registered; 98 percent of the firms sampled have five employees or fewer. In the analysis, the data are labeled "informal."

Enterprise Surveys—gender module. The gender module was one of two new surveys carried out for this study. For five countries that had completed an Enterprise Survey (Ghana, Mali, Mozambique, Senegal, and Zambia), we fielded an additional module to capture more information on the background of the entrepreneur, the motivation for starting a business, the means of starting or acquiring a business, and indicators of management techniques. The module also refined measures for the gender of both the principal owner and the person running the business, with this measure (but not the whole module) available for a sixth country, South Africa.

Surveys of new entrepreneurs. The second new survey carried out for this study was administered to new entrepreneurs in four countries (Côte d'Ivoire, Kenya, Nigeria, and Senegal). The survey covered firms in the formal and informal sectors (distinguished by

—Continued

BOX 1.3 *continued*

whether the enterprise is registered, not the extent of its compliance with tax laws or other regulations). It collected detailed background information on the entrepreneur, as well as the motivation for starting a business, the means of starting or acquiring a business, and the indicators of management techniques used. It also included some additional measures on the constraints of setting up a business.

The book also draws on two sets of surveys that sampled households and that were administered by national statistical offices.

Household surveys and labor force surveys. These have been compiled for 39 countries in Sub-Saharan Africa and 101 globally, drawing from each country's own national survey. They are not strictly comparable, because countries use different questionnaires (though most adhere to the International Labour Organization definitions of labor) and somewhat different sampling strategies. But they have been standardized for a core set of questions to allow cross-country patterns to be examined. These data provide the information of individuals' participation in the different employment categories.

Household surveys—enterprise modules. Those in the household who say they have an enterprise were asked additional questions in 20 Sub-Saharan African countries. These data can be used to examine firm performance (particularly for more informal businesses, such as those operating out of the house and those with household members working in them). The name does not mean that all the enterprises are run out of the home; indeed, many are not. It means that the basis for the sampling is the household.

Appendix A provides more details, including country coverage, and outlines the strengths and limitations of the different data sets.

a. "Enterprise Surveys" refers to the specific set of enterprise surveys run by the World Bank (see http://www.enterprisesurveys.org), and the term is therefore capitalized throughout.

Gender Differences in Labor Force Participation by Region

This section looks at household data to examine gender-disaggregated rates of entrepreneurship and to explore how entrepreneurship fits into the broader patterns of labor force participation. It begins by examining how Sub-Saharan Africa compares with other regions, and then examines how patterns vary by income.

Labor force participation is subdivided into five employment categories, with a sixth variable reflecting nonparticipation in the labor force. All the data look at individuals of working age, 16–60 years old, and give, for women and men, the average share of the population in each geographic region that is in each of the major employment categories (figure 1.1).[5] Employers are clearly a small share of the overall population for both women and men. Self-employment represents a larger share.

Figure 1.1 Women's Participation Rates Are Highest in Sub-Saharan Africa

a. Where women work

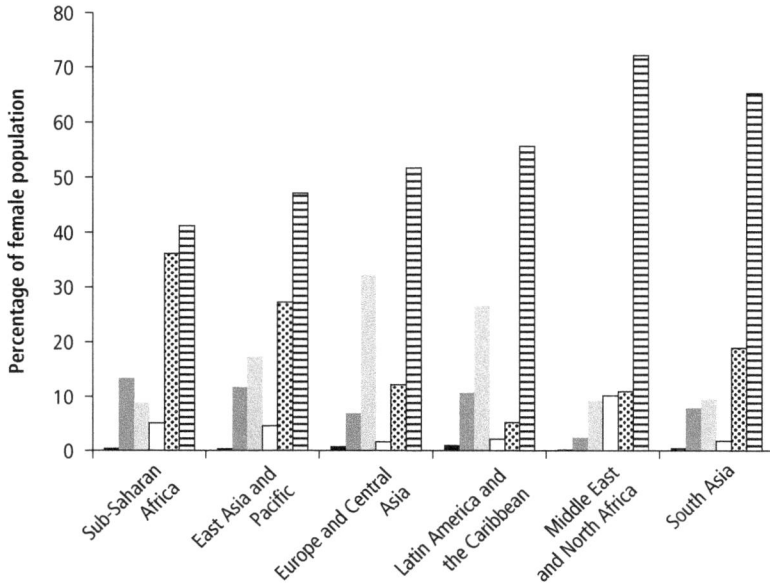

b. Where men work

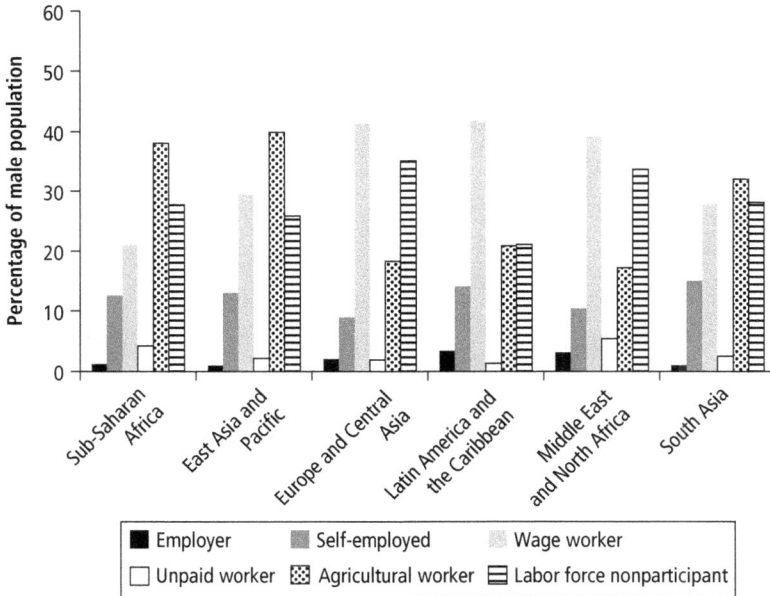

Legend:
- ■ Employer
- ▨ Self-employed
- ▨ Wage worker
- □ Unpaid worker
- ▨ Agricultural worker
- ☰ Labor force nonparticipant

Source: National household and labor force surveys for 101 low- and middle-income economies, most recent years (2000–10).

Entrepreneurship rates are affected by the overall shares of the population in agriculture or not participating in the labor force. Women are less likely than men to be in the labor force in every region. Men's labor force participation both is higher than women's and exhibits less variation across regions. Women's participation is highest in Sub-Saharan Africa (equivalently, nonparticipation is lowest there), and the gender gap in participation is lowest.

Agriculture is the most common labor activity in Sub-Saharan Africa, with little difference by gender. Excluding agricultural activities sees labor force participation fall the most there, to 25 percent for women (figure 1.2). In nonagricultural labor, only South Asia and the Middle East and North Africa have lower rates of female participation, and Sub-Saharan Africa no longer has the smallest gender gap in participation.

Entrepreneurship: Sub-Saharan Africa in a Global Context

Within nonagricultural employment, in the categories of self-employment, being an employer, or wage employment, Sub-Saharan Africa shows the highest

Figure 1.2 Sub-Saharan Africa Has the Biggest Difference between Women's Overall Labor Force Participation and Women's Nonagricultural Labor Force Participation

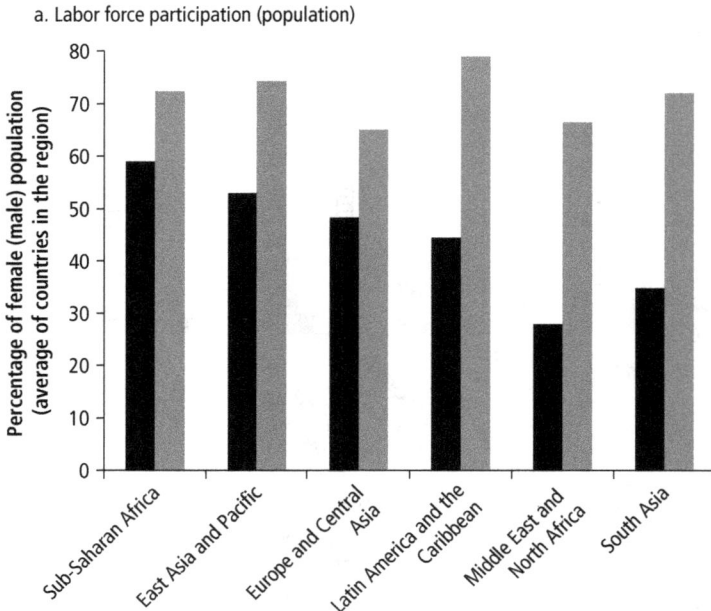

a. Labor force participation (population)

Figure 1.2 *(continued)*

b. Labor force participation in nonagricultural activities

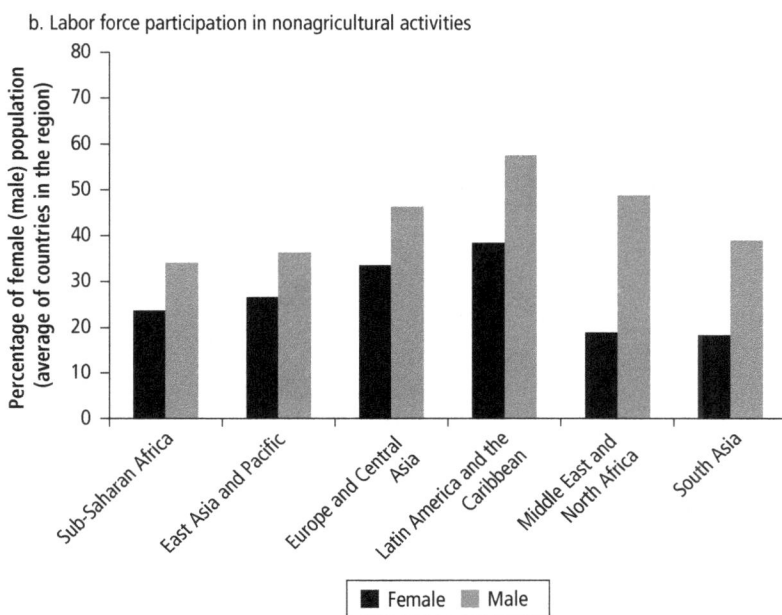

Source: National household and labor force surveys for 101 low- and middle-income economies, most recent years (2000–10).

self-employment rate and the lowest wage employment rate of all regions.[6] Three patterns of gender differences emerge:

- Sub-Saharan Africa is the only region where women's self-employment is more common than wage employment.
- The gender gap in the share in wage employment is the highest in Sub-Saharan Africa.
- Rates of being an employer are low across all regions, with variations greater for men than women. Among employers, the female share is generally 25–30 percent.

Self-Employment

Within nonagricultural employment, women's participation in self-employment is by far the highest in Sub-Saharan Africa (figure 1.3). Just more than half of all women are self-employed there.

Women represent half of those among the nonagricultural self-employed in Sub-Saharan Africa and the East Asia and Pacific region, but only 20 percent in the Middle East and North Africa (figure 1.4).[7]

Figure 1.3 Women's Nonagricultural Self-Employment Rate Is Highest in Sub-Saharan Africa

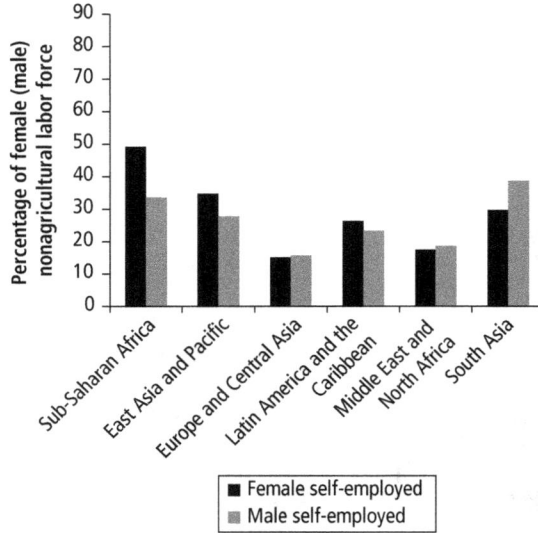

Source: National household and labor force surveys for 101 low- and middle-income economies, most recent years (2000–10).
Note: The figure shows the share within the nonagricultural labor force that is self-employed.

Figure 1.4 The Sub-Saharan Africa Region Leads in the Share of Nonagricultural Self-Employed Who Are Women

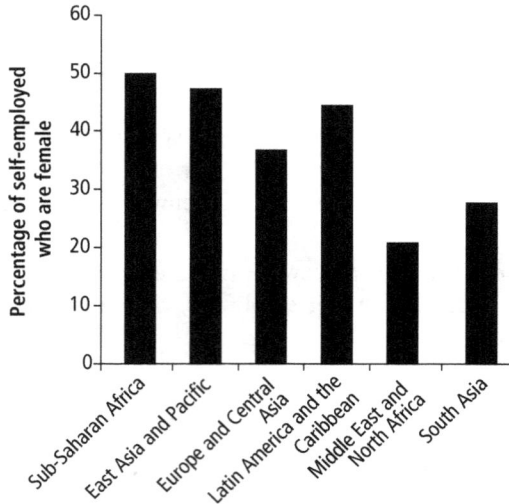

Source: National household and labor force surveys for 101 low- and middle-income economies, most recent years (2000–10).
Note: Analysis excludes agriculture.

Employers

The rates of being an employer are far smaller than those of self-employment (figure 1.5, which is not to scale with the previous charts). They vary considerably for men across regions (the rates in Latin America and the Caribbean and in the Middle East and North Africa are around twice those in Sub-Saharan Africa and East Asia and Pacific). For women the share is often half that of men, with less variation across regions.

A smaller share of employers is made up of women (25–30 percent); there is relatively little variation in this pattern except for in the Middle East and North Africa, where the share is 9 percent (figure 1.6).

Wage Employment

The share of wage employment, particularly for women, is lower in Sub-Saharan Africa than in any other region (figure 1.7). The share for women is more than twice as high in Europe and Central Asia as in Sub-Saharan Africa. The gender

Figure 1.5 Globally, Far Fewer Entrepreneurs Are Employers Than Are Self-Employed

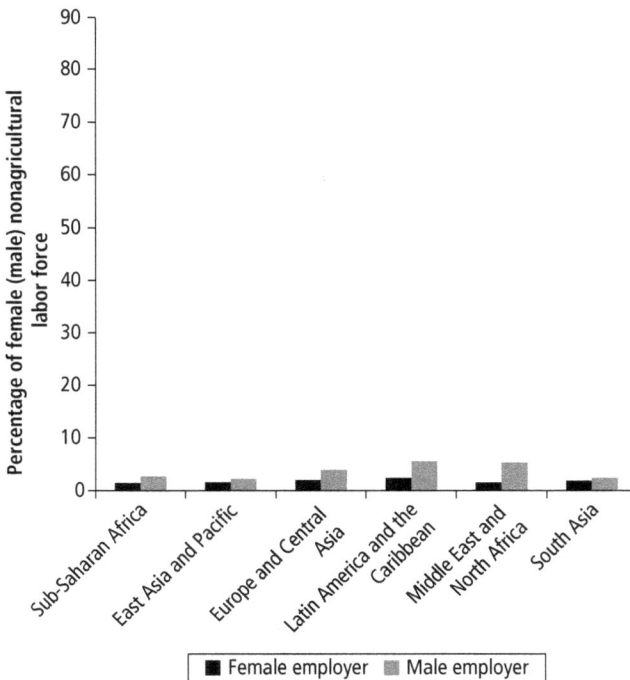

Source: National household and labor force surveys for 101 low- and middle-income economies, most recent years (2000–10).
Note: Analysis excludes agriculture.

Figure 1.6 The Share of Female Employers Is Lower Than for Self-Employment, but with Very Similar Rates for Five of the Six Regions

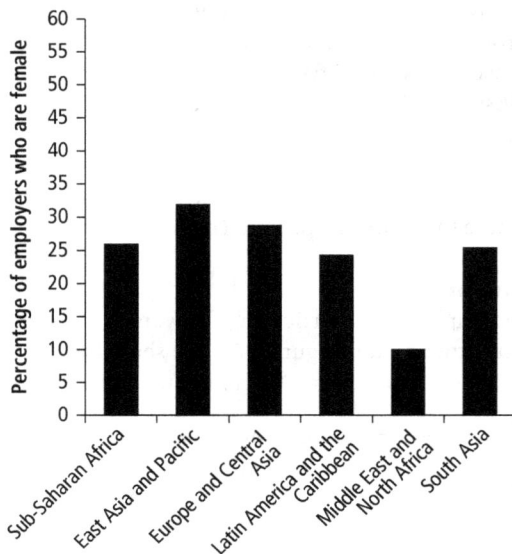

Source: National household and labor force surveys for 101 low- and middle-income economies, most recent years (2000–10).
Note: Analysis excludes agriculture. See figure 1.4 for the comparison with the self-employed.

gap is also widest in Sub-Saharan Africa. (Capturing gender gaps is discussed in box 1.4.)

Women are also a smaller share of wage earners than men, although wide variation exists across regions (figure 1.8).

The data show that the need to expand opportunities for entrepreneurs is particularly pressing in Sub-Saharan Africa. Entrepreneurship plays a bigger role in Sub-Saharan Africa than in any other region. Thus improving opportunities for entrepreneurs would affect a large portion of the population—many of whom do not have alternative forms of employment available. It is the region where the smallest share of the labor force is in nonagricultural wage employment. The gender dimension is also particularly striking, with gender gaps in wage employment the highest in Sub-Saharan Africa. If wage employment is scarce, running a business is the primary way of earning income.

"Running a business" encompasses a large range of activities, some of which are more likely to be successful and to earn higher returns than others. Thus it is important to look at the microdata on the types of enterprises women and men run. These data are discussed in the next chapter.

Figure 1.7 Of All Regions, Sub-Saharan Africa Has the Lowest Rate and Widest Gender Gap for Wage Employment

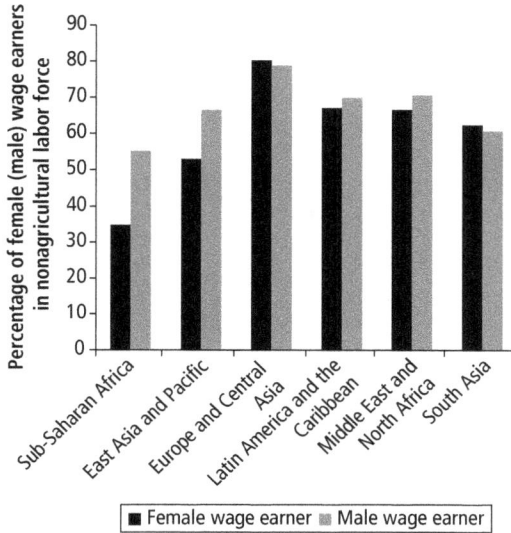

Female wage earner   Male wage earner

Source: National household and labor force surveys for 101 low- and middle-income economies, most recent years (2000–10).
Note: Analysis excludes agriculture.

Figure 1.8 The Regions Show a Wide Variation in the Share of Female Wage Earners

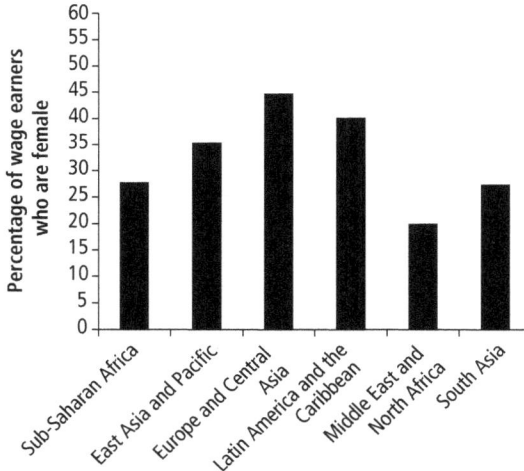

Source: National household and labor force surveys for 101 low- and middle-income economies, most recent years (2000–10).
Note: Analysis excludes agriculture.

BOX 1.4

How to Capture Gender Gaps

The gap of gender concentration *within* employment categories looks at the share of women compared with the share of men in that employment category.

For example, the gap of gender concentration *within* self-employment equals

$$\left(\frac{Self\text{-}employed\ women}{All\ women\ in\ nolabor\ force} - \frac{Self\text{-}employed\ men}{All\ men\ in\ nolabor\ force} \right),$$

where *nolabor* stands for nonagricultural labor.

Figure B1.4.1 graphs the share of men against the share of women in self-employment. If women and men sorted in the same proportions into the employment categories, the countries would line up along the 45 degree line. To the extent countries are below the line, women sort disproportionately into that employment category (and above the line, men). Figures B1.4.2 and B1.4.3 show the differences in the shares of women and shares of men as employers and as wage earners—or the vertical distance from the 45 degree line (those above the line are "negative" gaps, that is, women's shares are lower than men's).

In all three categories almost all countries are skewed the same way: there is a higher share of women among the self-employed, and higher shares of men among employers and wage earners.

Figure B1.4.1 Gender Gap in Self-Employment

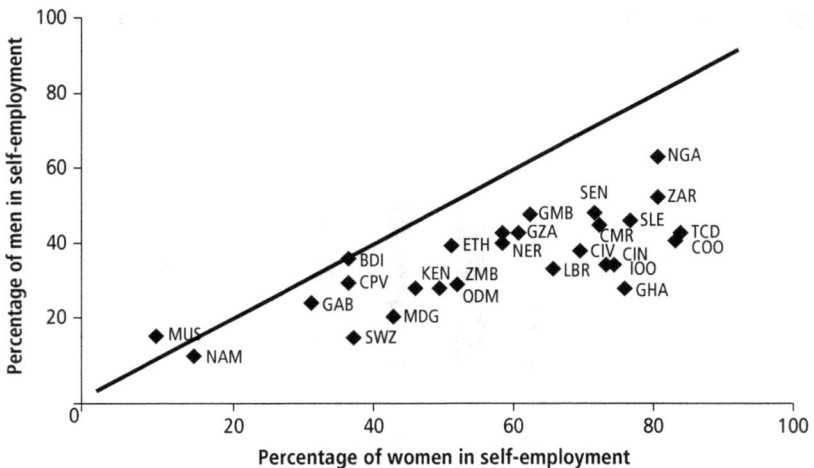

Source: National household and labor force surveys for 34 countries in Sub-Saharan Africa, most recent years (2000–10).
Note: Analysis excludes agriculture.

Figure B1.4.2 Gender Gap in Being an Employer

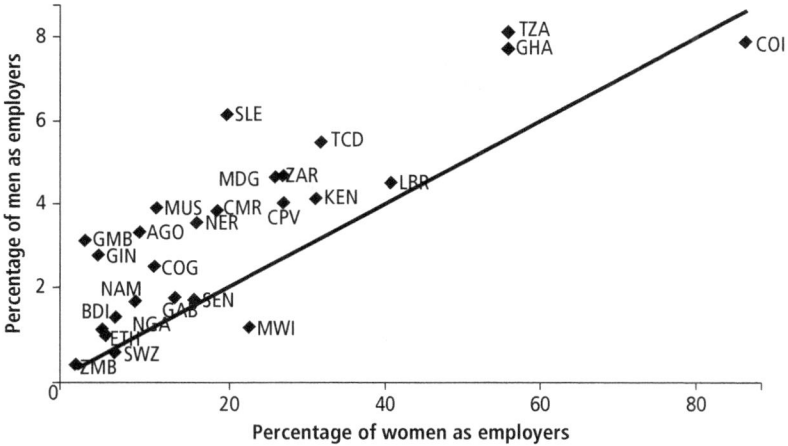

Source: National household and labor force surveys for 34 countries in Sub-Saharan Africa, most recent years (2000–10).
Note: Analysis excludes agriculture.

Figure B1.4.3 Gender Gap in Wage Workers

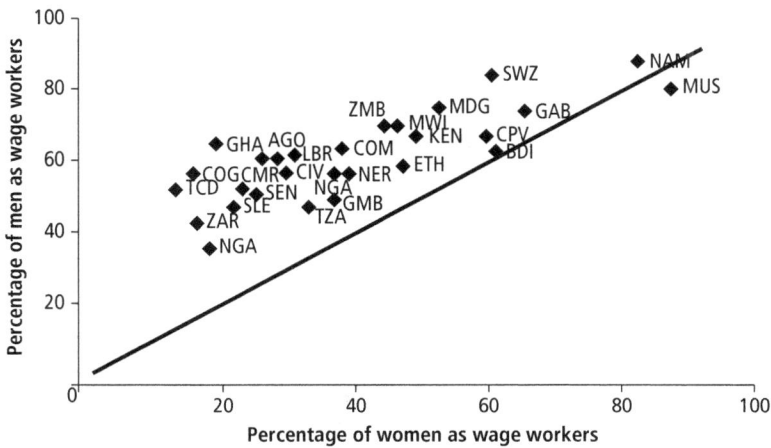

Source: National household and labor force surveys for 34 countries in Sub-Saharan Africa, most recent years (2000–10).
Note: Analysis excludes agriculture.

—Continued

BOX 1.4 *continued*

But if one compares the first two categories—that is, the gap in gender shares in self-employment versus the gender gap in being an employer—there does not appear to be a striking pattern (figure B1.4.4). It is not the case that, where there is a larger gender gap in self-employment, there is a larger—or smaller—gap in being an employer. This finding is important to the discussion in chapter 3, because it indicates that the two types of entrepreneurship are being driven by different sets of factors.

Figure B1.4.4 Degree of Correlation in Self-Employed and Employers

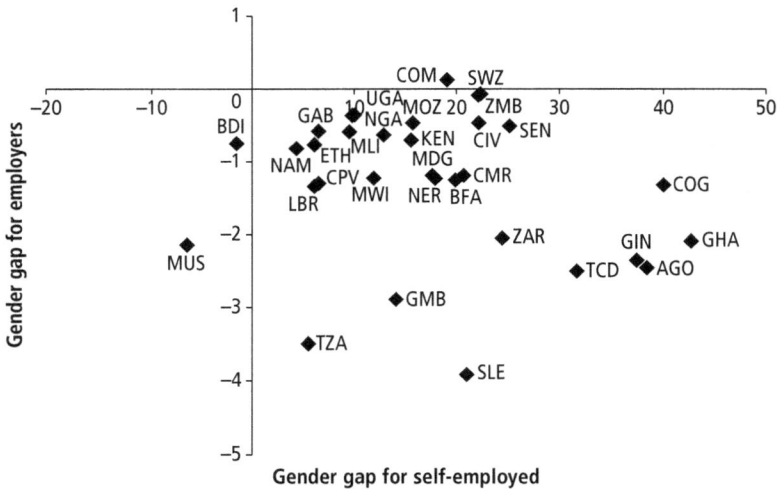

Source: National household and labor force surveys for 34 countries in Sub-Saharan Africa, most recent years (2000–10).
Note: Analysis excludes agriculture.

Notes

1. Other groups can be disadvantaged because of race, ethnicity, religious affiliation, disability, language, geographic location, sexual orientation, and so forth. Studies often find that women within these groups face particularly difficult challenges.
2. That work builds on a World Bank (2002) report, which provides a detailed review of the literature on gender equality and development, focusing on women's rights, access to resources, and voice.
3. There is a further debate as to the broader prospects for Africa's growth. The literature from the 1980s and 1990s was largely pessimistic. Higher growth rates in recent years have served to raise expectations, although growth rates vary across the region

and diversification remains a major challenge in most countries (Chuhan-Pole and Angwafo 2011; Collier and Gunning 1999; Tybout 2000; World Economic Forum, African Development Bank, and World Bank 2011).

4. More-recent survey data on backgrounds and motivations of entrepreneurs provide some insights, however (see chapter 3).

5. "Unemployed" is the omitted category. It is negligible in Sub-Saharan Africa.

6. We look at paid employment rather than labor force participation, as we cannot determine what sector the unemployed may be seeking work in. Unpaid workers are also not included.

7. The difference between figures 1.3 and 1.4 shows the stark effect of relative gender differences in nonagricultural labor force participation rates. For the Middle East and North Africa, for example, almost equal shares of men and women are self-employed (figure 1.3), but this translates into women being only a fifth of all the self-employed in the region (figure 1.4), given the region's wide gender gap in participation.

References

Arbache, J. S., A. Kolev, and E. Filipiak, eds. 2010. *Gender Disparities in Africa's Labor Market*. Washington, DC: World Bank.

Bigsten, A., P. Collier, S. Dercon, M. Fafchamps, B. Gauthier, J. W. Gunning, A. Oduro, R. Oostendorp, C. Patillo, M. Söderbom, F. Teal, and A. Zeufack. 2003. "Credit Constraints in Manufacturing Enterprises in Africa." *Journal of African Economies* 12 (1): 104–25.

Bigsten, A., and M. Söderbom. 2006. "What Have We Learned from a Decade of Manufacturing Enterprise Surveys in Africa?" *World Bank Research Observer* 21 (2): 241–65.

Chuhan-Pole, P., and M. Angwafo, eds. 2011. *Yes Africa Can: Success Stories from a Dynamic Continent*. Washington, DC: World Bank.

Collier, P., and J. W. Gunning. 1999. "Explaining African Economic Performance." *Journal of Economic Literature* 37 (1): 64–111.

Fafchamps, M., M. Söderbom, and N. Benhassine. 2009. "Wage Gaps and Job Sorting in African Manufacturing." *Journal of African Economies* 18 (5): 824–68.

ILO (International Labour Organization). 2002. "Women and Men in the Informal Economy: A Statistical Picture." Gender and Employment Sector, ILO, Geneva.

Kolev, A., and N. Sirven. 2010. "Gender Disparities in Africa's Labor Markets: A Cross-Country Comparison Using Standardized Survey Data." In *Gender Disparities in Africa's Labor Market*, ed. J. S. Arbache, A. Kolev, and E. Filipiak, 23–45. Washington, DC: World Bank.

Liedholm, C., and D. Mead. 1999. *Small Enterprises and Economic Development: The Dynamics of Micro and Small Enterprises*. London: Routledge.

Mammen, K., and C. Paxon. 2000. "Women's Work and Economic Development." *Journal of Economic Perspectives* 14: 141–64.

McPherson, M. A. 1996. "Growth of Micro and Small Enterprises in Southern Africa." *Journal of Development Economics* 48 (March): 235–77.

Mead, D. C. 1991. "Review Article: Small Enterprises and Development." *Economic Development and Cultural Change* 39 (January): 409–20.

———. 1994. "The Contribution of Small Enterprises to Employment Growth in Southern and Eastern Africa." *World Development* 22 (December): 1881–94.

Mead, D. C., and C. Liedholm. 1998. "The Dynamics of Micro and Small Enterprises in Developing Countries." *World Development* 26 (1): 61–74.

Nichter, S., and L. Goldmark. 2009. "Small Firm Growth in Developing Countries." *World Development* 37 (9): 1453–64.

Parker, S. C. 2004. *The Economics of Self-Employment and Entrepreneurship.* Cambridge: Cambridge University Press.

Sinha, A., and R. Kanbur. 2012. "Informality: Concepts, Facts and Models." *Journal of Applied Economic Research* 6 (2): 91–102.

Tybout, J. R. 2000. "Manufacturing Firms in Developing Countries: How Well Do They Do, and Why?" *Journal of Economic Literature* 28 (March): 11–44.

World Bank. 2002. *Engendering Development: Through Gender Equality in Rights, Resources and Voice.* Policy Research Report. Washington, DC: World Bank.

———. 2004. *World Development Report 2005: A Better Investment Climate for Everyone.* New York: Oxford University Press.

———. 2011. *World Development Report 2012: Gender Equality and Development.* Washington, DC: World Bank.

———. 2012. *World Development Report 2013: Jobs.* Washington, DC: World Bank.

World Economic Forum, African Development Bank, and World Bank. 2011. *African Competitiveness Report.* Geneva: World Economic Forum, African Development Bank, and World Bank.

Chapter 2

The Size, Formality, and Industry of Enterprises

Beyond knowing the rates of entrepreneurship and the breakdown of the self-employed and employers, it is important to understand the characteristics of enterprises run by women and by men. Clearly the efforts of the individual entrepreneurs affect the success of a business, but there are nonetheless very strong patterns of average returns and growth by types of enterprises. In this chapter we look at three dimensions: the size (number of employees) of the enterprise, the share of enterprises that are in the formal or informal sector, and the industry in which the enterprise operates.

For information on these dimensions we turn to microdata and the richness of the complementary enterprise and household surveys available. The analysis of these data sets corroborates the literature's findings:[1] women are more likely to be in small, informal firms and in traditional low-value-added industries.

Before showing the extent of gender sorting, however, there is a challenge of definition: identifying a "female" (or "women's") enterprise is not easy. "Female" could mean that the enterprise has one female owner among several owners, even though the woman may have no control; or that the enterprise has several owners, men and women, and a woman is the prime decision maker; or that the enterprise has a sole female proprietor.

The Enterprise Surveys focus on ownership rather than control, defining as female those enterprises where "any of the owners are female," not those where women are decision makers. Data from the six countries whose surveys included a specific gender module (see box 1.3) supplement this definition, as they identify firms where a woman is the main decision maker with certainty and so can flesh out the Enterprise Survey findings. Another approach to definition is to limit the sample to sole proprietors, on the assumption that single owners identified as women are most likely managers as well (box 2.1).

BOX 2.1

How to Designate "Female" and "Male" Enterprises: Ownership, Control, or a Mixture?

Identifying which enterprises are "female" is difficult because the data sets use different criteria.

Enterprise Surveys ask "Are any of the owners female?" and thus capture whether there is any female participation in ownership. But this is a very broad measure. In the five countries with a follow-up gender module, the data show the discrepancies between female participation in ownership and female decision making (figure B2.1.1). One-third of firms with some female ownership do not have women sharing in decisions, and one-half do not have women as the main decision maker.

For the vast majority of small firms, the same person is the owner, manager, and key decision maker, so knowing the gender of that person is sufficient. It is the larger, more productive multiple-owner businesses that tend to have women among the owners, but not as decision makers.

Figure B2.1.1 Up to Half of Firms with Some Female Ownership Are Not Run by Women

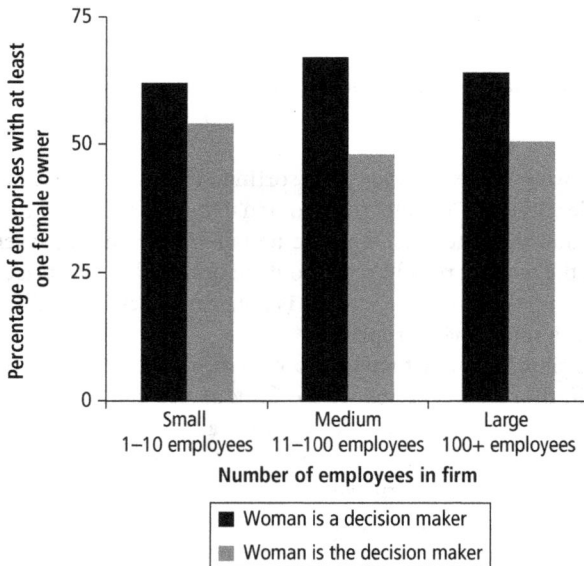

Sources: Enterprise Surveys' gender module, World Bank, http://www.enterprisesurveys.org; Aterido and Hallward-Driemeier 2011.
Note: Data are from 2010 for Sub-Saharan Africa. The figure shows a subset of firms in the gender module data that are not sole proprietorships, that have been identified as female using the definition "any female owner," and for which information is available on the decision makers.

We thus present results using three different measures of female enterprises:

- *Female participation in ownership.* This is the measure available for the larger Enterprise Survey sample of countries. Using it will likely make it harder to distinguish differences in either the constraints to or performance of businesses controlled by women, as many firms controlled by men but with at least one female partial owner will be included as female. As this measure may obscure potential gender gaps, it probably provides a lower bound on what gender gaps are likely to be found; but any gender gaps it captures are likely to be significant.

- *Women as prime decision maker.* This measure is available for a subset of six countries that have data about both ownership and the control of decisions.

Figure B2.1.2 Share of Formal Female Firms in Sub-Saharan Africa

a. Formal firms with female participation in ownership firms

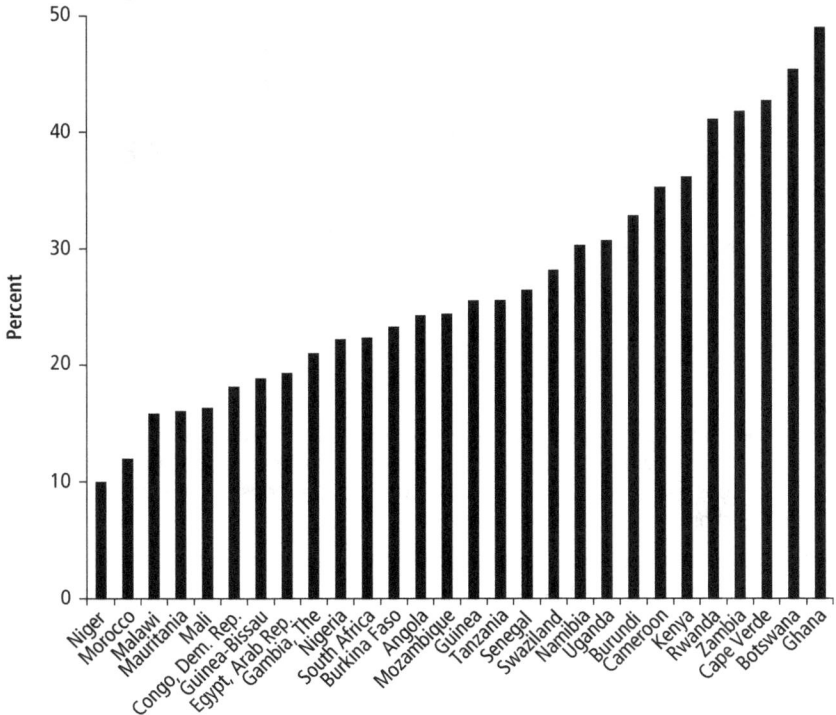

—Continued

BOX 2.1 *continued*

Figure B2.1.2 *(continued)*

b. Formal sole proprietors with female participation in ownership firms

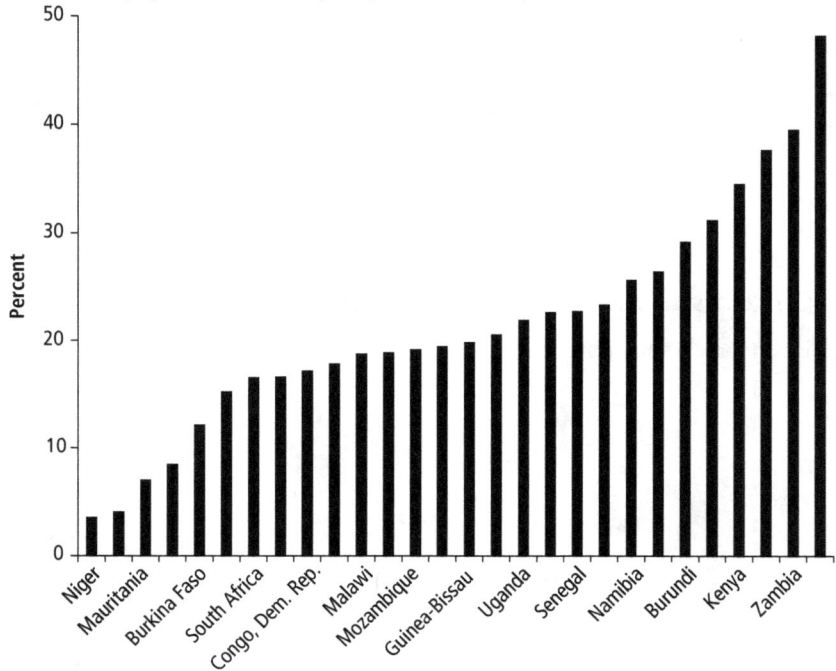

Source: Enterprise Surveys, World Bank, various years (2006–10), http://www.enterprisesurveys.org.

- *Women as sole owner and decision maker.* This approach restricts the sample to sole proprietorships where the owner and decision maker are the same person. It makes distinctions along gender lines much clearer, but the firms in the sample are often smaller than in the Enterprise Surveys.

The larger Enterprise Surveys' sample shows that the share of formal enterprises with female participation in ownership is higher than the share of sole proprietors who are women (figure B2.1.2). Averaging more than 25 percent in the region, female participation in ownership has wide variation across countries, from Niger (10 percent) to Ghana (nearly 50 percent).

Source: Aterido and Hallward-Driemeier 2011.

Enterprise Size

The size of an enterprise is at once a signal of past success and an indicator of future potential. Enterprises with many employees must have generated the revenue to pay their wages. Larger firms are more likely to be realizing economies of scale and thus to be more efficient. Larger firms are also likely better positioned to weather shocks; adjustments can be made that change the size of the firm, though not necessarily whether the firm remains in business (Bigsten and Gebreeyesus 2007; Bigsten and Söderbom 2006; Frazer 2005; Harding, Söderbom, and Teal 2006; Nichter and Goldmark 2009; Sleuwaegen and Goedhuys 2002; Söderbom and Teal 2004; Van Biesebroeck 2005). As an economy's income rises, the share of output and employment accounted for by larger firms rises. While larger firms are not necessarily likely to generate high rates of further employment growth, the number of jobs created can be substantial (Bartlesman, Haltiwanger, and Scarpetta, forthcoming).[2]

There are a number of key thresholds where size matters. The first is the basic move from having no employees to having at least one employee—that is, the move from self-employment to being an employer. This threshold is not merely an indication of scale; it involves a new set of processes and relationships—including the need to monitor efforts of employees and to specialize activities (Fafchamps and others 2010). Another important threshold is determined by a country's regulatory policies; an enterprise must register workers and meet certain other requirements (health and safety inspections, and so on) depending on the number of its employees. For many countries this threshold is 10 employees. A third threshold is somewhat more arbitrary, but tries to distinguish larger firms from smaller firms by looking at whether processes are automated or have dedicated staffs (such as inventory systems, marketing, human resources, and the like) and whether firms are more likely to be accessing larger markets. We have used 100 employees as the cutoff for this threshold (and occasionally use 500 to indicate the very largest firms).

On the broad criterion of female participation in ownership, Sub-Saharan Africa has lower female participation than other regions at all firm sizes, averaging 28 percent versus 39 percent—with the gap even greater among larger firms (figure 2.1). Within Sub-Saharan Africa, the gender composition of enterprises shows little difference by size until firms become fairly large.[3]

For sole proprietorships, the share of female enterprises is still lower in Sub-Saharan Africa than elsewhere, but the gaps with other regions are less pronounced (figure 2.2). Now the share of female enterprises declines with firm size, not simply among the largest firms, but even among smaller firms, too.

The enterprise module data from the household surveys show similar patterns of women tending to run smaller enterprises. Do the similarities stem from industry selection? With women tending to be concentrated in more labor-intensive activities, one might expect women's firms to be larger, since size is

Figure 2.1 Firms with Some Female Ownership Are Smaller in Sub-Saharan Africa Than in Other Regions

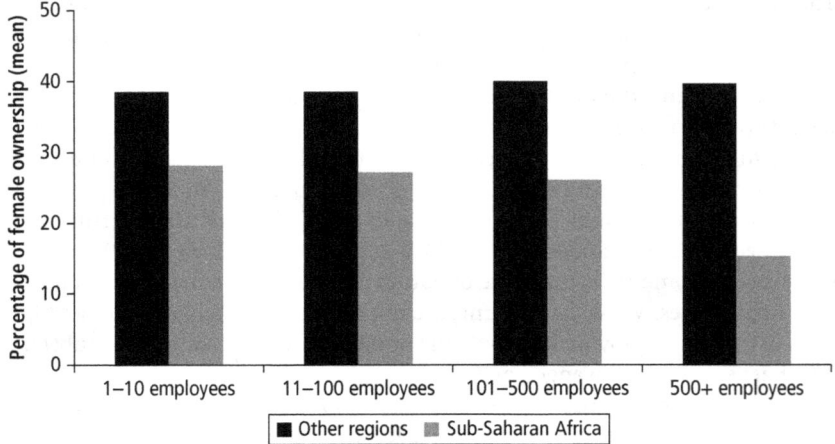

Source: Enterprise Surveys, World Bank, various years (2006–10), http://www.enterprisesurveys.org.

Figure 2.2 The Gender Ownership Gaps with Other Regions Are Smaller for Sole Proprietorships Than for All Firms

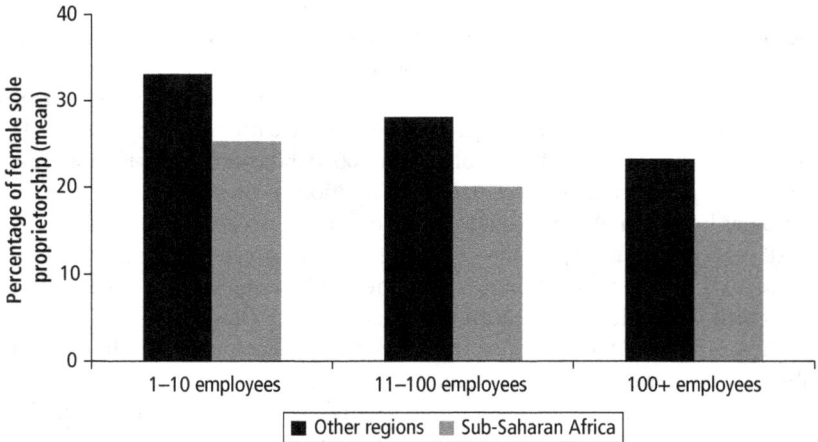

Source: Enterprise Surveys, World Bank, various years (2006–10), http://www.enterprisesurveys.org.

Figure 2.3 Women's Firms Are Smaller Than Men's (after controls for labor intensity)

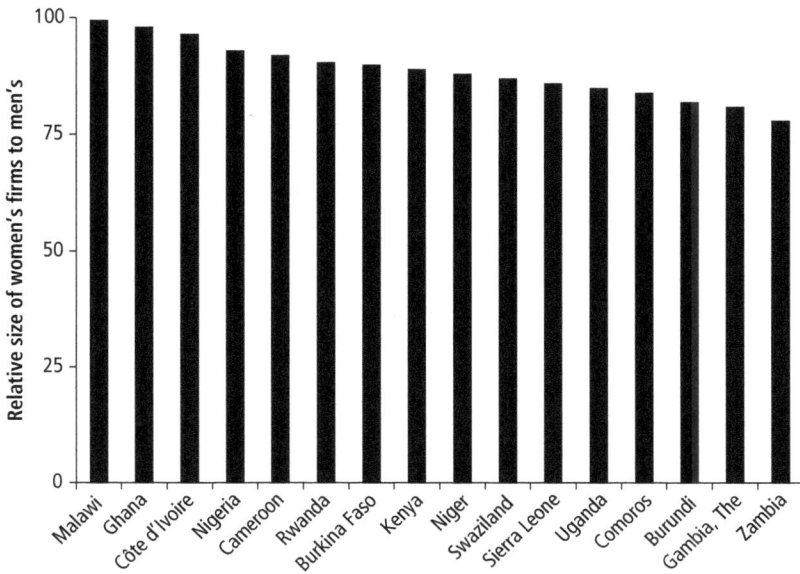

Source: Hallward-Driemeier and Rasteletti 2010.
Note: The relative size of firms is with respect to mean size in the sector. Data are from national representative household and labor force surveys in selected countries, most recent year (2000–10).

measured by the number of employees. So to control for the role of different labor intensity across industries, average deviations from the industry mean were calculated (figure 2.3). Even then, women's firms are smaller, in all countries.

Enterprise Formality

The standard used here for determining whether a firm is "formal" is its registration status. Whether a firm is registered does not only imply whether a firm pays taxes. It indicates whether it is protected by the formal system of property rights and the court system. It also indicates the market it operates in, the type of competition it faces, and thus the quality standards it is likely to meet. Formal firms are more likely to use contracts, thereby widening the extent of the market, as transactions do not need to be based on relationships. While some unregistered businesses have the potential to formalize, many others do not (de Mel, McKenzie, and Woodruff, forthcoming; La Porta and Shleifer 2011; McKenzie and Sakho 2010). While some informal firms are dynamic and profitable, formal firms are more likely to be so (Bigsten and Söderbom 2006; Falco and others 2009; Tybout 2000).

In all countries, the share of informal firms run by women is higher than the share of formal firms run by women; compare figure 2.4 and figure B2.1.2 in box 2.1 (see also Bardasi, Blackden, and Guzman 2007; ILO 2002; Liedholm and Mead 1999). These data use the criteria of female participation in ownership. Looking at sole proprietorship in the informal sector, the share that are run by women mirrors the share of women in the informal sector overall.

Similarly, according to the survey of new entrepreneurs (see box 1.3), women are more likely to be active in the informal sector: in the four countries sampled, women ran 27 percent of the informal firms and only 18 percent of the formal ones.

This difference persists even after distinguishing between entrepreneurs who are employers and those who are not. Employers are more likely to be registered than nonemployers, but no clear pattern emerges to show that the gender gap is significantly wider for either group (figure 2.5).

Enterprise Industry

Industries differ in their profitability, size, and opportunities for growth. Some industries earn higher profits than others; some industries are riskier than others, with greater swings in likely profits. It can be relatively easy to start

Figure 2.4 Informal Firms in Sub-Saharan Africa Are Often Female Run

a. All informal

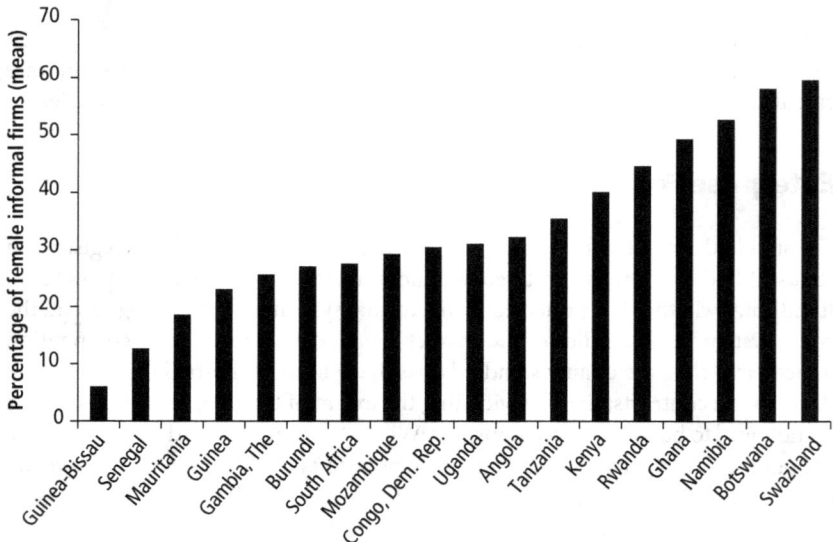

Figure 2.4 *(continued)*

b. Informal sole proprietors

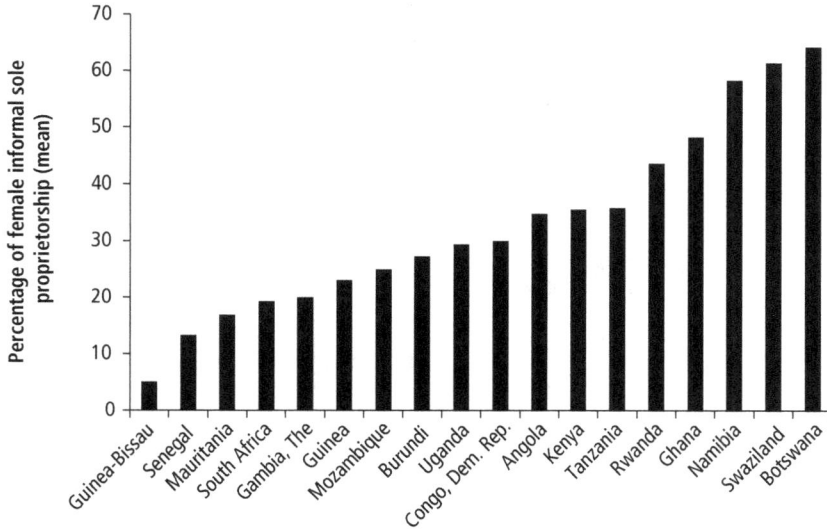

Source: Enterprise Surveys, World Bank, various years (2006–10), http://www.enterprisesurveys.org.

Figure 2.5 More Male-Owned Firms Are Registered—but with No Clear Difference in the Gender Gaps between the Self-Employed and Employers

a. Registered self-employed

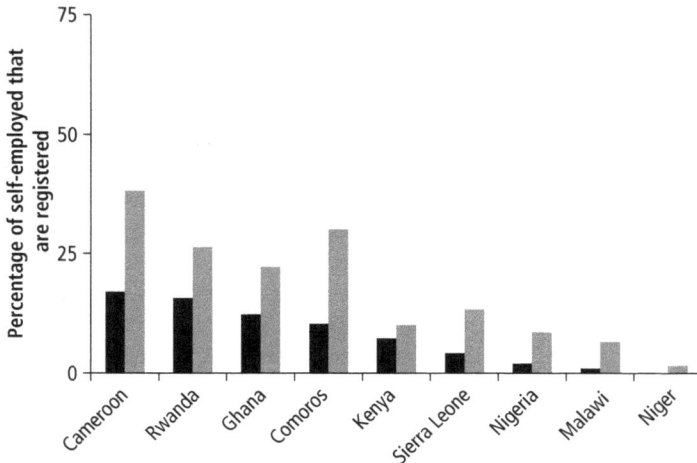

—*Continued*

Figure 2.5 *(continued)*

b. Registered employers

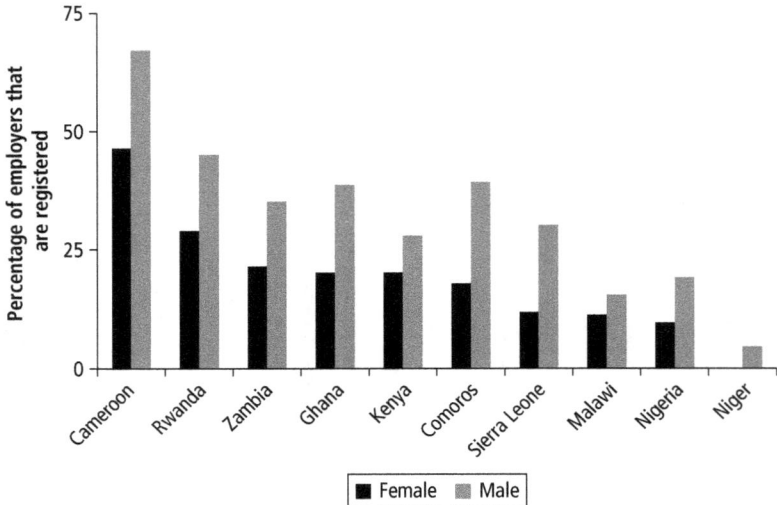

Source: Hallward-Driemeier and Rasteletti 2010.
Note: Registration is as reported in national representative household and labor force surveys for the most recent year (2000–10).

a business in some industries, but difficult in others. These features are often related. Higher-return activities are often harder to enter; if entry was easy the competition would increase and drive down profits. Factors that influence the ease of entry include the amount of capital that is needed in an industry, which affects the up-front investment needed to begin or expand operations. The availability of capital is also related to the efficient scale of operation and whether a small business is likely to be feasible or not. Industries also vary in the degree of specific knowledge that is needed to operate in them; a software designer, a tailor, and a metalworker have different skills that require different amounts time and effort to acquire (Tybout 2000; World Bank 2012).[4] Here, we look at broad groupings of industries, from garments, food preparation, retail, and other services that tend to be labor intensive and operate at small scale, to various metalwork, machinery, chemicals, and other kinds of manufacturing that tend to be capital intensive, formal, and larger scale. To the extent there is gender sorting across industries, on average, women and men are likely to earn different returns and face different prospects.

Unsurprisingly, female firms are not distributed uniformly across industries (figure 2.6). Women more than men concentrate in services and traditional, lower-value-added sectors such as the garment and food-processing sectors.

Figure 2.6 In Sub-Saharan Africa, Female-Owned Firms Are More Concentrated Than Men's in Lower-Value-Added Industries (formal sector)

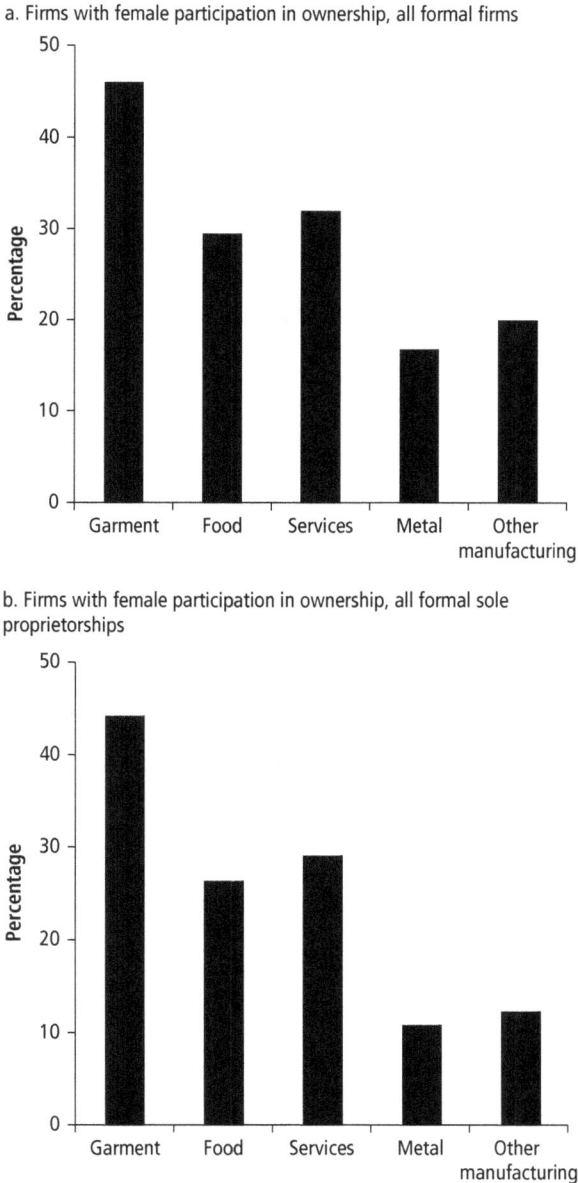

a. Firms with female participation in ownership, all formal firms

b. Firms with female participation in ownership, all formal sole proprietorships

Source: Enterprise Surveys, World Bank, various years (2006–10), http://www.enterprisesurveys.org.

Men concentrate more in other manufacturing and metals. Female sole proprietors show similar patterns.

The likely degree of formality within a sector can itself be a predictor of women's participation (figure 2.7). The industry with the lowest share of formal entrepreneurs (42 percent) is the textile and garment industry, with a female share of 35 percent. By contrast, the industry with the highest share of formal entrepreneurs is basic metal and metal products (85 percent), where the female share is only 3 percent.

Data from the household survey enterprise modules show similar trends of women concentrated in sectors with lower barriers to entry and higher labor intensity. In retail the share of female-headed firms tends to be much larger than that of male-headed firms (figure 2.8). The position is reversed for construction, transportation, and other services. Although in manufacturing the share of female-headed firms is relatively high, most female-headed businesses are clustered in food preparation, textiles, and garments—activities with low profit margins.

With women disproportionately running smaller, more informal enterprises in lower-value-added industries, women's economic opportunities are

Figure 2.7 The Degree of Formality Is a Good Predictor of Women's Participation in an Industry

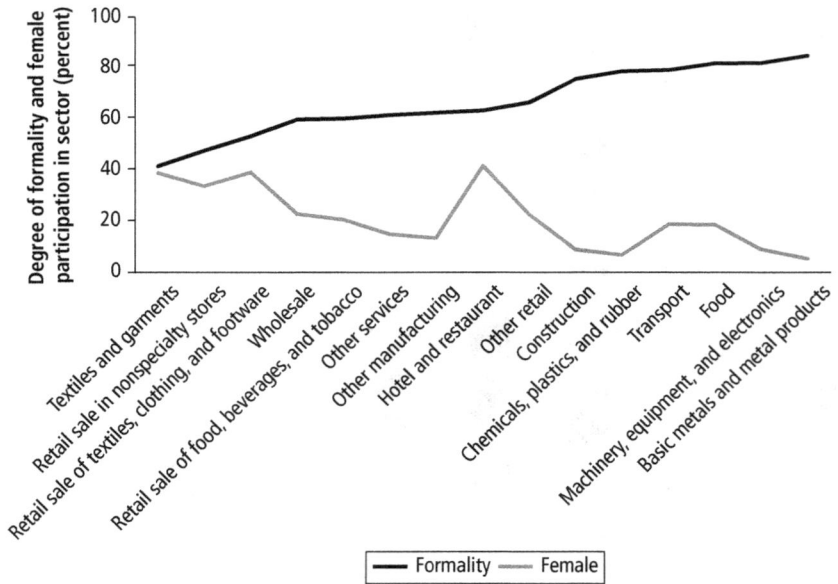

Source: Gajigo and Hallward-Driemeier 2010.
Note: Data are for newly established enterprises in Côte d'Ivoire, Kenya, Nigeria, and Senegal.

Figure 2.8 Retail, Food, and Textiles Attract Female Entrepreneurs

a. Female entrepreneurs—industry distribution

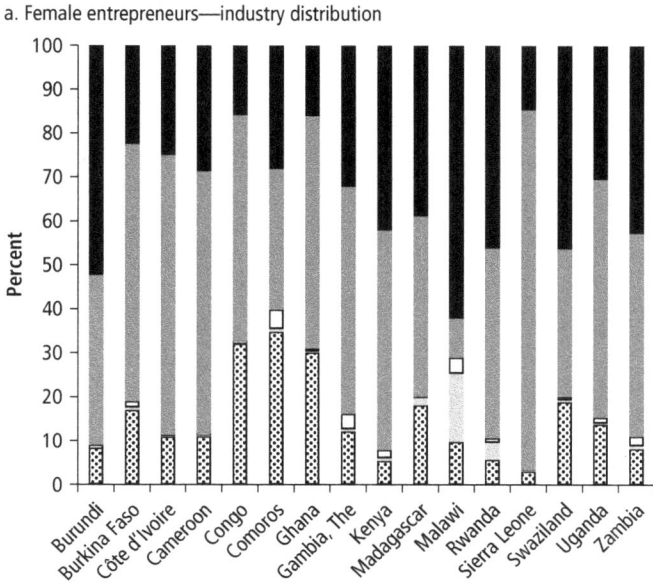

b. Male entrepreneurs—industry distribution

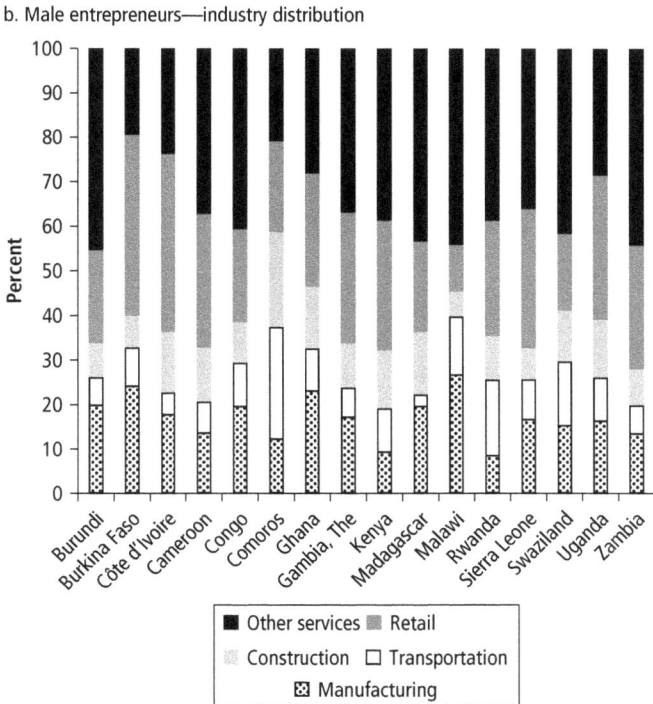

■ Other services ▨ Retail
▨ Construction ☐ Transportation
⊠ Manufacturing

—Continued

Figure 2.8 *(continued)*

c. Female-headed household enterprises—industry distribution

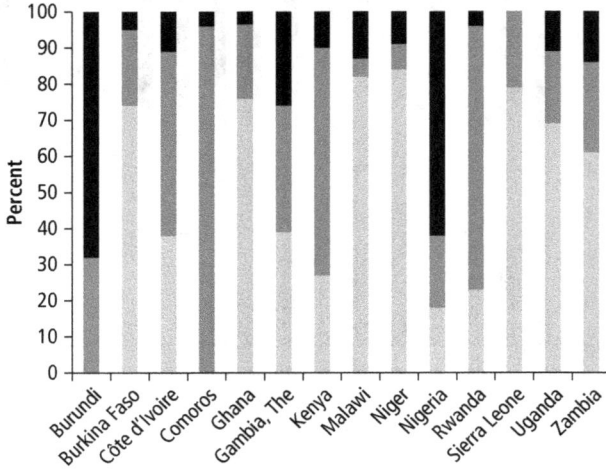

d. Male-headed household enterprises—industry distribution

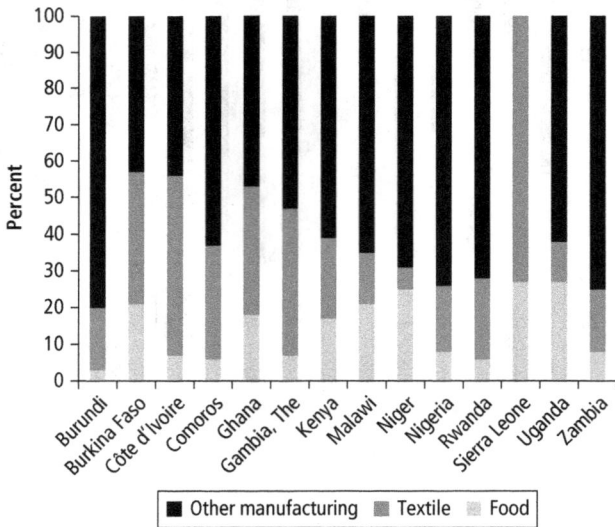

■ Other manufacturing   ■ Textile   ▧ Food

Source: Household surveys' enterprise modules, selected countries, various years (2000–10).

more limited than men's. Improving the conditions that face their existing businesses may help, but a more promising agenda is to enable more women to move into higher-return activities. Looking at how the extent of gender sorting in entrepreneurship varies across countries and by characteristics of the entrepreneur provides insights into what the constraints are and how they can be overcome.

Notes

1. See, for example, Mead and Liedholm (1998) and World Bank (2004).
2. The donor community traditionally focuses attention on small enterprises, heralding them as significant job creators. As the data here and in chapter 1 have demonstrated, micro and small enterprises can employ large numbers of people, but their potential to grow and become large firms is far more limited. See Page and Söderbom (2012) for a discussion.
3. For a discussion of women's enterprises in a different region, see Bruhn's (2009) analysis of women's enterprises in Latin America.
4. Industries can also vary in the extent of product differentiation, the importance of quality, the range of products within an industry, the importance of branding, and so on—issues for which we do not have good proxies in the available data.

References

Aterido, R., and M. Hallward-Driemeier. 2011. "Whose Business Is It Anyway?" *Small Business Economics* 37 (4): 443–64.

Bardasi, E., M. Blackden, and J. C. Guzman. 2007. "Gender, Entrepreneurship, and Competitiveness." In *Africa Competitiveness Report 2007*, edited by World Economic Forum, African Development Bank, and World Bank. Washington, DC: World Economic Forum, African Development Bank, and World Bank.

Bartlesman, E., J. Haltiwanger, and S. Scarpetta. Forthcoming. "Cross Country Differences in Productivity: The Role of Allocative Efficiency." *American Economic Review.*

Bigsten, A., and M. Gebreeyesus. 2007. "The Small, the Young, and the Productive: Determinants of Manufacturing Firm Growth in Ethiopia." *Economic Development and Cultural Change* 55 (4): 813–40.

Bigsten, A., and M. Söderbom. 2006. "What Have We Learned from a Decade of Manufacturing Enterprise Surveys in Africa?" *World Bank Research Observer* 21 (2): 241–65.

Bruhn, M. 2009. "Female-Owned Firms in Latin America: Characteristics, Performance, and Obstacles to Growth." Policy Research Working Paper 5122, World Bank, Washington, DC.

de Mel, S., D. McKenzie, and C. Woodruff. Forthcoming. "The Demand for, and Consequences of, Formalization among Informal Firms in Sri Lanka." *AEJ: Applied Economics.*

Fafchamps, M., D. McKenzie, S. Quinn, and C. Woodruff. 2010. "When Is Capital Enough to Get Female Microenterprises Growing? Evidence from a Randomized

Experiment in Ghana." NBER Working Paper 17207, National Bureau of Economic Research, Cambridge, MA.

Falco, P., A. Kerr, N. Rankin, J. Sandefur, and F. Teal. 2009. "The Returns to Formality and Informality in Urban Africa." CSAE Working Paper Series 2010-03, Centre for the Study of African Economies, Oxford, U.K.

Frazer, G. 2005. "Which Firms Die?: A Look at Exit from Manufacturing in Ghana." *Economic Development and Cultural Change* 53 (3): 585–617.

Gajigo, O., and M. Hallward-Driemeier. 2010. "Entrepreneurship among New Entrepreneurs." Working paper, World Bank, Washington, DC.

Hallward-Driemeier, M., and A. Rasteletti. 2010. "Women's and Men's Entrepreneurship in Africa." Working paper, World Bank, Washington, DC.

Harding, A., M. Söderbom, and F. Teal 2006. "The Determinants of Survival among African Manufacturing Firms." *Economic Development and Cultural Change* 54 (3): 533–56.

ILO (International Labour Organization). 2002. "Women and Men in the Informal Economy: A Statistical Picture." Gender and Employment Sector, ILO, Geneva.

La Porta, R., and A. Shleifer. 2011. "The Unofficial Economy in Africa." NBER Working Paper 16821, National Bureau of Economic Research, Cambridge, MA.

Liedholm, C., and D. Mead. 1999. *Small Enterprises and Economic Development: The Dynamics of Micro and Small Enterprises*. London: Routledge.

McKenzie, D., and Y. S. Sakho. 2010. "Does It Pay Firms to Register for Taxes? The Impact of Formality on Firm Profitability." *Journal of Development Economics* 91: 15–25.

Mead, D. C., and C. Liedholm. 1998. "The Dynamics of Micro and Small Enterprises in Developing Countries." *World Development* 26 (1): 61–74.

Nichter, S., and L. Goldmark. 2009. "Small Firm Growth in Developing Countries." *World Development* 37 (9): 1453–64.

Page, J., and M. Söderbom. 2012. "Is Small Beautiful? Small Enterprise, Aid and Employment in Africa." Working paper, Brookings Institutions, Washington, DC.

Sleuwaegen, L., and M. Goedhuys. 2002. "Growth of Firms in Developing Countries, Evidence from Côte d'Ivoire." *Journal of Development Economics* 68 (June): 117–35.

Söderbom, M., and F. Teal. 2004. "Size and Efficiency in African Manufacturing Firms: Evidence from Firm-Level Panel Data." *Journal of Development Economics* 73 (February): 369–94.

Tybout, J., R. 2000. "Manufacturing Firms in Developing Countries: How Well Do They Do, and Why?" *Journal of Economic Literature* 28 (March): 11–44.

Van Biesebroeck, J. 2005. "Firm Size Matters: Growth and Productivity Growth in African Manufacturing." *Economic Development and Cultural Change* 53 (3): 545–83.

World Bank. 2004. *World Development Report 2005: A Better Investment Climate for Everyone*. New York: Oxford University Press.

———. 2012. *World Development Report 2013: Jobs*. New York: Oxford University Press.

Part II

Why Women Work Where They Do

The gender sorting across types of entrepreneurial activities laid out in Part I is not uniform across countries or across all women within a country. This section looks at the factors associated with variations in the extent to which women operate enterprises that are smaller, more informal, and in traditional sectors. It examines key characteristics, both at the level of the country and of the individual. Two dimensions are particularly important: gender gaps in human capital, particularly access to managerial and business skills, and the ability to own and control assets. The entrepreneur's age, marital status, and prior work experience matter too.

Chapter **3**

Effect of Country Patterns in Income, Human Capital, and Assets on Where Women Work

This chapter examines what contributes to the gender-differentiated patterns of entrepreneurship across countries. It analyzes how much of the variation in women's overrepresentation in self-employment and relative underrepresentation among employers can be explained simply by a country's level of income. Do relatively more women move from self-employment to being an employer—or move into wage employment—as a country develops?

Beyond income, a range of country characteristics has been proposed to explain differences in income and growth, from geography to social capital to rule of law (see for example Acemoglu, Johnson, and Robinson 2002; Acemoglu and Johnson 2005; Hall and Jones 1999; Rodrik, Subramanian, and Trebbi 2004). Increasing attention is being paid to the magnitude and sources of frictions that lead to a misallocation of resources and thus reduce productivity (Hsieh and Klenow 2009); a range of empirical studies in Sub-Saharan Africa looks at the roles of the availability of infrastructure services, finance, the quality of governance, and business regulations in explaining differences in firm performance between and within countries (Aterido and Hallward-Driemeier 2010; Bigsten and Söderbom 2006; Bigsten and others 2003; Dollar, Hallward-Driemeier, and Mengistae 2005; World Bank 2004).[1] Many of these frictions or constraints in the investment climate are examined in the next chapters, but this chapter argues for the importance of looking at indicators of two critical inputs in running a business: human capital, and access to and control over assets.

The analysis here, using data from 37 Sub-Saharan African countries, finds that while country income is associated with some trends in entrepreneurship, it alone cannot explain all the differences in patterns across countries; there is a great deal of country variation in women's entrepreneurship at any given income level. Using adult literacy as a measure of basic human capital shows that where gender gaps in adult literacy are large, so too is the relative share of women in self-employment. Higher shares of female employers, on the other hand, are associated with greater legal protection of women's economic rights. What is particularly striking about this finding is that gender gaps in these legal protections are as prevalent in Sub-Saharan Africa's middle-income countries as low-income countries; closing the gender gaps in legal protections and strengthening women's property rights in particular will thus require active engagement and will not simply follow from increases in countries' income.

The discussion brings to the fore the importance of women's legal rights, and in particular, secure property rights, for women entrepreneurs (examined further in chapter 7) and the importance of human capital for expanding opportunity for women entrepreneurs (chapter 9). These factors, along with improved access to finance (chapter 8) and a greater voice for women in influencing the business environment (chapter 10), have a vital contribution to make in expanding opportunities for women entrepreneurs.

The Importance of Income: A Cross-Country Perspective

The next few figures are constructed using country data rather than regional averages. The patterns of entrepreneurship across income levels are traced out based on cross-country variations, not on changes in entrepreneurship as countries develop. Thus as any given country develops, it will not necessarily follow the relationships described here.

Putting Nonagricultural Employment in Context

Differences in income help explain much of the interregional variation in labor force participation and sector of employment (agriculture or nonagriculture) as described in chapter 1.[2] The share of women not in the labor force is lowest in low-income countries, rises with country income, and then declines a little (figure 3.1). For men the pattern is more muted (figure 3.2). Thus higher gross domestic product (GDP) per capita is associated with greater feminization of those not in the labor force (figure 3.3); among those not in the labor force, a higher share is female as incomes rise. Even taking into account Sub-Saharan Africa's many low-income countries, the region still has high rates of female labor force participation, so many of its countries actually lie below the fitted curve.

Female and male employment outside agriculture rises with income. Although the gap between them remains higher at higher incomes, the relative share of women among those in nonagricultural employment does not exhibit significant variation by income.

The rise in women's participation in nonagricultural employment is primarily driven by a steep decline in the share of women in agriculture—and despite a rising share of women not in the labor force, it rises until it reaches middle levels of income before flattening and then declining a little at higher levels of income.

Figure 3.1 Initially, the Share of Women Not in the Labor Force Rises Steeply with Country Income

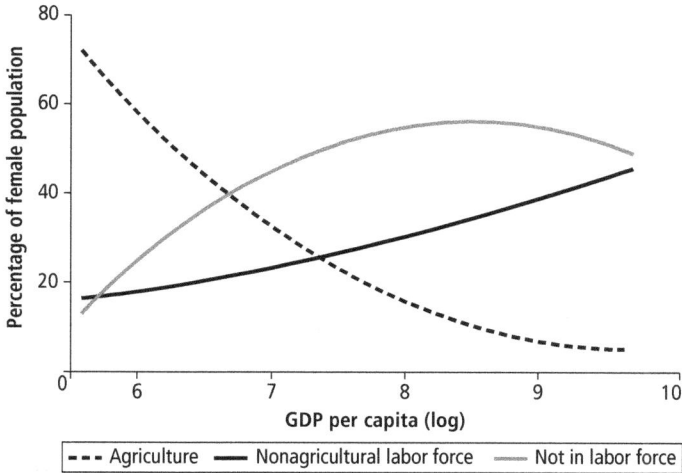

Source: Hallward-Driemeier and Rasteletti 2010.
Note: Analysis is based on national household and labor force surveys for 101 low- and middle-income economies, most recent years (2000–10).

Figure 3.2 The Share of Men Not in the Labor Force Shows Little Change as Country Income Climbs

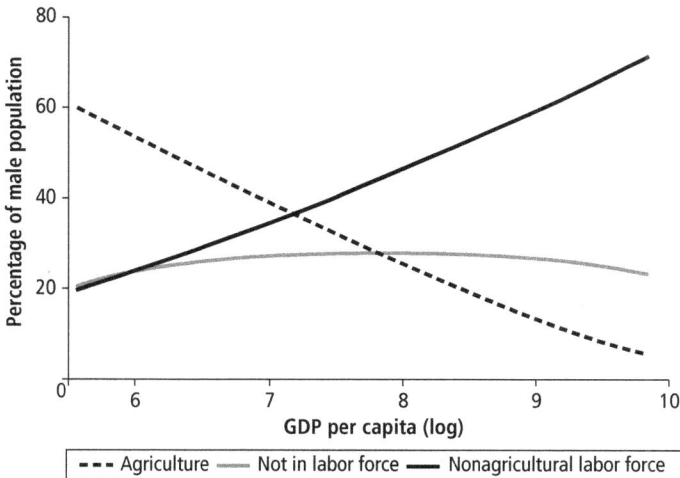

Source: Hallward-Driemeier and Rasteletti 2010.
Note: Analysis is based on national household and labor force surveys for 101 low- and middle-income economies, most recent years (2000–10).

Figure 3.3 The Share of Women in Nonagricultural Employment Changes Little as Country Income Rises

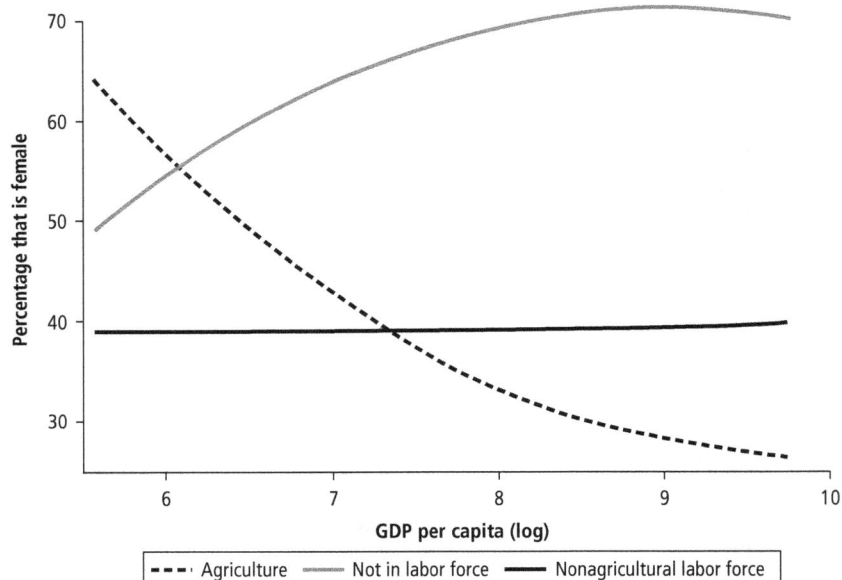

Source: Hallward-Driemeier and Rasteletti 2010.
Note: Analysis is based on national household and labor force surveys for 101 low- and middle- income economies, most recent years (2000–10).

Men's participation in agriculture is lower than women's at low incomes, and declines with income, but less steeply. Fewer men are not in the labor force, and the rate does not change much with income. The share of men in nonagricultural employment rises with income, proportionately faster than the comparable share for women, so the share of women in nonagricultural employment changes little, remaining at around 40 percent (figure 3.3).

Overall, therefore, as GDP per capita rises, the share of women falls in agriculture but shows little change in nonagricultural employment. These patterns also mask much variation among countries at any given level of GDP per capita. Clearly income does not explain the whole story.

Looking within Nonagricultural Employment
Within nonagricultural employment, self-employment generally falls as income increases, particularly for women (figure 3.4). At the lowest income levels, more than 60 percent of women are self-employed, and fewer than 20 percent are wage earners. At middle incomes the shares are closer to equal. The share of employers always tends to be low, changing little with country income.

Figure 3.4 Female Self-Employment Falls with an Increase in Country Income
(nonagricultural employment)

Where women work

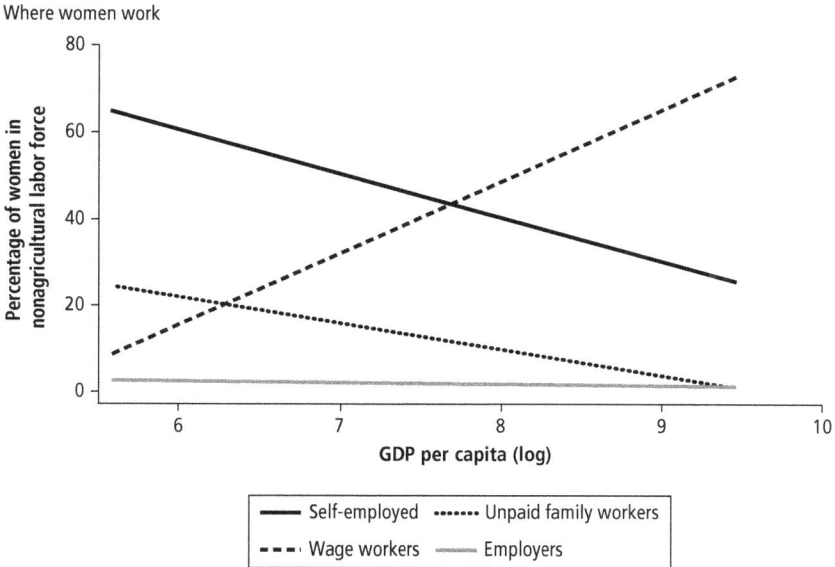

Source: Hallward-Driemeier and Rasteletti 2010.
Note: Analysis is based on national household and labor force surveys for 101 low- and middle-income economies, most recent years (2000–10).

Among men at low incomes, roughly equal shares are self-employed and wage earners, with the gap quickly widening to favor wage earners as incomes climb. As with women, a small but fairly consistent share consists of employers (figure 3.5).

The patterns in figures 3.4 and 3.5 are consistent and include a relatively large share of self-employed who are necessity entrepreneurs: where wage jobs are scarce, there are few alternatives to self-employment (chapter 1). Strikingly, even with such a large pool of self-employed at lower country incomes, the total share of those working outside agriculture who become employers climbs little as income rises. At higher incomes wage employment is more plentiful, self-employment is lower, and the share of necessity entrepreneurs is lower as employers represent a growing share of the self-employed.

By employment category, the share of self-employed who are women starts at nearly 50 percent at lower incomes, then falls approaching middle incomes (figure 3.6). The female share of wage earners, in contrast, starts low but rises smoothly with income. This pattern is consistent with self-employment falling, and wage employment rising, faster for women than men as income rises (see figures 3.4 and 3.5).

Figure 3.5 Male Wage Earners Gain as Income Improves (nonagricultural employment)

Where men work

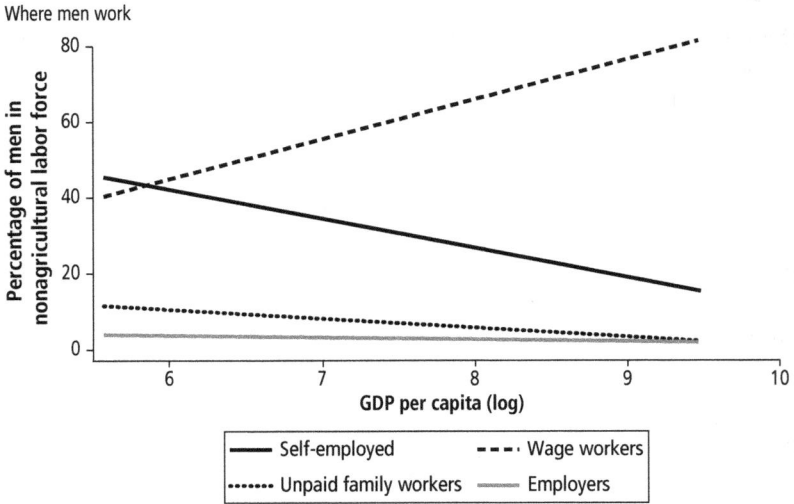

Source: Hallward-Driemeier and Rasteletti 2010.
Note: Analysis is based on national household and labor force surveys for 101 low- and middle-income economies, most recent years (2000–10).

Figure 3.6 Women Account for around a Quarter of Employers, Irrespective of Country Income (nonagricultural employment)

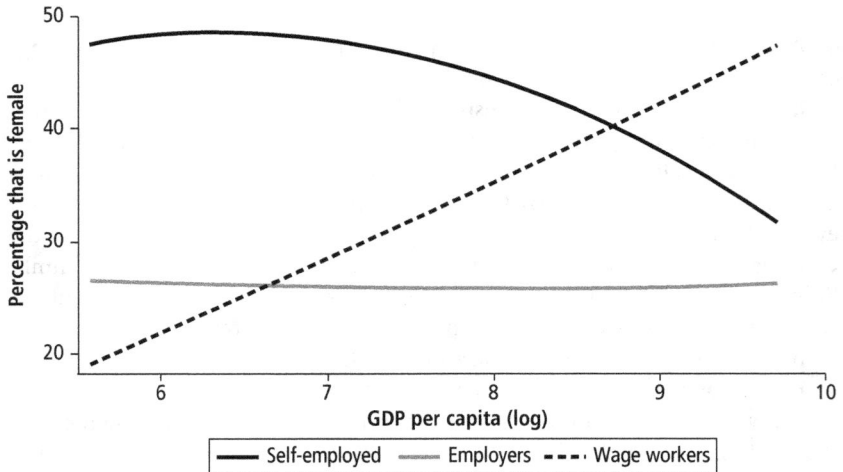

Source: Hallward-Driemeier and Rasteletti 2010.
Note: Analysis is based on national household and labor force surveys for 101 low- and middle-income economies, most recent years (2000–10).

A striking point is that the share of women as employers changes little as GDP climbs, with women representing just over a quarter of employers (figure 3.6).

Again, income accounts for some of the variation in labor force activities, but not all.[3] The next section looks at other country-level explanations. The next chapter then looks at factors at the individual level.

Cross-Country Patterns of Entrepreneurship: Human Capital (Literacy) and Access to Assets (Property Rights)

Various international organizations have computed composite indicators that try to capture gender equality and women's opportunities. These indicators show wide variation among countries, with some countries—including many in Sub-Saharan Africa—presenting substantial gender inequalities. The indicators also rank countries differently (though general correlations emerge) because each indicator focuses on different dimensions of gender equality, and country performance varies by dimension. A country may have low adult female literacy or high maternal mortality, for example, but also have high female political participation. Gender equality (or inequality) in one dimension does not necessarily imply gender equality (or inequality) across other dimensions.

Some of these dimensions are more relevant to entrepreneurship than others. Most relevant are measures of human capital and of access to and control over assets. But while almost all indicators include dimensions of human capital, not all of them have variables for access to and control over assets. To fill this gap, this chapter uses the Women's Legal and Economic Empowerment Database for Africa (Women–LEED–Africa).[4] That database contains information on constitutional provisions, ratified international conventions, and statutes (particularly family, inheritance, and land legislation) to capture where women's economic rights differ from men's.

Using female literacy as a measure of human capital and Women–LEED–Africa indicators, the chapter divides countries into four categories: small gender gaps in literacy, large gender gaps in literacy, small gaps in women's legal and economic rights, and large gaps in women's legal and economic rights. These four categories become a means of examining how country characteristics help explain variations in sorting and performance.

Indicators of Gender Equality and Opportunity—
From International Organizations

The organizations that compute indicators of gender equality and opportunity include the Economist Intelligence Unit, Organisation for Economic Co-operation and Development (OECD), United Nations Development Programme, World Bank, and World Economic Forum (figure 3.7 and appendix B).

Figure 3.7 Indicators of Equality and Opportunity Vary, but Most Show Sub-Saharan Women in a Challenging Environment

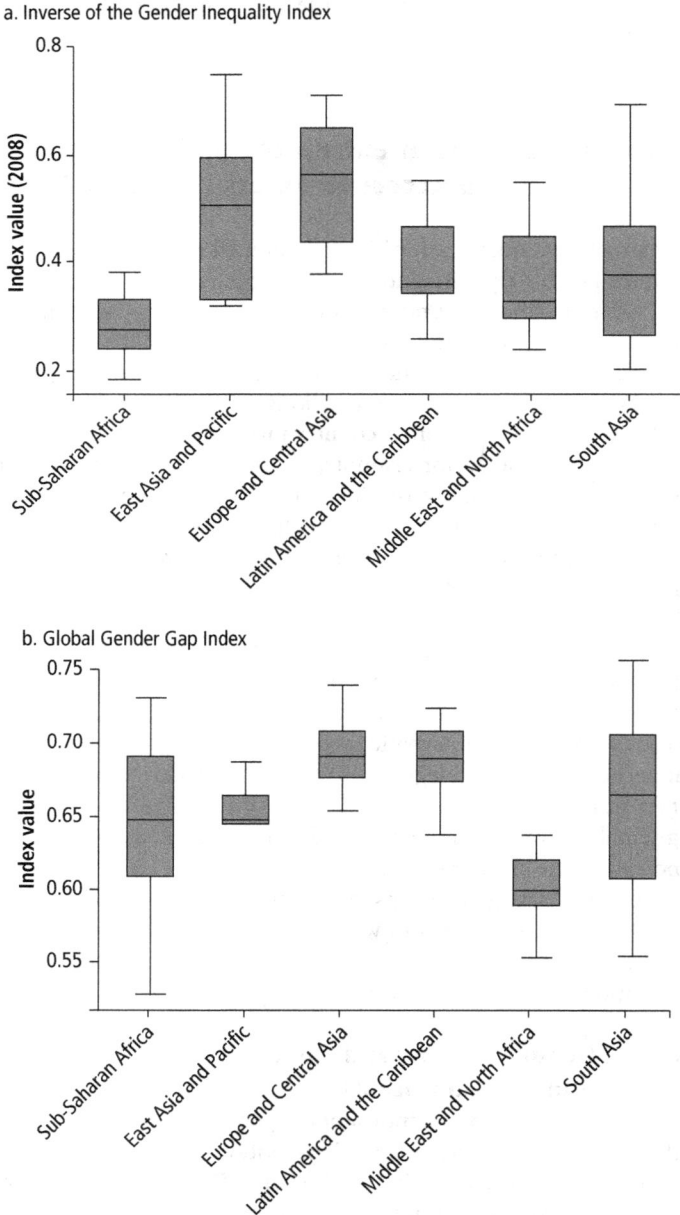

a. Inverse of the Gender Inequality Index

b. Global Gender Gap Index

Figure 3.7 *(continued)*

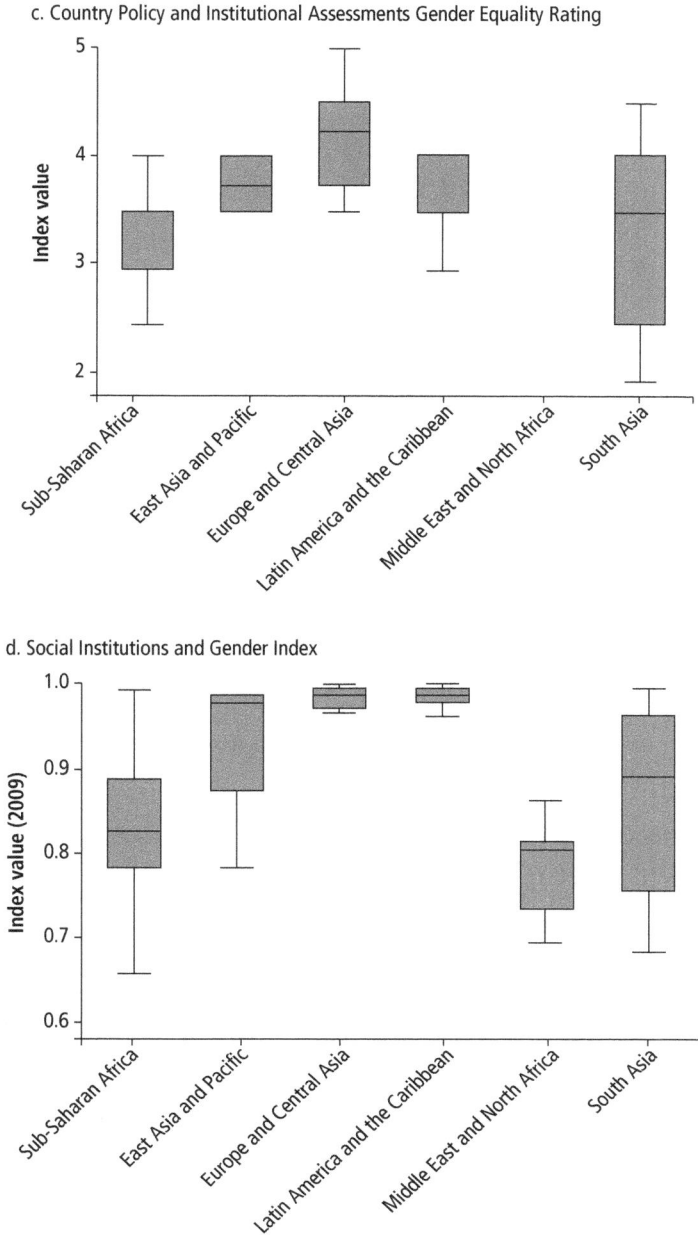

c. Country Policy and Institutional Assessments Gender Equality Rating

d. Social Institutions and Gender Index

—Continued

Figure 3.7 *(continued)*

e. Women's Economic Opportunity Index

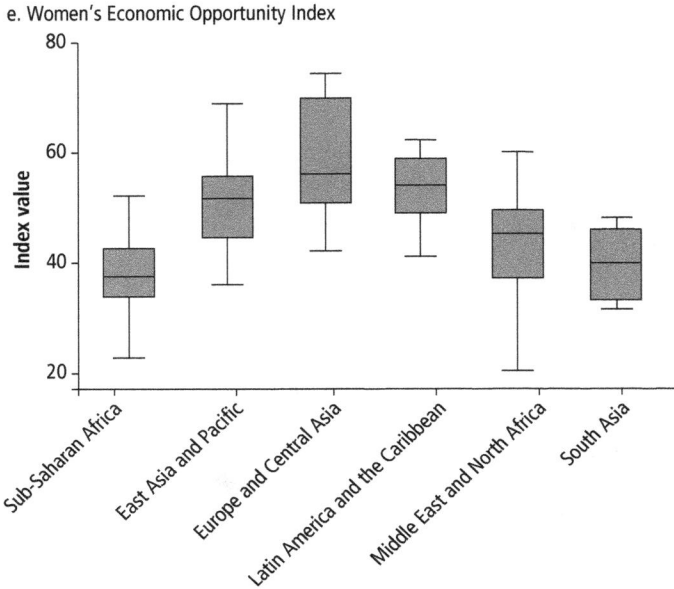

Sources: Figure 3.7a: United Nations Development Programme, Gender Inequality Index, 2010, http://hdr.undp
.org/en/statistics/gii/NDP; figure 3.7b: World Economic Forum, Global Gender Gap Index, http://www.weforum
.org/issues/global-gender-gap; figure 3.7c: World Bank, Country Policy and Institutional Assessments Gender
Equality Rating, http://www.worldbank.org/ida; figure 3.7d: OECD, Social Institutions and Gender Index,
http://www.oecd.org/dataoecd/52/33/42289479.pdf; figure 3.7e: Economist Intelligence Unit, Women's Economic
Opportunity Index, http://www.eiu.com/sponsor/WEO.
Note: As drawn, a higher index score indicates greater equality. See appendix B for descriptions of the indexes.
Figure 3.7e excludes outside values.

Their methodologies differ, providing an array of approaches and country
rankings. For example, indicators that emphasize levels of education or health
outcomes tend to rank low-income countries near the bottom—and Sub-Saharan
Africa performs poorly. Those with measures of political participation throw up
different rankings, given a weaker correlation between the number of women parliamentarians and economic development, gender gaps in health, or education.

These composite indicators are instructive in that they offer evidence of continuing gender gaps in constraints and opportunities across countries. But none
is fully appropriate for isolating the effects of particular dimensions of gender
inequality. Some include measures that are not of first-order importance to entrepreneurship. Female maternal mortality or gender gaps in child mortality may
indicate women's broader place in society, but they are not of direct relevance here.
Some measures do include labor force participation—that is, the share of women
in the nonagricultural labor force. There are two concerns about these measures.

First, it is unclear whether high rates of participation constitute a positive indicator—high rates of necessity entrepreneurs, for example, are not always a sign of women's empowerment. Second and more important, labor force participation rates are one of the outcomes we want to explain. So the outcome measure cannot be used as a source of the explanation for its variation across countries.

Another shortcoming of some measures is country coverage. Some institutions have greater coverage of Sub-Saharan Africa than others. The World Bank's Country Policy and Institutional Assessment covers 34 countries, the United Nations Development Programme's Gender Inequality Index 31, the World Economic Forum's Global Gender Gap Index 25, and the Women's Economic Opportunity Index of the Economist Intelligence Unit 22. The OECD's Social Institutions and Gender Index has 39 countries and thus the widest coverage, making it of particular interest. It also includes a wider set of measures that contain information about social institutions and women's rights, which could be relevant for entrepreneurship. Its measures are, however, based on largely subjective responses of experts in each country, rendering it harder to judge the comparability across countries and over time.

Two Indicators of Gender Equality and Opportunity: Women's Literacy, and Legal and Economic Rights

Given the foregoing limitations, we developed a different set of indicators to capture women's equality, using five criteria to select a narrower set of dimensions. The most important criterion was to capture the factors most relevant for entrepreneurship. Entrepreneurs run a business, and an enterprise's output is based on the quality and quantity of human capital and on the enterprise's assets.[5] The ability to control these resources and any resulting profits provide the incentives to grow. So, measures of human capital and measures of property rights are of prime interest.

The second criterion was to select measures that are not overly correlated with each other, because it is highly unlikely that a single dimension fully explains variations in country outcomes. The third was to preserve simplicity. Rather than use multiple dimensions to construct a single composite indicator, the aim was to have only a limited number of dimensions that could be examined together. The fourth criterion was to have adequate country coverage. The fifth was to have objective measures as much as possible rather than subjective assessments, which might reflect biases due to respondent selection or might be difficult to replicate.

Following these criteria, we selected two measures: adult female literacy, and a measure of gender gaps in women's legal and economic rights.

We opted for adult female literacy (among the potential human capital variables) because it is more appropriate for our purposes than current educational enrollment rates. Given the huge increase in enrollment in recent years, current enrollment levels or educational attainment of recent graduates is likely to be much higher than levels for older generations that are still economically active.

Adult literacy rates thus better capture the level of human capital across the full age spectrum of potential entrepreneurs.

Of the measures of female literacy, we had two choices. One was to look at female literacy within the adult population.[6] This approach measures the basic human capital available, but it does not capture a sense of potential gender gap. An alternative was to look at the gender gap between female and male literacy. These two measures have an extremely high correlation (figure 3.8).

In countries where women's literacy is high, gender gaps are quite small. Where female literacy is low, male literacy is generally not as low and the percentage gap between men and women is high. But the linearity of the relationship between the female level and gender gaps breaks down at the extreme low end, where Niger and Guinea-Bissau, and to a lesser extent Ethiopia, have low female literacy and particularly large gender gaps.

The choice of the measure for gender gaps in women's legal and economic rights raised more questions. Because we were interested in variables that were not simply correlated with income or the human capital measure, we reexamined indicators from international organizations (figure 3.9). After we controlled for GDP per capita, variation beyond literacy remained, so the indexes are capturing other sources of variation that could be meaningful.

Figure 3.8 The Correlation Is High between Low Levels of Women's Literacy and Large Gender Gaps in Literacy

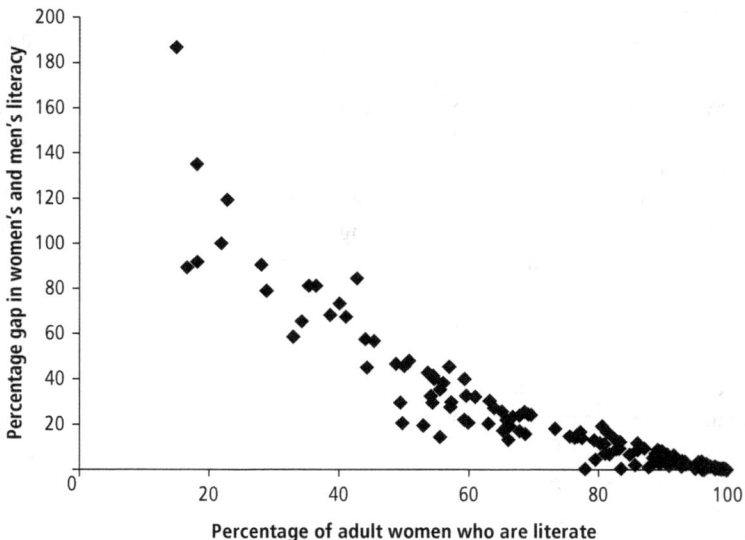

Percentage of adult women who are literate

Source: World Bank, World Development Indicators database, http://data.worldbank.org/indicator.

Figure 3.9 Variation beyond Literacy Remains after GDP per Capita Is Controlled for (using indicators from international organizations)

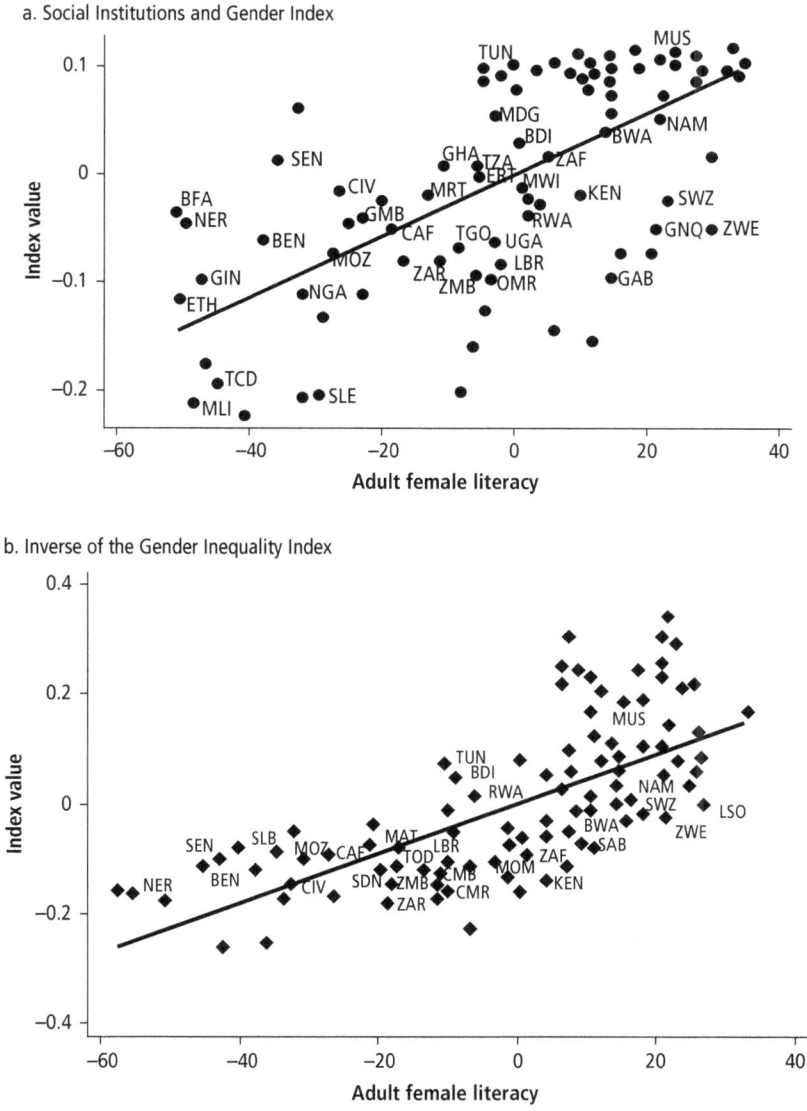

a. Social Institutions and Gender Index

b. Inverse of the Gender Inequality Index

Sources: Author's calculations using the database of national household and labor force surveys for 101 low- and middle-income economies, most recent years (2000–10); OECD, Social Institutions and Gender Index, 2010, http://www.oecd.org/dataoecd/52/33/42289479.pdf (figure 3.9a); and United Nations Development Programme, Gender Inequality Index, http://hdr.undp.org/en/statistics/gii/ NDP (figure 3.9b).
Note: Analysis controls for GDP per capita. See appendix B for more information on the indexes used.

These indicators were not, however, specifically focused on measures of property rights or the ability to own and control assets. Indicator subcomponents that had this focus were based on subjective rather than objective assessments (in, for example, the Social Institutions and Gender Index, the Gender Inequality Index, and the Women's Economic Opportunity Index).

The Women, Business, and the Law database, launched by the World Bank in March 2010, provided part of the answer (see appendix C). It assessed legal rights for 28 Sub-Saharan African countries, looking at whether property rights and women's legal capacity were the same as men's. But it did not go far enough. This study mainly used Women–LEED–Africa, which covers all 47 countries in the region.[7] It provides more-detailed indicators of where women's economic and legal rights can differ from men's, and it explicitly includes formal customary law. Because the indicators are based on the constitutions and laws on the books in these countries,[8] the measures are not subjective assessments or qualitative rankings. The categorization of countries can be replicated—and tracked consistently over time.[9]

Women–LEED–Africa focuses on constitutional protections of nondiscrimination based on gender. Every country in the region espouses this principle. However, despite the inclusion of nondiscrimination as one of the framing principles of each country's legal system, the majority of countries have formally recognized exceptions in key areas of women's economic rights. Twelve countries recognize in their constitution that customary law prevails over issues of marriage, property, and inheritance—and explicitly exempt customary law from nondiscrimination provisions. Twenty-two countries have head-of-household statutes that give husbands the legal authority to stop their wives from working outside the home or opening a bank account. Married women's ability to testify in court or to initiate legal proceedings can also be limited. Finally, some countries provide no statutory protections for women to keep a share of marital property on divorce or inheritance.

Some countries have only one such provision, some have several. To keep the groupings simple, we divided countries by whether they had any of these provisions.[10] The division is not quite equal: more countries have legal gaps in women's property and legal rights than have no or limited gender gaps in these rights.

It is particularly striking that the division has no link to income or female literacy—women's legal rights are not proxies for them (figures 3.10 and 3.11). Higher-income or more-developed countries—or ones that have closed the gender literacy gap—are not less likely to have gender gaps in legal rights. This finding implies that income growth alone is insufficient to close these legal gaps. More active measures are needed.

It is encouraging for this analysis that women's legal and economic rights do not appear correlated with income or literacy. It validates the selection of this indicator, as it means that the variation in rights is capturing a distinct dimension that should have explanatory power independent of income.

Figure 3.10 The Distribution of Income Is Very Similar across Countries with Weaker and Stronger Rights for Women

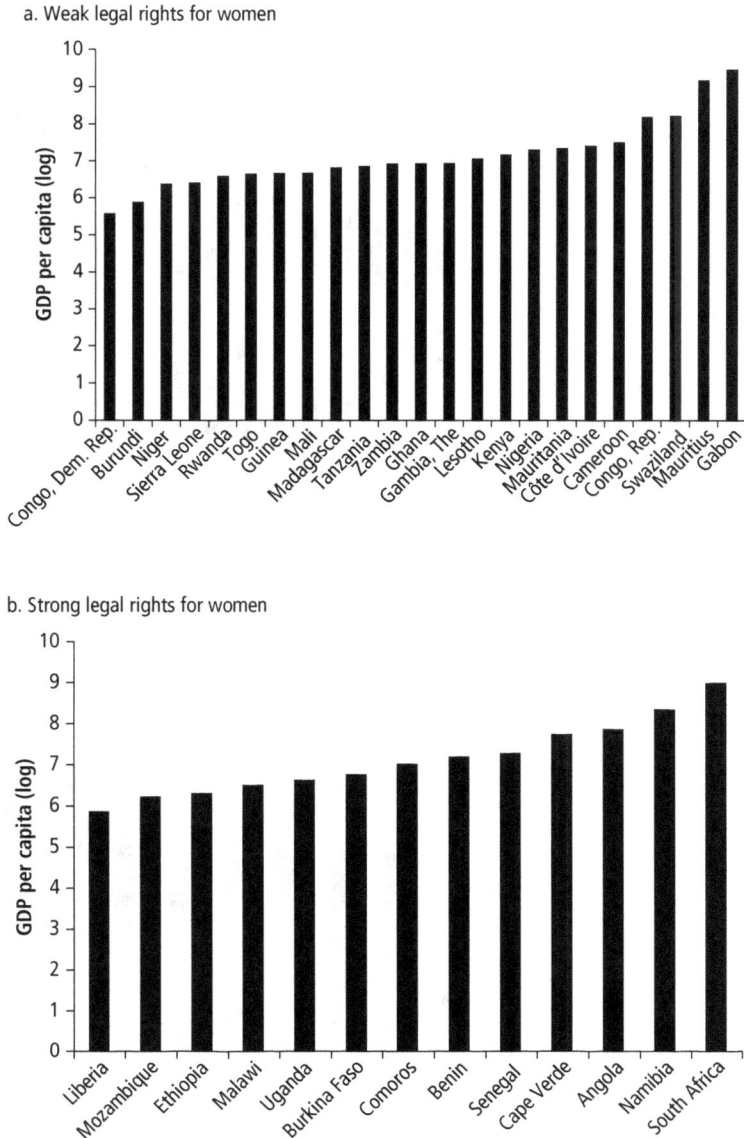

a. Weak legal rights for women

b. Strong legal rights for women

Sources: M. Hallward-Driemeier, T. Hasan, M. Blackden, J. Kamangu, and E. Lobti, Women's Legal and Economic Empowerment Database; World Bank, World Development Indicators database, http://data.worldbank.org/indicator.

Figure 3.11 The Distribution of Female Literacy Is Very Similar across Countries with Weaker and Stronger Rights for Women

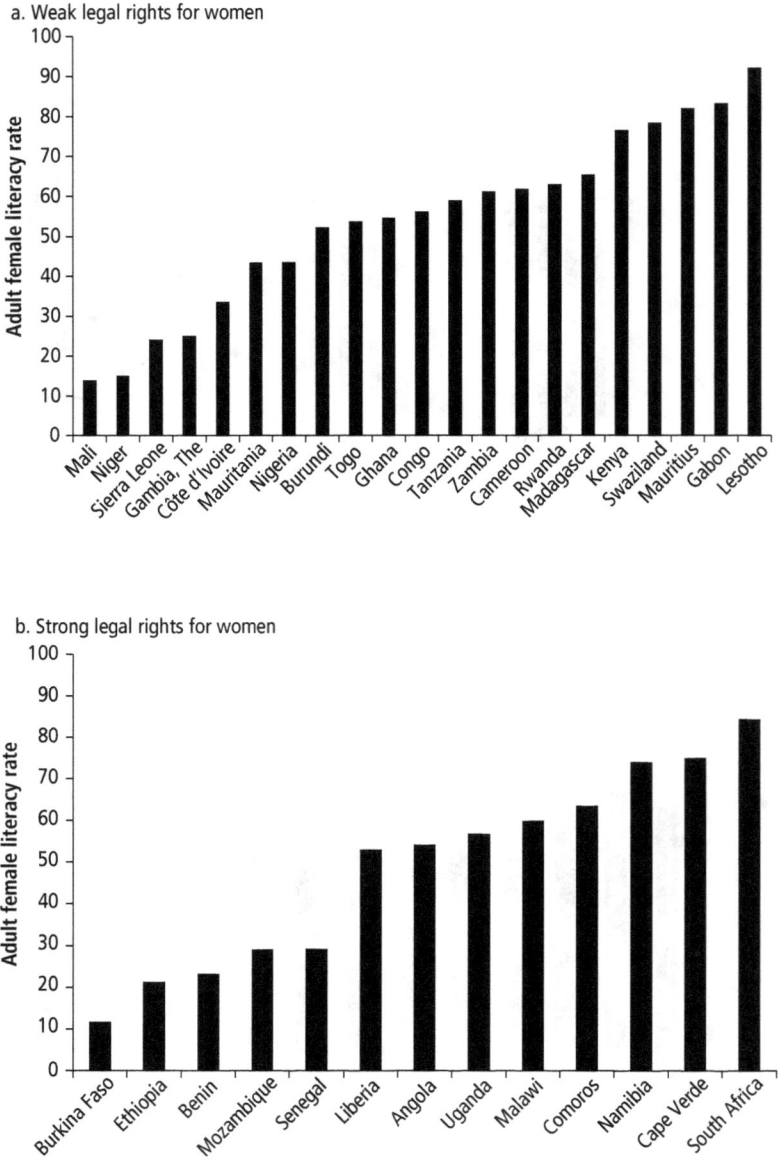

a. Weak legal rights for women

b. Strong legal rights for women

Sources: M. Hallward-Driemeier, T. Hasan, M. Blackden, J. Kamangu, and E. Lobti, Women's Legal and Economic Empowerment Database; World Bank, World Development Indicators database, http://data.worldbank.org/indicator.

That some countries have raised their incomes in a context of less secure legal and economic rights for women does not mean that women have benefited equally from higher incomes. Indeed, what is precisely of interest is to examine the effects that legal and economic rights have on the extent and composition of women's entrepreneurship.

The claim is not that formal laws are determinative, or that they are the only factor shaping how property rights are protected in practice. The institutional capacity of the legal system to enforce laws varies across all countries, and practical constraints to accessing the formal system can deter many (particularly poorer, less educated) women, from seeking the rights they have. Customs and traditions also set expectations for how property and other assets are to be controlled and passed on, regardless of formal laws. But the law still provides the final say in formal disputes, and the nature of the protections it provides affects people's ability to access and control resources and their incentives to expand their business. Particularly as economies develop and third-party transactions become a larger part of how business is conducted, the role of formal rules becomes all the more important.

Link between Entrepreneurship and Access to Human Capital and Assets

The chapter now develops country groups based on female literacy and measures of gender gaps in legal and economic rights. Using these two measures, countries are divided into four categories based on whether they have small or large gender literacy gaps and small or large gender gaps in legal and economic rights. We first compare gender gaps among these country groupings within each employment category, then across categories.

Gender Gaps in Participation within Employment Categories

For the self-employed there are clear patterns across higher and lower literacy groups, for both women and men (figure 3.12). Where gender literacy gaps are large, close to 60 percent of women are self-employed, compared with near 40 percent for men. Where gender literacy gaps are smaller, women's rates are now near 40 percent, while men's rates have fallen to 25–30 percent. The differences by legal status are much less significant. Strikingly, while the rates of self-employment are lower for both women and men in countries with higher rates of literacy, there is little difference in the percentage gap in rates between women and men across the four country groups. Women are more than 30 percent more likely to be in self-employment than men.

In contrast, when looking at gender gaps among employers, one finds the results are more sensitive to the extent of gaps in women's legal and economic

Figure 3.12 Gender Gaps in Literacy Are Correlated with Patterns in Self-Employment

a. Self-employment

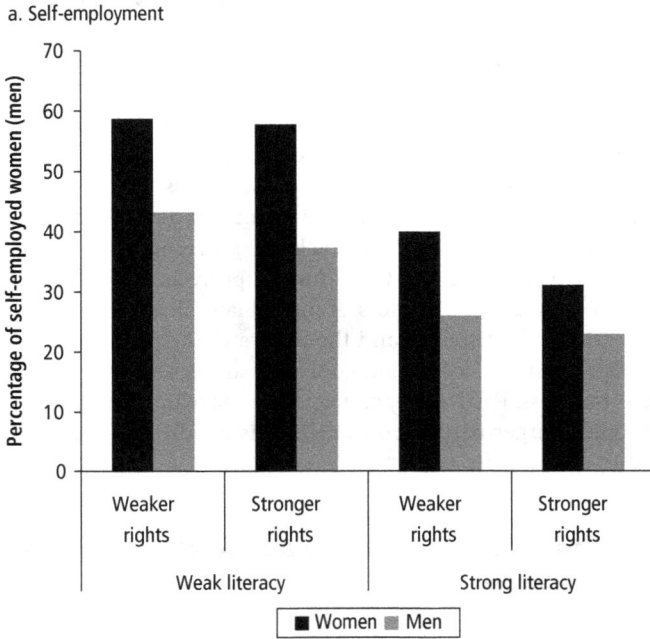

b. Gender gap among self-employed

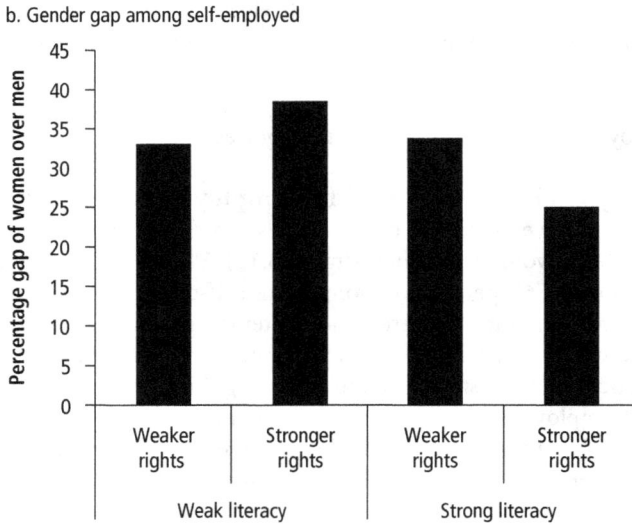

Sources: Women's Legal and Economic Empowerment Database; World Bank, World Development Indicators database, http://data.worldbank.org/indicator.

rights (figure 3.13). The share of women who are employers is about 1 percent where there are large literacy gaps, with the rate increasing by more than one-third in countries with smaller literacy gaps, and tripling where both literacy gaps and legal gaps are small. For men the rates of being an employer are much the same where there are legal gaps, lower where literacy gaps are large and legal gaps smaller (a bit of a puzzle), and larger again where literacy and legal gaps are both small. However, the changes are proportionally larger for women, so the gaps in figure 3.13b show how literacy and particularly greater legal protections close the gender gap in participating as an employer.

For wage earners, there are differences across all four groups (figure 3.14). Participation rates for women rise with smaller literacy gaps and with legal gaps, as do those for men. For both women and men, there is not a further increase associated with smaller gaps on both dimensions. However, looking at the proportional changes in figure 3.14b, the gender gaps decline as the differences in literacy and legal rights close (that is, moving to the right in the figures).

Gaps in Women's Participation across Employment Categories
Female shares in self-employment are significantly larger than female shares of employers in all four country categories, particularly where both rights and literacy are weaker (figure 3.15). Higher literacy rates close the gap between women who are self-employed and those who are employers, as do stronger women's legal rights. The effect of stronger legal rights is particularly noticeable where literacy is weaker.

For employers and wage earners, what is striking is that there is no average participation gap for women in countries with stronger literacy, though the extent of legal protection plays a significant role where larger literacy gaps exist (figure 3.16). Where gaps in rights are larger, women's share in wage earning is higher. Where gaps in rights are smaller, women's share as employers is higher.

So, legal rights are important not only in the trade-offs between being self-employed and being an employer, but also in the trade-offs between being an employer and being a wage earner.

To sum up, larger gender gaps in adult literacy are generally associated with women's greater involvement in self-employment, while greater legal protection is more associated with women having more opportunity to become employers. These results are consistent with self-employment relying mostly on the skills and human capital of the entrepreneur; they are also consistent with employers' need to sign contracts and have better control over assets, such that legal and economic rights are important.

These results rely on cross-country variation. Evaluations of legal reforms within a country also demonstrate the importance of stronger legal and economic rights on economic activities that are pursued. Box 3.1 discusses the case of Ethiopia. Chapter 7 provides additional discussion of these issues.

Figure 3.13 Gender Gaps among Employers Are Sensitive to Gaps in Women's Economic and Legal Rights

a. Employer

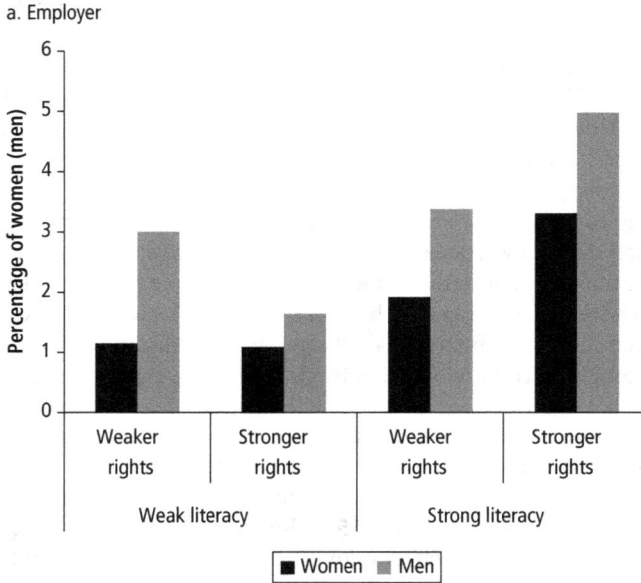

b. Gender gap among employers

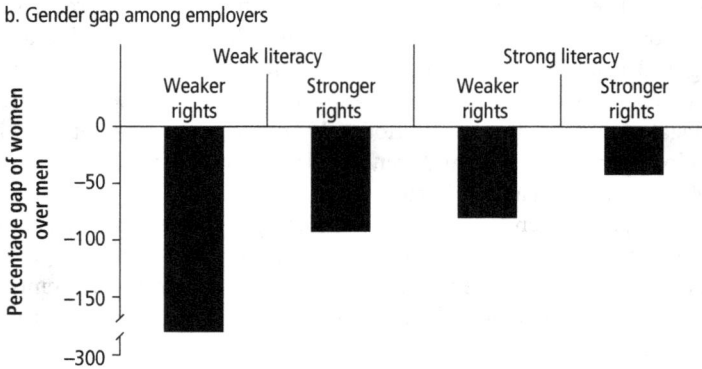

Sources: Women's Legal and Economic Empowerment Database; World Bank, World Development Indicators database, http://data.worldbank.org/indicator.

Figure 3.14 More Women Become Wage Earners Where Gaps in Literacy and Legal Rights Are Smaller

a. Wage earners

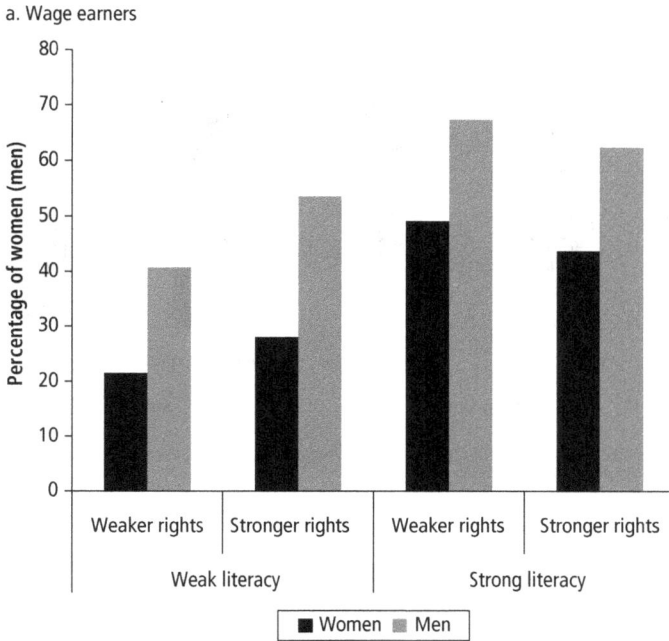

b. Gender gap among wage earners

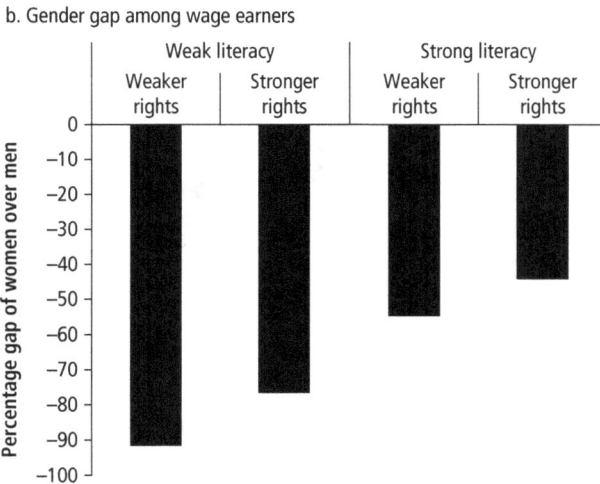

Sources: Women's Legal and Economic Empowerment Database; World Bank, World Development Indicators database, http://data.worldbank.org/indicator.

Figure 3.15 Stronger Literacy Closes the Employer–Self-Employed Participation Gap

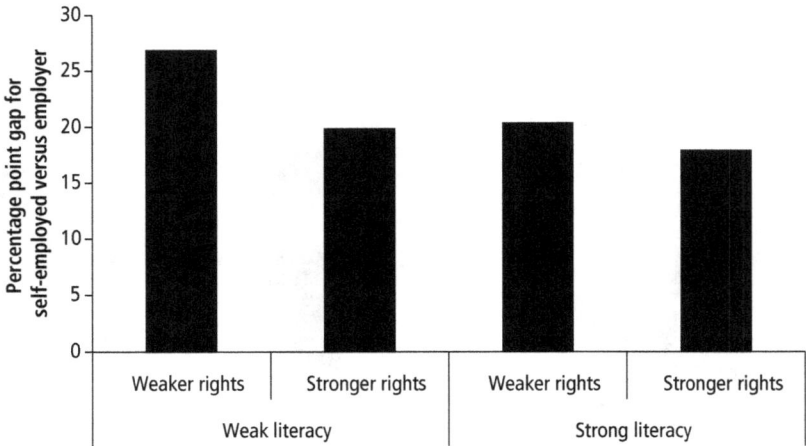

Sources: Women's Legal and Economic Empowerment Database; World Bank, World Development Indicators database, http://data.worldbank.org/indicator.

Figure 3.16 Stronger Literacy Shows Virtually No Employer–Wage Earner Participation Gap for Women

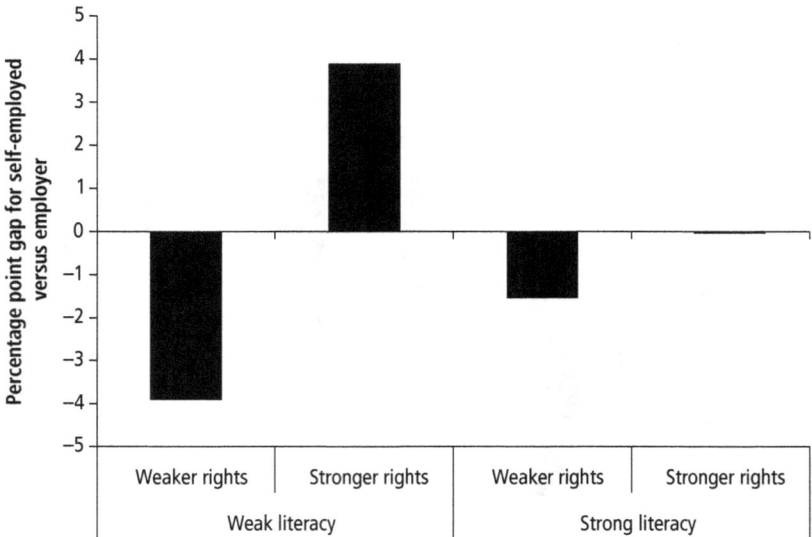

Sources: Women's Legal and Economic Empowerment Database; World Bank, World Development Indicators database, http://data.worldbank.org/indicator.

BOX 3.1

Strengthening Women's Property Rights Affects the Opportunities Women Pursue

Ethiopia changed its family law in 2000, raising the minimum age of marriage for women, removing the ability of the husband to deny permission for the wife to work outside the home, and requiring both spouses' consent in the administration of marital property. This reform, initially rolled out in selected regions and cities, now applies across the country.

Using two nationally representative household surveys, one in 2000 just prior to the reform and one five years later, we find a substantial shift in women's economic activities. In particular, women's relative participation in occupations that require work outside the home, full-time work, and higher skills rose more where the reform had been enacted (controlling for time and location effects).

Source: Hallward-Driemeier and Gajigo 2011.

Notes

1. Klapper and Parker (2010) provide a review of the broader literature on women's entrepreneurship and the business environment, but do not focus on Sub-Saharan Africa per se. Ayyagari, Beck, and Demirgüç-Kunt (2007) provide data and analysis of the share of firms around the world that are considered small and medium enterprises, but do not have information on the gender of the entrepreneur.
2. As in chapter 1, the figures do not include the shares of unemployed—shares that are very low in Sub-Saharan Africa.
3. Other authors also analyze how patterns of entrepreneurship vary across countries by income, but not disaggregated by gender (Bartlesman, Haltiwanger, and Scarpetta, forthcoming; Klapper, Amit, and Guillén 2008; Lerner 2007; Tybout 2000.)
4. M. Hallward-Driemeier, T. Hasan, M. Blackden, J. Kamangu, and E. Lobti, Women's Legal and Economic Empowerment Database. The database was developed for the companion volume (Hallward-Driemeier and Hasan 2012) and is further elaborated in chapter 7.
5. Access to technology could be a third dimension, but given the difficulty in measuring it, and the additional challenge of having an objective way to quantify gender differences in access to technology, we do not include it.
6. An alternative to using current literacy rates is to look at education completion rates of an earlier generation. Indeed, girls' completion of primary education in 1980 is very closely correlated with current literacy. However, as data on historical rates of girls' completion of primary education are available only for a few countries, we use the literacy rates here.
7. Note, however, that we could not find all the relevant family codes or land statutes for the Central African Republic, Chad, Equatorial Guinea, and São Tomé and Príncipe and so did not categorize them.

8. One exception is Kenya, whose new constitution came into force in August 2010. For categorizing the current situation, Kenya's new constitution provides the basis of the indicators. But in the analysis, the older constitution is used because it was in effect when the household and enterprise data were collected.

9. For more-detailed information on its construction, see Hallward-Driemeier and Hasan (2012). As a follow-up to the Women–LEED–Africa project, efforts are under way to build the database back over time to offer historical coverage of how countries have reformed laws affecting women's economic rights.

10. The one household-head provision we did not include was the right for the husband to choose the location of the marital domicile. If this involved moving, it could separate the wife from her business or client base. For three countries this is the only source of gender gaps in the categories we considered: Benin, Burkina Faso, and Senegal. The first two have made considerable progress in recent years, reforming their family codes to greatly strengthen women's rights. If this provision was the only source of gaps, the countries were not placed in the "weaker women's property rights" group.

References

Acemoglu, D., and S. Johnson. 2005. "Unbundling Institutions." *Journal of Political Economy* 113 (5): 949–95.

Acemoglu, D., S. Johnson, and J. Robinson. 2002. "Reversal of Fortune: Geography and Institutions in the Making of the Modern World Income Distribution." *Quarterly Journal of Economics* 117: 1231–94.

Aterido, R., and M. Hallward-Driemeier. 2010. "The Impact of the Investment Climate on Employment Growth: Does Sub-Saharan Africa Mirror Other Low-Income Regions?" Policy Research Working Paper 5218, World Bank, Washington, DC.

Ayyagari, M., T. Beck, and A. Demirgüç-Kunt. 2007. "Small and Medium Enterprises across the Globe." *Small Business Economics* 29: 415–34.

Bartlesman, E., J. Haltiwanger, and S. Scarpetta. Forthcoming. "Cross Country Differences in Productivity: The Role of Allocative Efficiency." *American Economic Review*.

Bigsten, A., P. Collier, S. Dercon, M. Fafchamps, B. Gauthier, J. Gunning, A. Oduro, R. Oostendorp, C. Pattillo, M. Söderbom, F. Teal, and A. Zeufack. 2003. "Credit Constraints in Manufacturing Enterprises in Africa." *Journal of African Economies* 12 (1): 104–25.

Bigsten, A., and M. Söderbom. 2006. "What Have We Learned from a Decade of Manufacturing Enterprise Surveys in Africa?" *World Bank Research Observer* 21 (2): 241–65.

Dollar, D., M. Hallward-Driemeier, and T. Mengistae. 2005. "Investment Climate and Firm Performance in Developing Economies." *Economic Development and Cultural Change* 54 (1): 1–32.

Hall, R., and C. Jones. 1999. "Why Do Some Countries Produce So Much More Output per Worker Than Others?" *Quarterly Journal of Economics* 114: 83–116.

Hallward-Driemeier, M., and O. Gajigo. 2011. "Strengthening Economic Rights and Women's Occupational Choice: The Impact of Reforming Ethiopia's Family Law." Paper presented at Centre for the Study of African Economics annual conference, St. Catherine's College, Oxford, March 20–22.

Hallward-Driemeier, M., and T. Hasan. 2012. *Empowering Women: Legal Rights and Economic Opportunities in Africa*. Washington, DC: World Bank and Agence Française de Développement.

Hallward-Driemeier, M., and A. Rasteletti. 2010. "Women's and Men's Entrepreneurship in Africa." Working paper, World Bank, Washington, DC.

Hsieh, C.-T., and P. J. Klenow. 2009. "Misallocation and Manufacturing TFP in China and India." *Quarterly Journal of Economics* 124 (4): 1403–46.

Klapper, L., R. Amit, and M. F. Guillén. 2008. "Entrepreneurship and Firm Formation across Countries." Working paper, World Bank, Washington, DC.

Klapper, L., and S. Parker. 2010. "Gender and the Business Environment for New Firm Creation." *World Bank Research Observer* 26 (2): 237–57.

Lerner, J., ed. 2007. *International Differences in Entrepreneurship*. Chicago: University of Chicago Press.

Rodrik, D., A. Subramanian, and F. Trebbi. 2004. "Institutions Rule: The Primacy of Institutions Over Geography and Integration in Economic Development." *Journal of Economic Growth* 9 (2): 131–65.

Tybout, J. R. 2000. "Manufacturing Firms in Developing Countries: How Well Do They Do, and Why?" *Journal of Economic Literature* 28 (March): 11–44.

World Bank. 2004. *World Development Report 2005: A Better Investment Climate for Everyone*. Washington, DC: World Bank.

Chapter 4

Sorting into Entrepreneurial Activities: Individual Patterns

The earlier chapters emphasize the gender patterns across employment categories and types of enterprise. A key finding here is that enterprise characteristics often swamp gender differences within similar types of activities; formal firms share more characteristics, regardless of the gender of the entrepreneur, than do formal and informal women's enterprises. The same is largely true of large and small enterprises, and high- and low-value-added lines of business. So the question becomes, what accounts for individuals' choice of enterprise?

Chapter 3 points to some broad features of the economy that can matter, including average income and (to a greater degree) gender gaps in access to education and property rights. This chapter examines differences among entrepreneurs themselves, focusing on individual characteristics and how they affect the choice of activity (box 4.1). Studies that look at women entrepreneurs have raised several issues as being important, from the division of household responsibilities, to differences in risk taking, to differences in "entrepreneurial spirit," to differences in ability to navigate the business environment; for reviews of the literature see Klapper and Parker (2010); Mammen and Paxon 2000; Minniti (2009); and Parker (2004). The emphasis here is on more observable characteristics of age, education, marital status, prior work experience, and family background. Measures of motivations and attitudes are included, but are not found to have much explanatory power, particularly once the observable characteristics are taken into account. This finding is also consistent with those of other authors, such as Blanchflower and Oswald (1998), who emphasize that access to capital rather than personality is the best predictor of whether an individual will become an entrepreneur, or Djankov and others (2005 and 2006), who emphasize the importance of a tradition of entrepreneurship within the family.

Deciding whether to be an entrepreneur and what type of business to run is a multistage process, discussed here as consisting of four choices: participating in the nonagricultural labor force, becoming an entrepreneur, operating in the formal or informal sector, and choosing the line of business.

BOX 4.1

Choice of Activity—Externally Constrained or Internally Preferred?

One of the central debates in the sociological literature on women's entrepreneurship is whether different outcomes between men and women reflect different constraints or different preferences. Unfortunately, no definitive answer has appeared.

Legal restrictions on women's participation in certain activities are an obvious constraint on options. But different responsibilities outside work (for example, care within the home) or differences in preferences may also reduce options, as may cultural norms.

In this chapter, to see how much "choice" women actually have, we draw on surveys that ask entrepreneurs what motivated them to become an entrepreneur and why they chose the activity they did.

In examining these choices, this chapter analyzes individuals of working age (16–60 years) who are not attending school. The analysis mostly considers individuals making autonomous decisions, but also allows that some decisions are made jointly with the spouse—and that decisions may not represent a choice if there are no alternatives available. The analysis requires comparisons with people who are not in business (unlike many of the comparisons in the earlier chapters). Thus it looks at household surveys from 39 countries in Sub-Saharan Africa, comparing the characteristics of those who did and did not become entrepreneurs. There is room, though, for strengthening data collection (box 4.2).

Education is a key determinant in these choices, with smaller roles played by prior work experience, marital status, motivation, age, and relevant business skills. More specifically, education, prior experience, and age help predict whether an individual joins the formal or informal sector and the size of the enterprise. This holds for women and men. But while the effect of education on entrepreneurial performance is almost always positive, its effect on selection into entrepreneurship is more ambiguous (given the high variability in returns not only within the entrepreneurial sector but also within competing occupations in the wage sector).

Strikingly, characteristics of female and male entrepreneurs within a sector are much more similar than characteristics of female or male entrepreneurs across sectors. Thus many of the observed gender gaps in entrepreneurship stem from deeper gender gaps in education and access to alternative wage employment.

BOX 4.2

Strengthening Data Collection

This chapter's analysis could be improved in two ways, but both would require more data.

The first would be to track individuals over time. Such panel data sets allow use of more-sophisticated estimation methods and can take into account how changing conditions affect decisions. Unfortunately, the household surveys are repeat cross-section surveys. National statistical offices should be encouraged to collect more panel data.

The second would be to collect more information on types of constraints that might affect decisions. More information on access to assets, control of income, and time use, for example, would enable us to examine how decisions are made in the household and in turn how this process affects outcomes. A few countries collect data on these variables, but the data are rarely comparable across countries.

Prior work experience is important, particularly with respect to the performance of the enterprise. Indeed, entrepreneurship-related experience can be a bigger determinant of productivity than nonspecialized formal education. The sector (formal or informal) in which the prior work experience occurred matters—most individuals open their business in the same sector they had worked in before. This finding has a gender dimension: because women are more likely to work in the informal sector, they are more likely to run informal enterprises if they become entrepreneurs.

Marital status, more for women than men, determines legal standing, property rights, and ability to engage in business (as discussed further in chapter 7). The time demands for men and women at home can also vary, leading to different elasticities of labor supply. The effect of marital status is greatest for women's decision to participate in the labor force and for their decision to operate in the informal or formal sector.

In a few of the reasons for going into entrepreneurship cited by survey respondents there are discernible gender and sector differences. Among those who cite the possession of business skills as an important motivation for becoming an entrepreneur, the proportions of male and formal entrepreneurs are higher than those of female and informal entrepreneurs. A similar pattern is evident for those who profess to have knowledge about their particular line of business. This difference likely reflects the higher average human capital of male entrepreneurs, who also dominate in the formal sector.

Choice 1: Participating in the Nonagricultural Labor Force

Five individual or household characteristics weigh heavily in the initial decision to join the nonagricultural labor force:

- *Age.* The probability of participating increases with age, if at a decreasing rate.[1]
- *Education.* Those with more education are more likely to join. The effect is much stronger for women than men.
- *Head-of-household status.* Heads of household are more likely to participate, particularly women.
- *Marital status.* Married women are much less likely to participate than either married men or unmarried women.
- *Urban-rural location.* Living in an urban area increases the chances of participating. The effect is larger for men than women.

To explore some of the cross-country variation in the effects of individual characteristics on a person's decision to participate, we now allow some of the effects of certain characteristics to matter more in some environments than others. The results thus combine differences within and across countries.

We focus on the effects of gross domestic product (GDP) per capita, higher education, property rights, and governance. We focus on the Organisation for Economic Co-operation and Development's Gender-related Development Index, with its relative weight on human capital, and the Worldwide Governance Indicators (WGI) project's overall indexes as our measures for social inclusion and governance quality, respectively. Given that the literature highlights the importance of ownership rights and corruption for economic outcomes, we also present results using the Social Institutions and Gender Index subindicator on ownership rights and the WGI indicator on control of corruption (for more on the indexes see appendix B).[2]

With respect to the effects of GDP per capita, most of the effects of workers' characteristics on participation in the nonagricultural labor force tend to be smaller in absolute terms in countries with higher GDP per capita. Specifically, being older, more educated, and married have a smaller impact on the decision to participate in the nonagricultural labor force in more-developed economies.

Greater female education and property rights and the quality of governance also play important roles. They are associated with higher rates of women's participation in the nonagricultural labor force. In addition to this level effect, these country characteristics also affect the relative importance of an individual's education and marital status. The effect of an individual's level of education on participation in the nonagricultural labor force is larger in those countries with smaller gender gaps in education and property rights and where there is better governance. Women married to a working spouse are also more likely to participate in the nonagricultural sector in environments with larger gender gaps and stronger governance.

Choice 2: Becoming an Entrepreneur (Self-Employed or Employer)

Within the nonagricultural labor force, individuals have various options (boxes 4.3 and 4.4): entrepreneurship (self-employment or being an employer), wage work, unpaid work, and (perhaps less of a free choice) unemployment. Some of these types of employment are not always available; they may not be "options" or "choices" in many cases (Banerjee and Newman 1993; Iyer and Schoar 2010). At issue here are the prevalence of the categories and the types of individuals most likely to be working in each one. Again, our population of interest consists of those ages 16–60 who are not currently attending school. The two characteristics most strongly associated with choosing entrepreneurship are education and marital status.

Education

Earlier studies have found that education has a significant effect both on the decision to become an entrepreneur and on the level of entrepreneurial productivity once an entrepreneur has started a business (Blau 1985; Parker and van Praag 2006; Van der Sluis, van Praag, and Vijverberg 2008). The latter effect is almost invariably positive. The former effect is more ambiguous, given the high variability in returns not only within entrepreneurship but also within competing occupations in wage work. More-educated workers are more likely to take wage jobs (usually in urban areas) than to become an entrepreneur, and entrepreneurship is likely to be more attractive where the main alternative livelihood is farming. These trade-offs vary by level of income, with the gap between the attractiveness of wage earning relative to entrepreneurship being highest in Sub-Saharan Africa's low-income countries.

Three patterns emerge in most countries for education among male and female entrepreneurs. First, men tend to be more educated than women. Second, employers are more educated than the self-employed. Third, the second pattern is particularly true within gender (that is, male employers are more educated than male self-employed, and women employers are more educated than female self-employed), but not between genders. In some countries, female employers on average have less education than self-employed men; these are countries with more pronounced gender gaps in education and adult literacy. Self-employed women are almost always the least educated (figure 4.1).

BOX 4.3

Motivation: Necessity or Opportunity?

Does the motivation of the entrepreneur matter—beyond the gender patterns across types of activities seen in enterprises' external characteristics? Are those individuals who claim that they are pursuing an opportunity different from those who claim to be default or necessity entrepreneurs?

The gender module of existing formal enterprises and the survey of new entrepreneurs (see box 1.3) asked questions to capture the motivation for becoming an entrepreneur. Some respondents were entrepreneurs who had been "pulled" into starting a business to take advantage of an opportunity, while others had been "pushed" into it out of necessity, perhaps for lack of alternative wage jobs, loss of a job, or household shocks (such as illness, death, or divorce). These two broad lines have long been recognized in the enterprise literature.

The survey data find job loss, household shock, family traditions, or unavailability of attractive wage jobs significantly less common than other reasons (figure B4.3.1).

Figure B4.3.1 The Reason for Starting a Business Varies Little by Gender or Formality

Source: Gajigo and Hallward-Driemeier 2010; see also Aterido and Hallward-Driemeier 2011.
Note: Data are for newly established enterprises in Côte d'Ivoire, Kenya, Nigeria, and Senegal.

This is unlike findings in the literature, which cites household shocks as a frequent reason for becoming an entrepreneur. It may be that the entrepreneurs in this sample—completely urban—are less likely to go into entrepreneurship out of necessity than rural entrepreneurs. The sample also has few household-based enterprises, again likely affecting the share of reported necessity entrepreneurs. Of less interest here is the comparison of necessity and opportunity entrepreneurs per se; of more interest is whether there are any significant gender differences in the reasons given for starting a business.

When one divides answers depending on whether necessity or opportunity is most important, the clearest pattern is that all four groups of respondents tend to track each other relatively well. Motivation does not differ dramatically for women versus men, or for those in the informal versus the formal sector.

No tight relationships are evident between education and motivation, although those who had no better alternative jobs, had lost their job, were in business to follow family tradition, or had felt a shock were less likely to have high education (university and graduate school). Similarly, differences across motivations for starting a business are not large for work experience.

Using the above motivations, the analysis shows that around 60 percent of new entrepreneurs in the four countries surveyed (Côte d'Ivoire, Kenya, Nigeria, and Senegal) are necessity entrepreneurs (figure B4.3.2). The informal sector shows no gender difference, but the formal sector has more female than male necessity entrepreneurs.

Figure B4.3.2 Gender Plays Some Role among Necessity Entrepreneurs in the Formal Sector

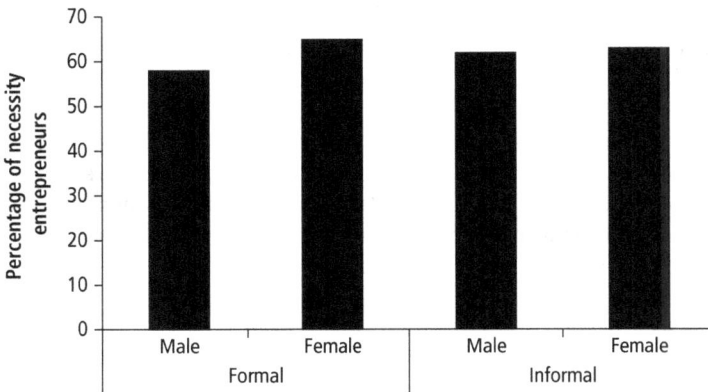

Source: Gajigo and Hallward-Driemeier 2010.
Note: Data are for newly established enterprises in Côte d'Ivoire, Kenya, Nigeria, and Senegal, 2010.

—Continued

BOX 4.3 *continued*

Regression results (probit) for the determinants of necessity entrepreneurs show that on average, females are more likely to be necessity entrepreneurs. However, once we control for previous employment background, the significance level for this result disappears. Among previous employment experiences, having been a worker in a nonenterprise organization reduces the likelihood of being a necessity entrepreneur for men but increases it for women. By marital status, married women are significantly less likely to become a necessity entrepreneur. Educational level is a strong predictor of opportunity entrepreneurship, especially at the highest levels (university and graduate school). More–highly educated individuals would have the opportunity to engage in highly remunerative and less risky wage employment. Other characteristics that reduce the likelihood of being a necessity entrepreneur are having a background as an employee in a nonbusiness entity and being financially literate. Older entrepreneurs are more likely to be necessity entrepreneurs.

Note: Because of the gender division of labor, even female entrepreneurs are responsible for most household work. Thus for a woman who also does significant household work, entrepreneurship is preferable to wage work, since it does not require such regular working hours. In analyzing job growth among Guatemalan entrepreneurs, Kevane and Wydick (2001) found that young female entrepreneurs are especially constrained in generating employment compared to young males and older women, and they attribute this gender difference to the higher opportunity time cost for younger women during their childbearing years.

The probability of being an entrepreneur has an inverted-U relationship with education; individuals are more likely to become an entrepreneur as their education increases, but at a certain level of education, the probability starts to decline. For age, the probability is increasing and concave: it rises with age, but at a decreasing rate.

These patterns show some variation by income. At higher incomes, more-educated women are more likely to become entrepreneurs, particularly employers. The marginal effect of additional education in encouraging women's entrepreneurship is also larger in countries that have lower gender gaps in property rights and stronger governance.

Marital status

Women could also face constraints arising from their marital status. Women's marital status, more so than men's, determines their legal standing, property rights, and ability to engage in business activity (discussed further in chapter 7). For example, a married woman could be more restricted than a single woman in her ability to be an entrepreneur, because, under the law, she may be unable to access or control assets, or make autonomous business

BOX 4.4

Entrepreneurship: An Opportunity That Varies with Income and Education

Among entrepreneurs the average education of employers is higher than that of the self-employed, though to a striking degree the gap closes as national income rises. Wage earners are more educated than the self-employed in almost all countries—that is, the education gap on the y-axis is almost always positive (figure B4.4.1 shows this for women; the pattern is similar for men). The gap in education for wage earners and the self-employed is greatest in low-income countries and where self-employment is higher.

In low-income Sub-Saharan African countries, wage earners are more educated than employers—thus in figure B4.4.2, most of the diamonds are in the upper right quadrant. In higher-income countries, many employers are more educated than wage earners—that is, the squares are primarily in the bottom left quadrant. The gap

Figure B4.4.1 Gaps in Education for Female Wage Earners versus Female Self-Employed Rise as the Share of Women in Self-Employment Rises

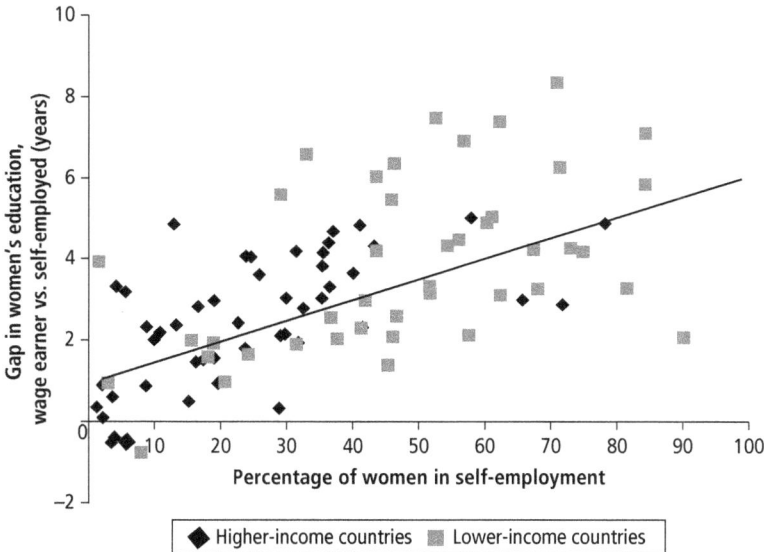

Source: Based on national household and labor force surveys for 101 low- and middle-income economies, most recent years (2000–10).

—Continued

BOX 4.4 *continued*

in education for female wage earners and employers is greater than that for male wage earners and employers in low-income countries (the diamonds are above the 45 degree line).

Figure B4.4.2 Gap in Education for Wage Earners versus Employers Is Higher for Women Than Men

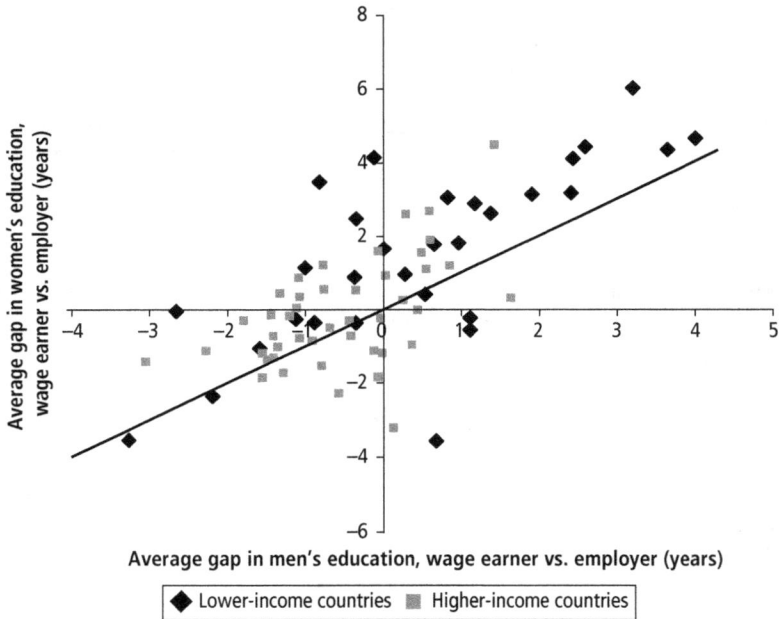

Average gap in men's education, wage earner vs. employer (years)

◆ Lower-income countries   ▪ Higher-income countries

Source: Based on national household and labor force surveys for 101 low- and middle-income economies, most recent years (2000–10).

decisions. Among self-employed women, on average, more than 60 percent are married, 15 percent are single, and 10 percent are widowed or divorced. Female employers are twice as likely to be divorced or widowed as women overall.[3]

Married women are 55 percent of the female population, and they make up 50 percent of wage earners and more than 60 percent of female self-employed and employers.[4] However, for divorced women, the distribution across activities is more dramatic. While 5 percent of women are divorced, they make up 10 percent, or twice as large a share, of female employers,

Figure 4.1 Self-Employed Women Are the Least Educated among Male and Female Entrepreneurs

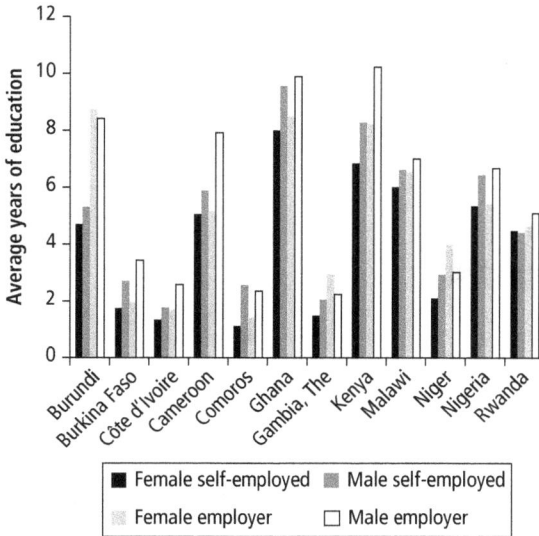

Source: Hallward-Driemeier and Rasteletti 2010.
Note: Data are from enterprise modules of household surveys in selected countries, various years (2000–10).

self-employed, and wage earners. Some of the jump is clearly due to divorced women's increased need to earn income (since they generally no longer have the income contributions of their spouse to their household). However, the variation in the extent of concentration of divorced versus married women in entrepreneurship varies by certain country characteristics, in particular the extent of gaps in legal capacity and property rights for married and nonmarried women. Figure 4.2 shows one of the more extreme examples: Swaziland. It is among the most restrictive countries where rights for married women are concerned.

Switching the perspective to look within each marital status category at the shares of entrepreneurs, we see that rates of self-employment and rates of being an employer are highest among divorced women. It is also well established that marital status has a significant effect in the labor market: one of the most consistent findings is that married men have higher returns (Goldin 1990). Another important gender difference is that female divorced and widowed entrepreneurs are more common than male, especially in informal activities, suggesting that they face much higher barriers to entry into the formal sector than other categories of marital status (Gajigo and Hallward-Driemeier 2010).

Figure 4.2 Where Married Women Have Fewer Economic Rights, Employers Are More Likely to Be Divorcees or Widows: The Case of Swaziland

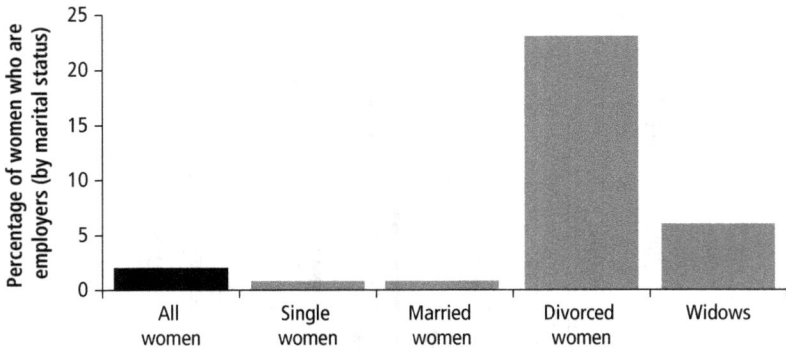

Source: Gajigo and Hallward-Driemeier 2010.

The occupation of the spouse also shows a pattern. Those with a wage-earning spouse are less likely to be entrepreneurs. Those married to an entrepreneur are more likely to be entrepreneurs themselves, which could be because many household enterprises engage multiple members of the same family. These two effects are particularly large for women relative to men, consistent with women being more likely to help operate their husband's enterprises than vice versa.

Choice 3: Formal or Informal Sector

A strong predictor of an enterprise's productivity and size is whether the enterprise is registered or is operating in the informal sector (ILO 2002). This section looks in more detail at individual characteristics and how they correlate with choice of sector. It should be kept in mind that working in the informal sector may be seen as more desirable for some entrepreneurs, particularly if flexible hours or the ability to work close to home are valued (Heintz 2012; Maloney 2004). At the same time, for many, the option to operate in the formal sector may not be feasible given the resources available.

Education
Patterns of education are far more similar for women and men within the informal (or formal) sector than they are between the sectors, based on data from surveys of new entrepreneurs in Côte d'Ivoire, Kenya, Nigeria, and Senegal (figure 4.3). Among informal entrepreneurs, only 17–18 percent

Figure 4.3 Education Varies More by Sector Formality Than by Gender

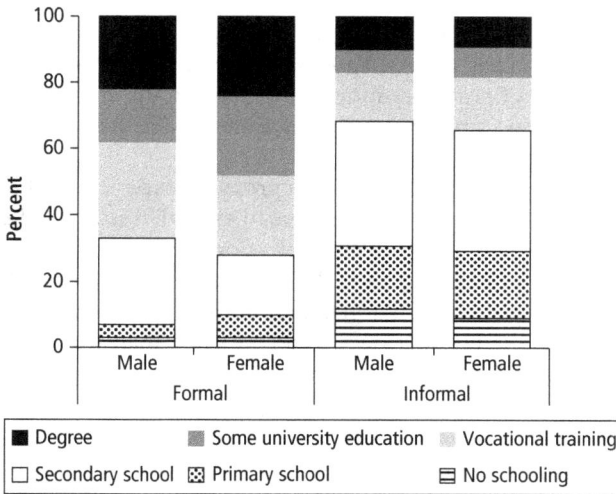

Source: Gajigo and Hallward-Driemeier 2010.
Note: Data are for newly established enterprises in Côte d'Ivoire, Kenya, Nigeria, and Senegal, 2010.

have some postsecondary education, compared with more than 40 percent of formal entrepreneurs (almost 50 percent of women and 40 percent of men).

Still, some gender differences emerge, more so in the formal sector. Female entrepreneurs are more likely to have completed or to have had some university education, and men are more likely to have completed vocational or secondary school. This finding would indicate that women who have made it into the formal sector are on average more educated than their male counterparts.

Age
Enterprise modules in household surveys indicate that the average age of entrepreneurs is 35 for the self-employed and 37 for employers. Employers also tend to be older than wage employees. Gender differences within a sector are smaller than the differences across sectors.

Age is also a significant predictor of productivity, using revenue per worker as the metric. This difference is robust to controlling for education, sector (formal sector), country, and industry dummies. The effect does not increase monotonically—the positive effect does not persist past age 30. Further, there is no gender gradient to the effect of age on productivity when the above variables are controlled.

The finding that age is a significant predictor of productivity is not new. While numerous studies have shown negative association between age and productivity among workers (including Aubert, Cavoli, and Rogers 2006; Behagel and Greenan 2005; Haltiwanger, Lane, and Spletzer 1999), some have shown that older managers (a category more comparable to the entrepreneurs in our sample) do better on some practical management skills than younger workers (Colonia-Willner 1998).

The age of the entrepreneur could be a proxy for experience. The data from the surveys of new entrepreneurs allow us to explore this possibility in more detail because we know both the years of prior experience and the sector in which the experience was gained. Among new entrepreneurs from Côte d'Ivoire, Kenya, Nigeria, and Senegal, men in the formal sector are distinctly older than men in the informal sector and are older than women in both the formal and informal sectors (figure 4.4). And these older entrepreneurs who are starting new businesses tend to show better performance. However, age itself is not the reason: older individuals who start a business tend to come from backgrounds that allowed them to accumulate more experience. The selection effect is at work: former employees who saw an opportunity and left their job to start a business have a higher likelihood of running a productive firm than those who

Figure 4.4 Women Entrepreneurs Tend to Be Younger Than Their Male Colleagues—Particularly in the Formal Sector

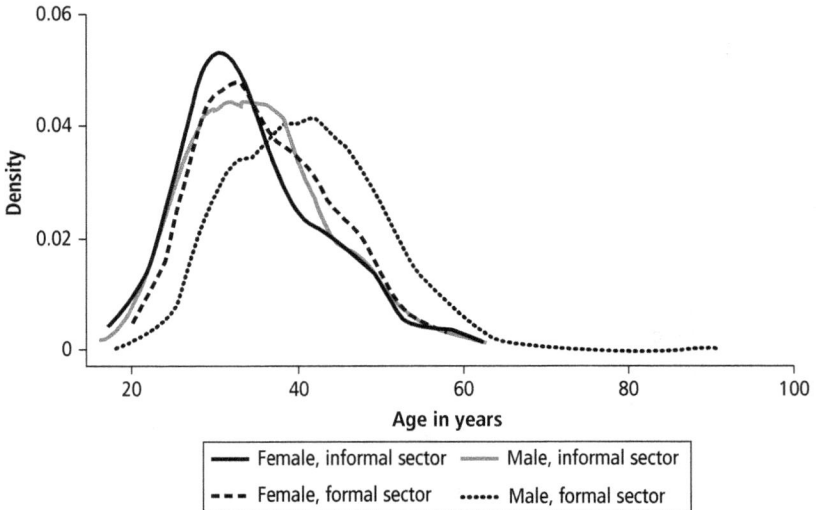

Source: Gajigo and Hallward-Driemeier 2010.
Note: Kernel = Epanechnikov; bandwidth = 2.0347. Data are for newly established enterprises in Côte d'Ivoire, Kenya, Nigeria, and Senegal, 2010.

started a business many years earlier (for opportunity or necessity) and are still in business years later. And many of the older entrepreneurs starting businesses came from the public sector or formal private sector.

Prior Labor Market Experience

Beyond education, experience is another important human capital variable in the choice of formal or informal sector work. (Experience matters for enterprise size, too; see box 4.5.) Gender is likely to affect work experience, since the time demand for men and women at home can vary, leading to different elasticities of

---

BOX 4.5

Scale of Enterprise

The measures of human capital most strongly correlated with business size are the education and the experience of the senior manager. The more-educated and more-experienced managers are more likely to be in the formal sector and run a large business. The patterns by education are stronger than those by experience (figure B4.5.1). While there is little difference in education between women and men in the informal sector and in smaller formal firms, women who run firms with 50 or more employees are progressively more educated than their male counterparts.

Figure B4.5.1 Managers' Education Is More Strongly Correlated with Business Size Than Managers' Experience

a. Managers' Education and Firm Size

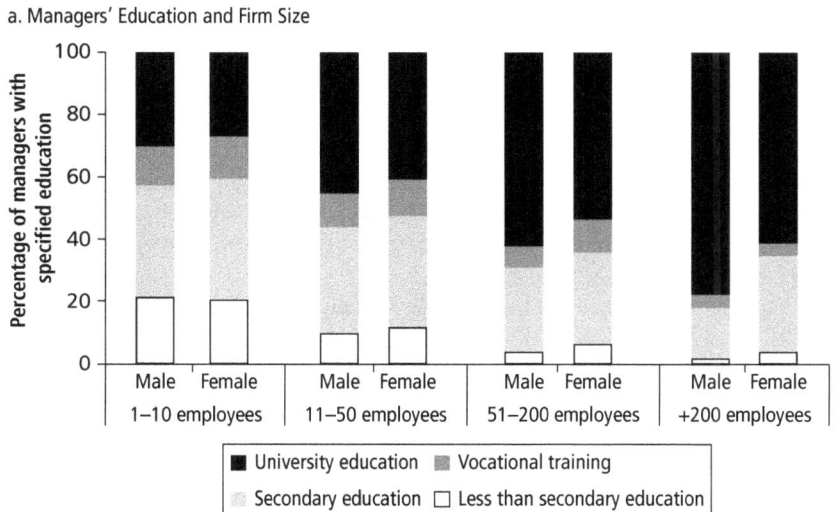

—Continued

BOX 4.5 *continued*

Figure B4.5.1 *(continued)*

b. Managers' Experience and Firm Size

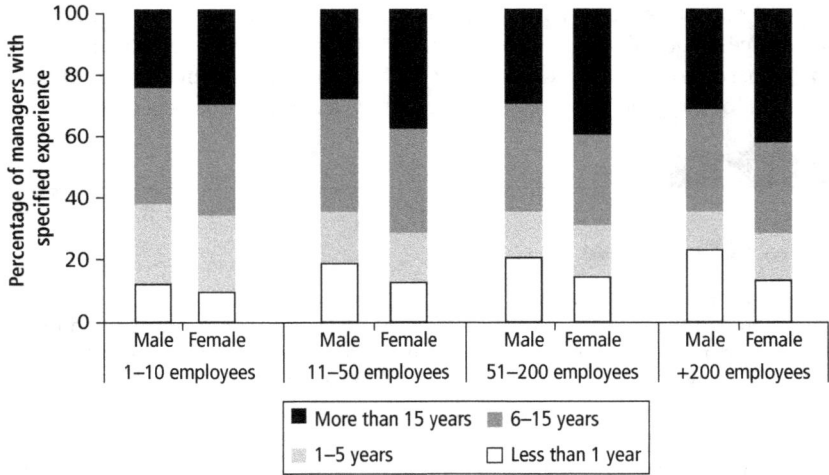

Source: Enterprise Surveys, World Bank, various years (2006–10), http://www.enterprisesurveys.org.
Note: Percentages are means for each group.

---

labor supply. Consequently, both the duration and type of experience may differ by gender (Dessing 2002; Grossbard-Shechtman and Neuman 1998).

Roles within the family can also affect the extent to which a family background of entrepreneurship helps predict whether individuals become entrepreneurs. In our samples, having a father who was an entrepreneur was a strong predictor, particularly for men. Men were more likely to have worked in the enterprise, reinforcing family and prior labor experience in entrepreneurship (Aterido and Hallward-Driemeier 2011).

Heterogeneity in prior work experience is likely to be important in influencing the choice of sector. Two entrepreneurs may each have 10 years of work experience, one in the formal sector, one in the informal. These different backgrounds have different effects on the probability of entrepreneurship and thus on the relative representation of different backgrounds among current entrepreneurs.

The surveys of new entrepreneurs show that the owners of formal and informal enterprises are heavily drawn from former employees of firms within the same sector. More than half of all formal entrepreneurs (57 percent) were wage-earning, formal enterprise workers before starting their current enterprises. Similarly, the most common former employment type among informal

Figure 4.5 Differences in Prior Experience Are Greater between the Sectors Than between Genders within Sectors

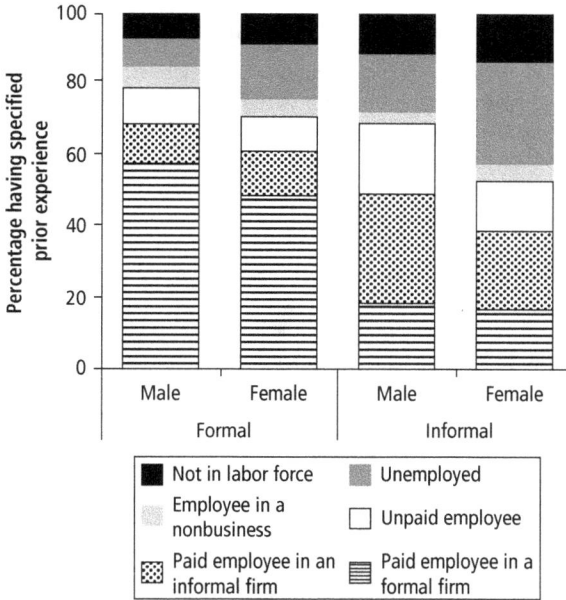

Source: Gajigo and Hallward-Driemeier 2010.
Note: Data are for newly established enterprises in Côte d'Ivoire, Kenya, Nigeria, and Senegal, 2010.

entrepreneurs (29 percent) is as paid workers in other informal firms. The vast majority of individuals do not move between sectors.

Thus, like education, the background of the entrepreneur is a strong predictor of whether the enterprise will be formal or informal, and, again, the differences between men and women within each sector are much smaller than the differences between the sectors (figure 4.5).

Despite the greater degree of difference by sector, some gender difference in background is apparent, especially in the informal sector (see box 4.6). Women there are much more likely than informal sector males to have been looking for a job in the months before they became entrepreneurs (29 percent versus 16 percent). And the 50 percent share of men in the informal sector who used to be paid employees (formal and informal, significantly exceeds the 39 percent of women in the informal sector who used to be paid employees.

Marital Status

Significantly independent of gender and sector is the predominance of married people among the ranks of new entrepreneurs surveyed in the four countries

BOX 4.6

Relationship between Education and Work Experience

The type of experience that is most correlated with work in the formal sector is previous working experience with a formal sector firm (figure B4.6.1).

Entrepreneurs with this background are among the most educated group. About 42 percent of the entrepreneurs in this group have at least some university education— a proportion superseded only by individuals who used to be employees in nonbusiness areas (for example, teachers and nurses).

At the other end of the spectrum, entrepreneurs who used to work as paid employees for informal firms have educational attainment very similar to that of unpaid workers in general.

Even though previous work experience in the formal sector is a strong predictor of formal sector entrepreneurship, a nontrivial percentage of formal entrepreneurs used to work in the informal sector. The entrepreneurs who made this transition tend to be divorced and men, and to have larger start-up capital. They also depend heavily on trade credit and microfinance institutions relative to other sources at start-up.

Figure B4.6.1 Education and Work Experience Are Linked

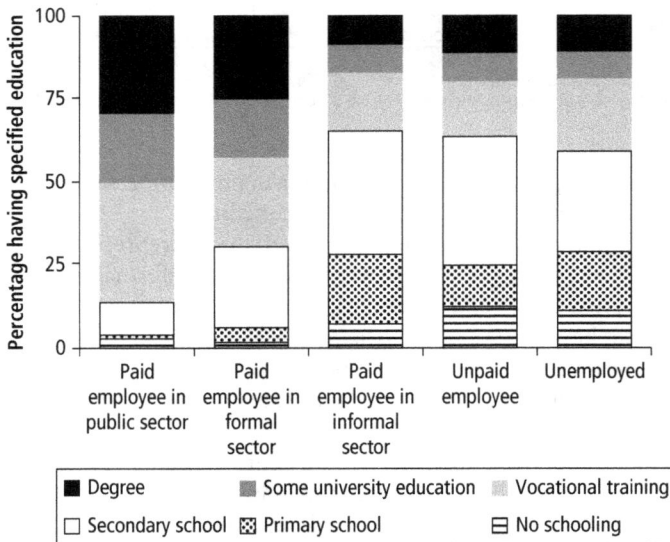

Source: Gajigo and Hallward-Driemeier 2010.
Note: Data are for newly established enterprises in Côte d'Ivoire, Kenya, Nigeria, and Senegal, 2010.

Figure 4.6 Married People Predominate among New Entrepreneurs

Marital status by gender and formality

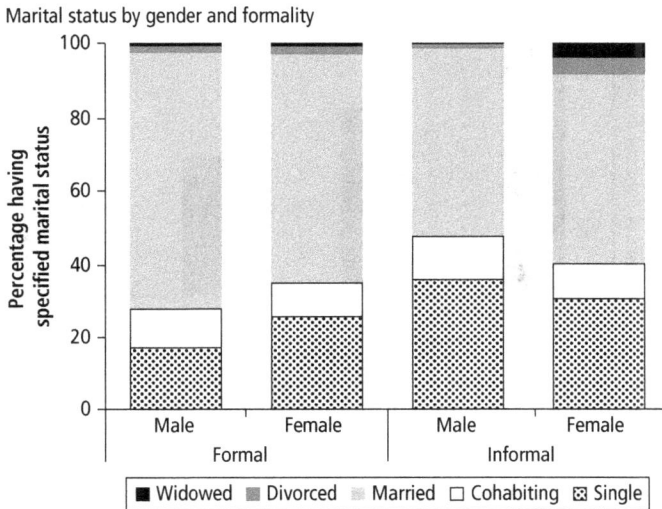

Source: Gajigo and Hallward-Driemeier 2010.
Note: Data are for newly established enterprises in Côte d'Ivoire, Kenya, Nigeria, and Senegal, 2010.

(figure 4.6). This is unsurprising because the average age of entrepreneurs is far higher than that of the general population. Over half of male and female entrepreneurs are married. For both genders, the share of married people is higher among those in the formal sector.

Along gender lines, one difference is that the share of men in the formal sector is higher than that of women. Given that the time demand of entrepreneurship is likely to be higher in the formal sector than in the informal sector, the relatively higher presence of married men than of married women likely reflects the greater time demand on women at home. One further difference is that, in the formal sector, the share of single women is higher than that of single men.

Another important gender difference is that the divorced and widowed are more represented among female than male entrepreneurs, especially in the informal sector. Their informal sector prevalence suggests that they face particularly high barriers to entering the formal sector.

Enterprise Formation

The four-country survey of entrepreneurs who recently started a business shows that 86 percent of enterprises are newly created, rather than old enterprises in a different guise. This dominance holds true for male and female entrepreneurs,

Figure 4.7 Very Few Enterprises Are Set Up from Existing Outfits

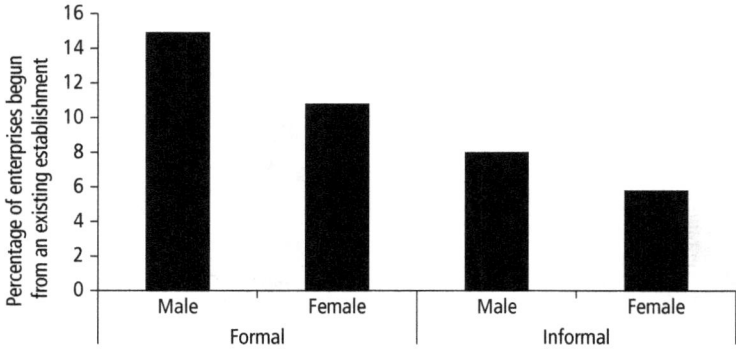

Source: Gajigo and Hallward-Driemeier 2010.
Note: Data are for newly established enterprises in Côte d'Ivoire, Kenya, Nigeria, and Senegal, 2010.

and for the formal and informal sectors (figure 4.7). Most of the difference is along sector lines (formal or informal) rather than gender lines.

Those starting a new enterprise tend to have different prior work experience from those acquiring or expanding an existing family business. Those who had previously been unpaid, unemployed, or not in the labor force were twice as likely to start a new business as those who had been paid employees.

Gender differences as well as sector differences are apparent in acquiring or expanding an existing enterprise—or creating a new one. For men, newly created businesses tend to be smaller (in terms of employees or start-up capital) than those created from an existing enterprise. For women the two types of businesses showed much less difference (figure 4.8).

What about differences in how women and men see "success"? Women in the formal sector appear to place more value on remaining in business and expanding their customer base than in raising profits per se (see box 4.7).

Choice 4: Line of Business

All entrepreneurs face the twin decisions—whether sequential or simultaneous—of starting a business and choosing a line of business. The choice of business line is affected by profit opportunities and by limitations stemming from, for example, time, expertise, and access to finance (Jones and Barr 1996). Familiarity with a business line gained from prior work experience or a prior family enterprise can also be influential. So too can cultural

Figure 4.8 New Businesses Started by Women Average Less Capital and Fewer Initial Employees—Regardless of Whether the Business Was Acquired or a Start-Up

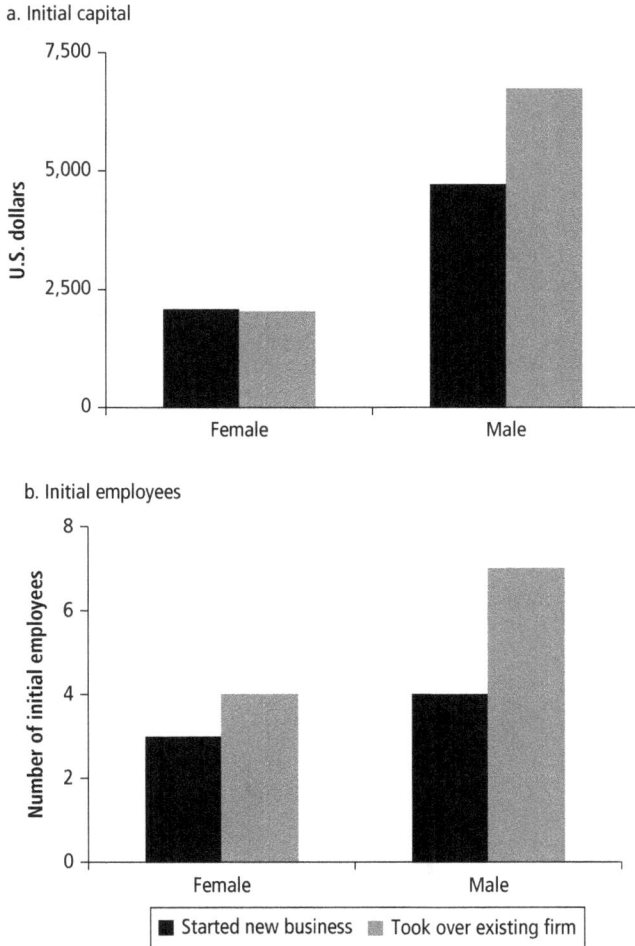

a. Initial capital

b. Initial employees

■ Started new business   ■ Took over existing firm

Source: Gajigo and Hallward-Driemeier 2010.
Note: Data are for newly established enterprises in Côte d'Ivoire, Kenya, Nigeria, and Senegal, 2010.

expectations, particularly regarding gender roles (Chitsike 2000; Fafchamps 2001; Farré and Vella 2007; Fogli and Veldkamp 2001; Gneezy, Leonard, and List 2009; World Bank 2002, 2011). The three factors influencing the line of business that are cited most often in the surveys of new entrepreneurs are identifying a new market, seeing an inspiring case, and having prior

BOX 4.7

Do Entrepreneurs' Reported Criteria for Success Reflect Effort and Performance?

While more traditional variables such as value added and labor productivity are the most common criteria used for measuring success, entrepreneurs themselves may have different conceptions of success. It is important to find out if possible differences in their criteria for success reflect differences across sectors (formal or informal) or in gender, as different conceptions of success could influence their effort and thus their performance.

The two most common criteria for success cited by respondents to the survey of new entrepreneurs are attaining some preset profit and expanding the number of customers (see figure B4.7.1). Among informal entrepreneurs, men and women rate these criteria almost identically. In the formal sector more male than female entrepreneurs cite attaining a preset profit, but male entrepreneurs cite expanding the customer base less often than female entrepreneurs.

Expanding their range of products or services and remaining in business for at least 10 years are the next two most common criteria. In formal and informal sectors the gender differences are fairly small. And for all entrepreneurs such criteria as providing employment for family or expanding the number of employees are not important. Thus the differences by level of formality or gender are relatively few.

Figure B4.7.1 New Entrepreneurs' Criteria for Success Differ Only Slightly by Gender and Registration Status

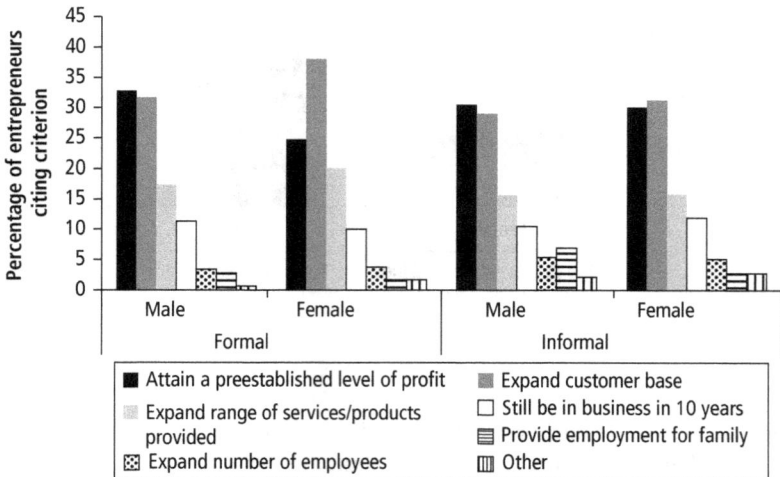

Source: Gajigo and Hallward-Driemeier 2010.
Note: Data are for newly established enterprises in Côte d'Ivoire, Kenya, Nigeria, and Senegal, 2010.

Figure 4.9 Prior Experience, New Market Opportunities, and Inspiring Cases Prompt Entrepreneurs to Select Their Line of Business

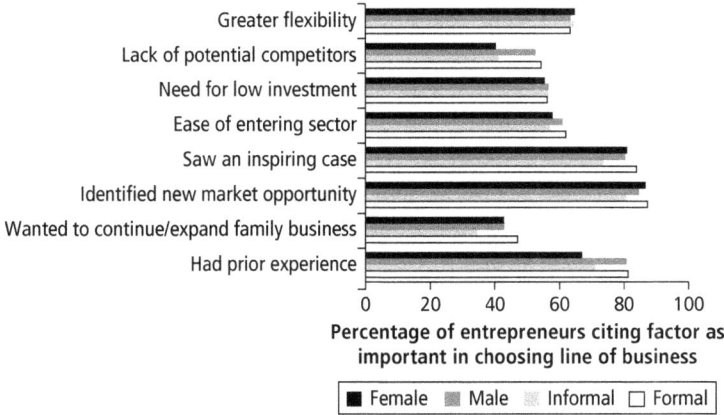

Source: Gajigo and Hallward-Driemeier 2010.
Note: Data are for newly established enterprises in Côte d'Ivoire, Kenya, Nigeria, and Senegal, 2010.

experience in a particular line (figure 4.9). Informal entrepreneurs cite these three factors less often.

Entrepreneurs motivated by confidence in their own skills and by optimism about future profitability are more likely to be influenced by some market opportunity in choosing their product line. Those looking for flexibility in choosing their product line tend also to claim flexibility as a major factor in their decision to become an entrepreneur.

For two factors (flexibility and easy entry due to low investment), no gender or sector differences are discernible. But such differences are evident in the importance attached to prior experience and the lack of potential competitors: male and formal entrepreneurs are more likely to cite them than female and informal entrepreneurs. Further, the gender difference holds even after controlling for other individual and enterprise characteristics. For experience, this pattern likely reflects the fact that the occupational history of entrepreneurs is a significant determinant of their sector choice. As shown previously, formal entrepreneurs are likely to be drawn from the ranks of paid employees of other formal firms. And the finding on the presence of potential competitors no doubt reflects a formal entrepreneur's superior advantage in being less financially constrained or burdened by other obstacles such as registration. In fact, entrepreneurs who cite prior experience and presence of competitors are likely to have more start-up capital and be initially registered at start-up.

Options Not Pursued

Fewer than a quarter of entrepreneurs gave much consideration to pursuing a different business line. Of these, the overwhelming share were men (87 percent of those in the formal sector and 71 percent of those in the informal sector).

The four most common reasons for not pursuing other business lines are shown in figure 4.10. Male and formal entrepreneurs are more likely than their female and informal counterpart to rate issues as important in the decision to discard other lines. The exception is high upfront investment (slightly more important to women than men). This finding is a concern because it would be consistent with more limited access to finance, which constrains not only the size of firms, but firms' distribution across sectors and business lines.

Concerns about the high upfront investments needed to go into an alternative business line could be an indicator of risk aversion—about sinking in high fixed costs without knowing whether the business is profitable. It could also reflect inadequate access to finance among many potential entrepreneurs.

Part II has shown the extent of gender sorting across activities. A major finding is that within similar enterprises, women and men have similar characteristics. So gender gaps in education, work experience, and access to assets are important in explaining the sorting. How to address these underlying gaps

Figure 4.10 Both Opportunities and Constraints Play a Role in New Entrepreneurs' Decision Not to Pursue Other Business Lines

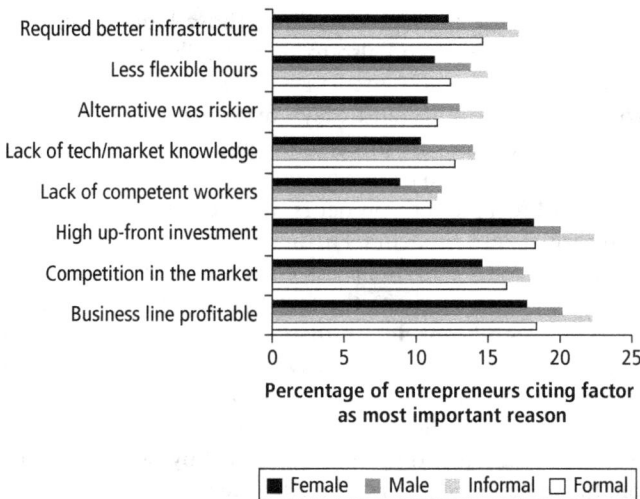

Source: Gajigo and Hallward-Driemeier 2010.
Note: Data are for newly established enterprises in Côte d'Ivoire, Kenya, Nigeria, and Senegal, 2010.

is addressed in part IV. Before turning to that agenda, we look in part III at whether the sorting matters for outcomes and opportunities.

Notes

1. Even though the data estimates suggest an inverted-U shape for such probability, the peaks for men and women are at 79 years of age, outside our population of interest.
2. An alternative measure would look at the legal economic rights. However, this approach involves a series of dichotomous variables and so does not provide the same degree of variation to exploit.
3. Percentages cited here and in the next paragraph are from national representative household surveys for 34 economies in Sub-Saharan Africa, most recent year (2000–10).
4. But there is wide variation between countries. For Ethiopia, Rwanda, and São Tomé and Príncipe, the share of married self-employed women is below 50 percent, while for Benin, Burkina Faso, and Senegal, the share is 80 percent or above.

References

Aterido, A., and M. Hallward-Driemeier. 2011. "Whose Business Is It Anyway?" *Small Business Economics* 37 (4): 443–64.

Aubert, P., E. Cavoli, and M. Rogers. 2006. "New Technologies, Organisation and Age: Firm-Level Evidence." *Economic Journal* 116 (509): 73–93.

Banerjee, A., and A. Newman. 1993. "Occupational Choice and the Process of Development." *Journal of Political Economy* 101: 274–98.

Behaghel, L., and N. Greenan. 2005. "Training and Age-Biased Technological Change: Evidence from French Microenterprises." Working Paper 2005–06, Centre de Recherche en Économie et Statistique, Paris.

Blanchflower, D. G., and A. J. Oswald. 1998. "What Makes an Entrepreneur?" *Journal of Labor Economics* 16 (10): 26–60.

Blau, D. 1985. "Self-Employment and Self-Selection in Developing Country Labor Markets." *Southern Economic Journal* 52 (2): 351–63.

Chitsike, C. 2000. "Culture as a Barrier to Rural Women's Entrepreneurship: Experience from Zimbabwe." *Gender and Development* 8 (1): 71–77.

Colonia-Willner, R. 1998. "Practical Intelligence at Work: Relationship between Aging and Cognitive Efficiency among Managers in a Bank Environment." *Psychology and Aging* 13 (1): 45–57.

Dessing, M. 2002. "Labor Supply, the Family and Poverty: The S-Shaped Labor Supply Curve." *Journal of Economic Behavior and Organization* 49 (4): 433–58.

Djankov, S., E. Miguel, Y. Qian, G. Roland, and E. Zhuravskaya. 2005. "Who Are Russia's Entrepreneurs?" *Journal of the European Economic Association* 3 (2–3): 587–97.

Djankov, S., Y. Qian, G. Roland, and E. Zhuravskaya. 2006. "Who Are China's Entrepreneurs?" *American Economic Review* 96 (2): 348–52.

Fafchamps. M. 2001. "Networks, Communities, and Markets in Sub-Saharan Africa: Implications for Firm Growth and Investment." *Journal of African Economies* 10 (Suppl. 2): 109–42.

Farré, L., and F. Vella. 2007. "The Intergenerational Transmission of Gender Role Attitudes and Its Implications for Female Labor Force Participation." Discussion Paper Series 2802, Institute for the Study of Labor, Bonn.

Fogli, A., and L. Veldkamp. 2001. "Nature or Nurture? Learning and the Geography of Female Labor Force Participation." *Econometrica* 79 (4): 1103–38.

Gajigo, O., and M. Hallward-Driemeier. 2010. "Entrepreneurship among New Entrepreneurs." Working paper, World Bank, Washington, DC.

Gneezy, U., K. L. Leonard, and J. A. List. 2009. "Gender Differences in Competition: Evidence from a Matrilineal and a Patriarchal Society." *Econometrica* 77 (5): 1637–64.

Goldin, C. 1990. *Understanding the Gender Gap: An Economic History of American Women.* Oxford: Oxford University Press.

Grossbard-Shechtman, S., and S. Neuman. 1998. "Women's Labor Supply and Marital Choice." *Journal of Political Economy* 96 (6): 1294–302.

Hallward-Driemeier, M., and A. Rasteletti. 2010. "Women's and Men's Entrepreneurship in Africa." Working paper, World Bank, Washington, DC.

Haltiwanger, J. C., J. I. Lane, and J. R. Spletzer. 1999. "Productivity Differences across Employers: The Roles of Employer Size, Age and Human Capital." *American Economic Review* 89 (2): 94–98.

Heintz, J. 2012. "Why Do People Work in Informal Employment? Determinants of Selection into Self-Employment in Ghanaian Labor Markets." *Journal of Applied Economic Research* 6 (2): 181–209.

ILO (International Labour Organization). 2002. "Women and Men in the Informal Economy: A Statistical Picture." Gender and Employment Sector, ILO, Geneva.

Iyer, R., and A. Schoar. 2010. "Are There Cultural Determinants of Entrepreneurship?" In *International Differences in Entrepreneurship*, edited by J. Lerner, 209–40. Chicago: University of Chicago Press.

Jones, P., and A. Barr. 1996. "Learning by Doing in Sub-Saharan Africa: Evidence from Ghana." *Journal of International Development* 8 (3): 445–66.

Kevane, M., and B. Wydick. 2001. "Microenterprise Lending to Female Entrepreneurs: Sacrificing Economic Growth for Poverty Alleviation." *World Development* 29 (7): 1225–36.

Klapper, L., and S. Parker. 2010. "Gender and the Business Environment for New Firm Creation." *World Bank Research Observer* 26 (2): 237–57.

Maloney, W. 2004. "Informality Revisited." *World Development* 32 (7): 1159–78.

Mammen, K., and C. Paxon. 2000. "Women's Work and Economic Development." *Journal of Economic Perspectives* 14: 141–64.

Minniti, M. 2009. "Gender Issues in Entrepreneurship." *Foundations and Trends in Enterpreneurship* 5 (7–8): 497–621.

Parker, S. C. 2004. *The Economics of Self-Employment and Entrepreneurship*. Cambridge: Cambridge University Press.

Parker, S. C., and M. van Praag. 2006. "Schooling, Capital Constraints, and Entrepreneurial Performance." *Journal of Business and Economic Statistics* 24 (4): 416–31.

Van der Sluis, J., M. van Praag, and W. Vijverberg. 2008 "Education and Entrepreneurship Selection and Performance: A Review of the Literature." *Journal of Economic Surveys* 22 (5): 795–841.

World Bank. 2002. *Engendering Development*. Policy Research Report. Washington, DC: World Bank.

_____. 2011. *World Development Report 2012: Gender Equality and Development*. Washington, DC: World Bank.

Part III

How Women Perform—and the Constraints They Face

Does the gender sorting across types of enterprises matter for economic outcomes? This section looks at the extent of gaps in productivity between enterprises run by women and men, and how constraints in the business environment can vary by gender. A central question is the extent to which gender matters directly— or indirectly, because of the differences in economic activities where women and men are active. For example, do women have a harder time accessing finance because they are women, or because they are running smaller, informal firms that are perceived to be less creditworthy?

Chapter 5

How Sorting Affects Gender Gaps in Productivity and Profits

Part I showed that women entrepreneurs are more concentrated in self-employment, in smaller firms, in the informal sector, and in more traditional sectors. The questions for this chapter are these: Are women's enterprises less productive or profitable than men's enterprises? If so, are productivity gaps due to differences in sorting across types of entrepreneurial activities, or are they present between women and men engaged in the same activity?

The literature on firm performance focuses on differences across firms mainly by size and secondarily by sector (Aterido, Hallward-Driemeier, and Pages 2011; Ayyagari, Beck, and Demirgüç-Kunt 2007; Beck, Demirgüç-Kunt, and Maksimovic 2005; Falco and others 2009; Tybout 2000). Liedholm and Mead (1999), McPherson (1995), and Mead (1994) provide some of the earlier literature, with an explicit focus on micro and small firms. Large firms are not included as comparators, however. Even so, size and age emerge as important explanatory variables of growth and profitability, though they are less important for survival. On this last point, later work by Frazer (2005) and Harding, Söderbom, and Teal (2006) confirms the result that size affects performance, but that larger firms are also more likely to survive. Indeed, this work raises the question of what it means that so many small and productive firms exit: is it due to an inability to weather adverse shocks, or is it a sign that successful entrepreneurs are offered more lucrative and steady wage employment opportunities elsewhere? Sleuwaegen and Goedhuys (2002) in Côte d'Ivoire and Van Biesebroeck (2005) in nine countries find important contributions to productivity from large firms, arguing that the region displays evidence of a missing middle. Bigsten and Gebreeyesus (2007) also find that age matters as well as size, as does Söderbom (2012) and Söderbom and Teal (2004). These latter papers, however, do not include gender as a significant part of their analysis.

This chapter finds that the choice of industry, the size of the enterprise, and the decision about whether to operate in the formal sector markedly affect performance patterns. It also finds a gap in average productivity between men's and women's enterprises. But controlling for formal enterprise characteristics, industry, and size of business—thereby comparing like with like—shrinks productivity gaps and can remove them altogether.

Particularly among registered enterprises, gender in itself does not account for productivity differences among similar types of enterprises. Instead, gender gaps exist in that women account for such a small share of formal entrepreneurs. In the informal sector, other enterprise and entrepreneur characteristics account for most of the productivity gap. Similar patterns are found using earlier rounds of the Enterprise Surveys, in Sub-Saharan Africa as well as in Eastern Europe and Central Asia, with gender gaps persisting only among the smallest enterprises (Bardasi, Blackden, and Guzman 2007; Bardasi and Sabarwal 2009; Sabarwal and Terrell 2008). Indeed, this chapter finds that the type of enterprise where gender gaps persist, even controlling for other characteristics, is informal home-based enterprises. Differences in hours of operation seem to account for much of the productivity gap, though the scarcity of data makes it hard to substantiate this claim.

Examining the extent to which country characteristics affect enterprise performance—notably income, governance, and indexes of gender equality—this chapter finds that countries with higher incomes tend to have firms with higher value added per worker, but also larger gender gaps in average performance measures. In these environments women's continued higher concentration in traditional lower-value-added industries keeps them from benefiting from the opportunities at the top end. Controlling for size and industry still has the effect of making gender insignificant as an explanatory variable for performance measures; not taking these enterprise characteristics into account shows that gender differences can actually rise with income.

Still, a country's income, governance, and indexes of gender equality tend to have weaker explanatory power than enterprise characteristics: the type of enterprise matters more in explaining patterns of performance (see Hallward-Driemeier and Rasteletti [2010] for more details).

It is encouraging that there are few or no significant differences between female and male entrepreneurs in the productivity of their businesses (after controlling for other key enterprise characteristics). It confirms that Sub-Saharan Africa has considerable hidden growth potential in its women, and that tapping that potential—such as improving women's choices of where to be economically active—can boost the region's economic growth (World Bank 2011). This finding underscores the importance of analyzing where obstacles to women and men have gender differences (undertaken in this chapter), and why the patterns of entrepreneurship persist (undertaken in part IV).

Productivity and Gender Gaps

We use value added per worker as the base measure of performance among registered firms. Simply comparing women and men points to a gender gap in labor productivity of about six percentage points, but comparing them in enterprises of the same industry, size, and capital intensity shows no productivity gap (figure 5.1). So the productivity gap stems from women operating in lower-value-added sectors and smaller firms, rather than from gender itself. In other words, controlling for enterprise characteristics, among registered firms at least, explains the unconditional gender gap (Hallward-Driemeier and Rasteletti 2010).

With no control for any enterprise characteristics, value added per worker averages 5.8 percent less in female enterprises (figure 5.1, top bar). The size of the gap closes somewhat when the industry of operation is controlled (middle bar). Adding firm size, measured by the number of employees, reduces the gap to 3.9 percentage points, and the gap is no longer statistically significant. Finally, also controlling for the capital intensity of the enterprise makes the coefficient on gender completely insignificant.[1]

Figure 5.1 Controlling for Enterprise Characteristics Removes the Gender Gap in Productivity (registered firms)

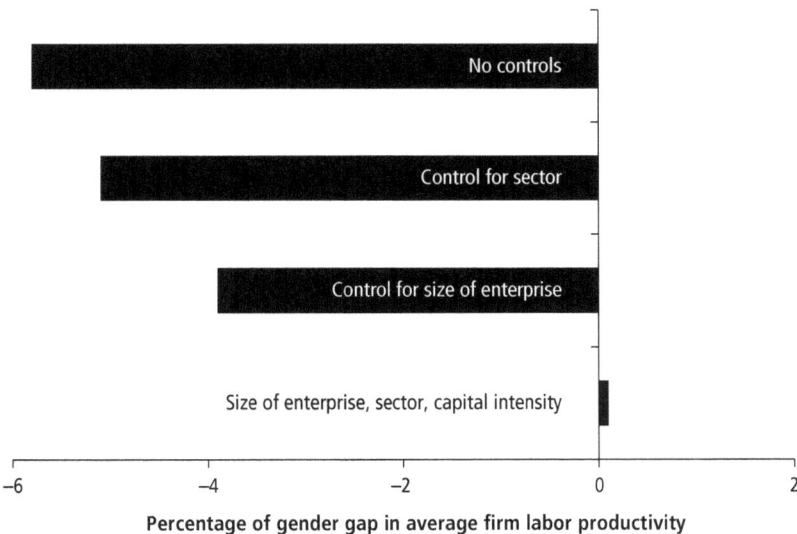

Percentage of gender gap in average firm labor productivity

Source: Hallward-Driemeier and Rasteletti 2010.
Note: Analysis is based on regressions using data from 37 Sub-Saharan countries, with country dummies included to capture country-invariant effects. Thus the results are all based on within-country differences. A dummy is included for whether there is female participation in ownership.

One question is whether these results are also robust to different measures of defining "women's enterprises." For the four countries with additional information on the main decision maker (Côte d'Ivoire, Kenya, Nigeria, and Senegal), the unconditional gender gap is more than 1.5 times as large, at 10 percent. But here again, once enterprise characteristics are controlled for, the gap shrinks considerably. And once measures of the entrepreneur's human capital are included, the gap becomes insignificant (Aterido and Hallward-Driemeier 2011).

Similar patterns hold for new entrepreneurs and formality. (Here we have less information on material inputs, so our metric for enterprise productivity is revenue per worker.) Differences are accounted for by formality rather than gender (figure 5.2).

Among the newly created enterprises, median revenue per worker in the formal sector is more than three times that in the informal sector (figure 5.3). In fact, female entrepreneurs' median productivity in the formal sector is actually higher than that of their male counterparts, but no significant difference exists in the informal sector (Gajigo and Hallward-Driemeier 2010).

The data can be further disaggregated by industry. An industry's formality and its median revenue per worker have a close positive relationship (figure 5.4).

On the other hand, the correlation between an industry's degree of formality and its share of enterprises run by women is significantly negative (figure 5.5).

Figure 5.2 New Entrepreneurs in the Formal Sector Have Significantly Higher Revenue per Worker Than Their Informal Counterparts

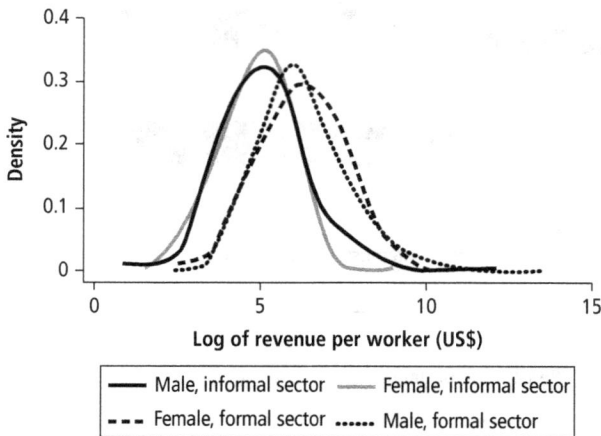

Source: Gajigo and Hallward-Driemeier 2010.
Note: Kernel = Epanechnikov; bandwidth = 0.2725. Data are for newly established enterprises in Côte d'Ivoire, Kenya, Nigeria, and Senegal, 2010.

Figure 5.3 New Entrepreneurs' Median Revenue per Worker Is Higher for Women Than Men in the Formal Sector

Median productivity by sector and gender

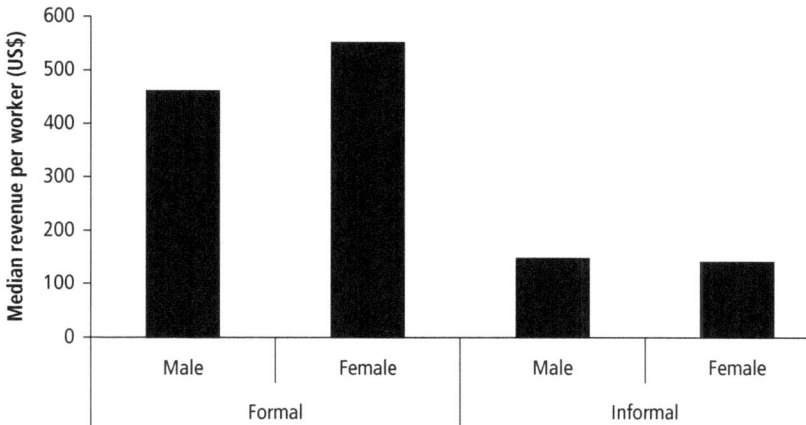

Source: Gajigo and Hallward-Driemeier 2010.
Note: Data are for newly established enterprises in Côte d'Ivoire, Kenya, Nigeria, and Senegal, 2010.

Figure 5.4 Median Revenue per Worker Trends Higher in Formal Sector Industries

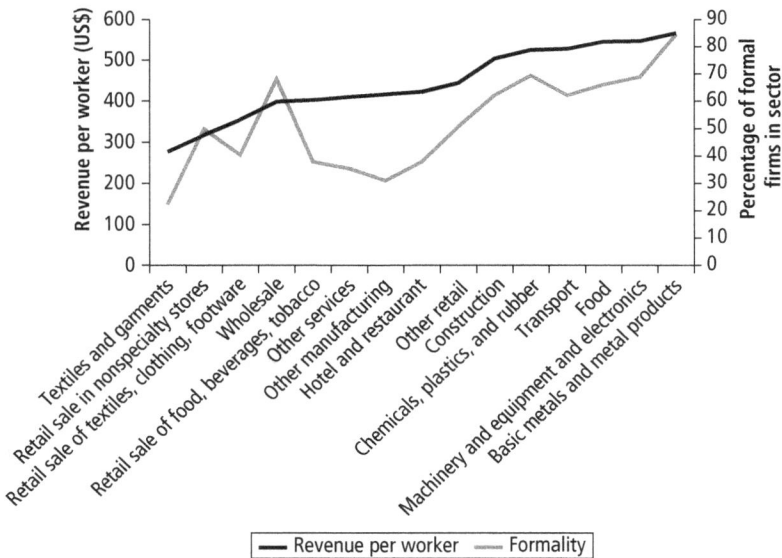

Source: Gajigo and Hallward-Driemeier 2010.
Note: Data are for newly established enterprises in Côte d'Ivoire, Kenya, Nigeria, and Senegal, 2010.

Figure 5.5 Median Revenue per Worker Tends to Be Lower in Sectors with Greater Female Ownership

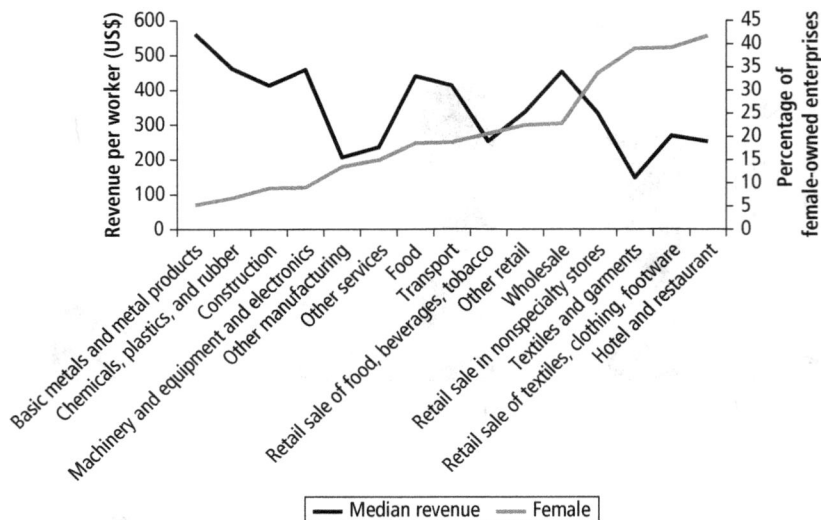

Source: Gajigo and Hallward-Driemeier 2010.
Note: Data are for newly established enterprises in Côte d'Ivoire, Kenya, Nigeria, and Senegal, 2010.

A simple comparison of women and men shows women's enterprises as less productive, but a large share of the measure of productivity is really due to women's concentration in informal industries.

The average firm size in Sub-Saharan Africa is smaller than in other regions, though not always significantly so. Aterido, Beck, and Iacovone (forthcoming) test whether women's enterprises are smaller than men's on average and how this pattern may vary in Sub-Saharan Africa using the database of Enteprise Surveys. Controlling for firm size, sector, location, export status, legal status, and ownership, firms with female participation in ownership tend to be 7.6–10.3 percent smaller. But women's enterprises are not disproportionately smaller in Sub-Saharan Africa (the coefficient on "female" is negative and significant, showing the effect ranges from −7.6 to −10.3 percent. But the coefficient on "female_Africa" is not significant; see Aterido, Beck, and Iacovone 2011 for more details).

Among household enterprises, more evidence of gender gaps in performance emerges, though this must be seen in a context of additional data challenges. The surveys do not consistently ask for the time spent working in the enterprise, either as hours a week or weeks a year. The Enterprise Surveys limit themselves to full-time enterprises, but many of the household enterprises are run only part-time. Not being able to control for that fact is a concern, particularly because the countries with measures of time spent show that women are more likely to work part-time or seasonally. One option is that we restrict the sample to urban settings, which are less likely to be affected by strong seasonal patterns. Another is to distinguish comparisons of enterprises run out of the house from those operated in a separate location. The assumption is that the former may be more likely to be operating fewer hours.

Among household enterprises, the unconditional gender gap—at 50 percent—is considerably larger than in the Enterprise Survey data. The majority of household enterprises are in the informal sector. Controlling for whether the enterprise is registered reduces the gap by half, with productivity rising as much for women as men among registered businesses.[2] The effects of industry and size also serve to reduce the gap. Looking at the subset of countries that have information on the number of months of operation, we find that controlling for the time spent working in the enterprise greatly narrows the gender gap. This indicates the importance of taking into account the time spent in an enterprise, information not always available in the household surveys. It also cautions against simple, unconditional comparisons of women's and men's enterprises.

Controlling for physical capital is also very important in looking at household enterprises, because once we do this, the gap in performance of female-headed firms is no longer significant.

Country Characteristics' Effect on Potential Gender Gaps

Constraints to improving the performance of women's enterprises exist at several levels. In looking at the effect of country-level constraints on potential gender gaps in performance, we review income per capita, quality of governance, and indexes of gender equality constructed by international organizations.

Income per capita reflects the country's overall development status. It is often highly correlated with the quality of the country's infrastructure and institutions, both of which should have general positive effects on business. The question is whether they have a gender dimension in affecting people's ability to operate their business and improve its performance. The answer: they do. And, perhaps surprisingly, not in women's favor (box 5.1).

Beyond income, several other indicators of country characteristics could affect firm performance. One is the quality of governance, measured through, for example, control of corruption, political stability, or the rule of law (usually in combination). Better governance is generally associated with better private outcomes. A mild gender effect is also apparent—women's performance is closer to men's in better-governed countries.

BOX 5.1

Gender Gaps in Labor Productivity and in Firm Size Can Rise with Income

Countries with higher incomes tend to have firms with higher value added per worker. The share of informal businesses tends to decline. Is the gender gap smaller in high-income countries? No. The effects of industry selection there are even more pronounced (Hallward-Driemeier and Shah 2009). Top performers earn high rates of return and operate high-value-added businesses. In these environments women's continued higher concentration in traditional lower-value-added industries keeps them from benefiting from these opportunities.

In average firm size, too, gender gaps can open at higher levels of development in Sub-Saharan Africa (figure B5.1.1). The average size of female-owned firms rises gently with income, but that of male-owned firms rises faster. Some of this difference is again explained by industry differences: in more-developed countries, the more capital-intensive sectors operate at larger economies of scale. This finding makes clear that the need to increase women's participation in higher-end entrepreneurial activities is relevant across the income spectrum.

Figure B5.1.1 The Sector-Selection Effects of Average Firm Size Appear Greatest in More-Developed Countries

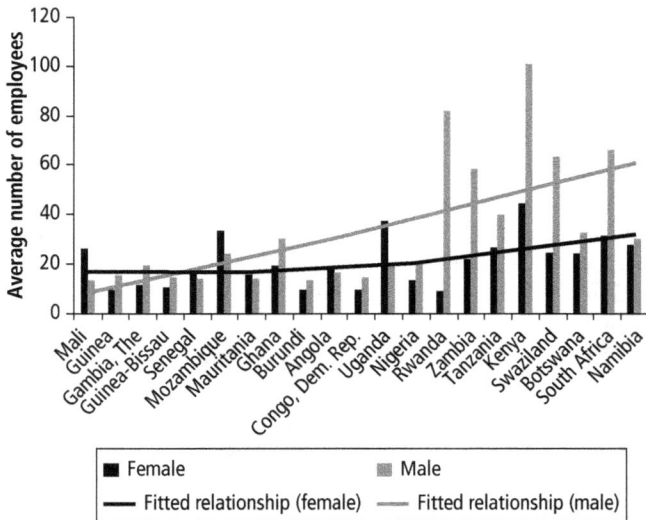

Source: Hallward-Driemeier and Shah 2009.
Note: The relationship is fitted with a polynomial rather than a straight line.

Figure 5.6 Gender Gaps in Revenue per Worker Are Affected by Country Characteristics

Development (GDP per capita) Controlling for sector selection is important in high-income countries; women's lower participation in capital- and technology-intensive sectors becomes relatively more costly in more sophisticated markets.	**Social/Gender Inclusion** More inclusion is associated with smaller performance gaps.
Governance (control of corruption; government effectiveness) Good governance reduces gender performance gaps; women benefit disproportionately from it.	**Human Capital** (educational attainment) Declines in gender education gaps are associated with declines in performance gaps—particularly when governance is strong.

Source: Hallward-Driemeier and Rasteletti 2010.

Finally, we consider aggregate measures collected by various international organizations with a focus on gender equality and women's empowerment (appendix B). Most of these measures suggest that women may face particularly challenging environments in Sub-Saharan Africa (figure 3.7). Indeed, we find that countries with weaker institutions of gender inclusion or equality tend to have slightly wider gender gaps in performance (figure 5.6).

Yet despite the evidence that income, governance, and gender inclusion can affect gender performance gaps, they tend to have smaller explanatory power than enterprise characteristics. What kind of enterprise an entrepreneur runs matters more than where it is located—although location or country characteristics are significant in that they enable different types of enterprises to thrive.

Notes

1. As capital intensity is available only for manufacturing firms, which are just under half of the sample, repeating the initial specification shows that the same unconditional gender gap exists within manufacturing; the lack of a significant gender gap once the enterprise characteristics are controlled for is thus not due to any selection issue or special characteristics of the subset of firms with capital stock information available.
2. Thus, the coefficient on "registered" is large and positive, and the gender-registration interaction term is small and insignificant.

References

Aterido, R., T. Beck, and L. Iacovone. Forthcoming. "Gender and Finance in Sub-Saharan Africa: Are Women Disadvantaged?" *World Development.*

Aterido, R., and M. Hallward-Driemeier. 2011. "Whose Business Is It Anyway?" *Small Business Economics* 37 (4): 443–64.

Aterido, R., M. Hallward-Driemeier, and C. Pages. 2011. "Big Constraints to Small Firms' Growth? Business Environment and Employment Growth across Firms." *Economic Development and Cultural Change* 59 (3): 609–47.

Ayyagari, M., T. Beck, and A. Demirgüç-Kunt. 2007. "Small and Medium Enterprises across the Globe." *Small Business Economics* 29: 415–34.

Bardasi, E., M. Blackden, and J. C. Guzman. 2007. "Gender, Entrepreneurship, and Competitiveness." In *Africa Competitiveness Report 2007*, edited by World Economic Forum, African Development Bank, and World Bank, 69–86. Geneva: World Economic Forum, African Development Bank, and World Bank.

Bardasi, E., and S. Sabarwal. 2009. "Gender, Access to Finance, and Entrepreneurial Performance in Sub-Saharan Africa." Working paper, World Bank, Washington, DC.

Beck, T., A. Demirgüç-Kunt, and V. Maksimovic. 2005. "Financial and Legal Constraints to Growth: Does Firm Size Matter?" *Journal of Finance* 60 (1): 137–77.

Bigsten, A., and M. Gebreeyesus. 2007. "The Small, the Young, and the Productive: Determinants of Manufacturing Firm Growth in Ethiopia." *Economic Development and Cultural Change* 55 (4): 813–40.

Falco, P., A. Kerr, N. Rankin, J. Sandefur, and F. Teal. 2009. "The Returns to Formality and Informality in Urban Africa." Working Paper Series 2010-03, Centre for the Study of African Economies, Oxford, U.K.

Frazer, G. 2005. "Which Firms Die? A Look at Exit from Manufacturing in Ghana." *Economic Development and Cultural Change* 53 (3): 585–617.

Gajigo, O., and M. Hallward-Driemeier. 2010. "Entrepreneurship among New Entrepreneurs." Working paper, World Bank, Washington, DC.

Hallward-Driemeier, M., and A. Rasteletti. 2010. "Women's and Men's Entrepreneurship in Africa." Working paper, World Bank, Washington, DC.

Hallward-Driemeier, M., and M. Shah. 2009. "Female Entrepreneurship in Sub-Saharan Africa: Differences across Sub-Regions and Sizes of Firms." Working paper, World Bank, Washington, DC.

Harding, A., M. Söderbom, and F. Teal 2006. "The Determinants of Survival among African Manufacturing Firms." *Economic Development and Cultural Change* 54 (3): 533–56.

Liedholm, C., and D. Mead. 1999. *Small Enterprises and Economic Development: The Dynamics of Micro and Small Enterprises.* London: Routledge.

McPherson, M. 1995. "Growth of Micro and Small Enterprises in Southern Africa." *Journal of Development Economics* 48: 253–77.

Mead, D., C. 1994. "The Contribution of Small Enterprises to Employment Growth in Southern and Eastern Africa." *World Development* 22 (December): 1881–94.

Sabarwal, S., and K. Terrell. 2008. "Does Gender Matter for Firm Performance? Evidence from Eastern Europe and Central Asia." Policy Research Working Paper 4705, World Bank, Washington, DC.

Sleuwaegen, L., and M. Goedhuys. 2002. "Growth of Firms in Developing Countries, Evidence from Côte d'Ivoire." *Journal of Development Economics* 68 (June): 117–35.

Söderbom, M. 2012. "Firm Size and Structural Change: A Case Study of Ethiopia." *Journal of African Economies* 21: ii126–51.

Söderbom, M., and F. Teal. 2004. "Size and Efficiency in African Manufacturing Firms: Evidence from Firm-Level Panel Data." *Journal of Development Economics* 73 (February): 369–94.

Tybout, J. R. 2000. "Manufacturing Firms in Developing Countries: How Well Do They Do, and Why?" *Journal of Economic Literature* 28 (March): 11–44.

Van Biesebroeck, J. 2005. "Firm Size Matters: Growth and Productivity Growth in African Manufacturing." *Economic Development and Cultural Change* 53 (3): 545–83.

World Bank. 2011. *World Development Report 2012: Gender Equality and Development.* Washington, DC: World Bank.

Chapter 6

How Sorting Affects Constraints

The analysis in chapter 5 compared the performance of women's and men's enterprises. This chapter turns to the constraints on entrepreneurs in operating and expanding their business. Are they different for men and women?

The literature points to constraints in the business environment or investment climate in which a firm operates as significantly affecting firm profitability and growth (Aterido and Hallward-Driemeier 2010; Aterido, Hallward-Driemeier, and Pages 2011; Bardasi, Blackden, and Guzman 2007; Batra, Kaufmann, and Stone 2003; Bigsten and others 2003; Dollar, Hallward-Driemeier, and Mengistae 2005; McCormick, Kinyanjui, and Ongile 1997; Ramachandran, Gelb, and Shah 2009; World Bank 2004). However, the severity and relative importance of any given constraint can vary by type of enterprise or by the gender of the entrepreneur. Improving the investment climate may not necessarily succeed in leveling the playing field. If there are systematic differences by type of enterprise or by the gender of the entrepreneur in which constraints are binding, then reforms that address those constraints will be disproportionately beneficial for those enterprises or entrepreneurs. In setting priorities for reforms of the business environment, a disaggregated approach to understanding constraints is clearly needed.

The chapter uses surveys of entrepreneurs to understand the types and severity of such obstacles. Enterprise Surveys are the primary data source. The gender modules and the surveys of new entrepreneurs allow finer-grained analysis, making it possible to capture different definitions of "female" or "woman's" business. The Enterprise Surveys provide two types of data on constraints. The first are subjective rankings of the degree to which specific issues constrain operating and expanding a business; they are responses to questions such as "How constraining is access to finance to the growth of your firm?" The second are quantitative measures of the time and costs associated with particular types of transactions; they are responses to questions such as "Do you have a loan? What are the terms of the loan?"

Issue areas will likely vary in whether there is a gender dimension to them, and whether any gender dimension is direct or indirect. Access to finance is one area that is often reported to pose greater challenges for women. Interactions with officials and access to land are others. Other issues of infrastructure, such as access to reliable electricity or to roads, are less likely to have a direct gender impact, but may reveal some gender differences based on choice of sector or size of the enterprise.

The survey evidence in this chapter shows patterns similar to the performance outcomes discussed in chapter 5: once the characteristics of the enterprise are controlled for, gender differences are not significant.[1] That is, while there are some gender gaps, they are largely explained once enterprise characteristics are taken into account; in similar industries and at similar firm sizes, women and men report similar constraints. If women have a harder time accessing land, for example, it is largely because small firms report this as a greater constraint, and women are more likely to be in smaller firms. What remains at issue is how much the original sorting into smaller and more informal firms itself reflects gender differences in constraints.

These findings hold on average across Sub-Saharan Africa, but some countries show more persistent gaps. Indeed, the quality of a country's governance and of its broad institutions of social inclusion is associated with smaller gender gaps in performance. Still, the effect of country characteristics is generally small compared with that of enterprise characteristics.

Four caveats bear repeating. First, the definition of female ownership can underestimate some of the gender differences in constraints. If some of these firms have a female owner but are otherwise run by men, counting them as women's enterprises masks differences between the genders. In this case, focusing on sole proprietors gives a cleaner look at the role of gender and reveals larger gender gaps in reported constraints in access to finance and as a result of corruption.

Second, we do not have the data to fully analyze how constraints affect the entry decision or the choice of formality, industry, or size itself. We can look at the effects of gender within various firm sizes and conclude that size, rather than gender, is the main determinant. But we cannot assess how much gender differences in the constraints explain why women are more likely to run smaller firms to begin with. The data needed to extend this analysis are lacking: gender-disaggregated data remain scarce on potential entrepreneurs. Those who faced conditions so constraining that they could not enter or remain in business are not included.[2]

Third, reforms to address constraints may not always have the intended consequences or be effective at increasing women's empowerment, and in some cases they could even be detrimental. Even if a constraint is identified as having a gender dimension, such as women having a harder time qualifying for credit, increasing the credit that goes to women may not necessarily improve their entrepreneurial outcomes or even their intrahousehold bargaining power.

There are positive examples, but some evidence is more mixed (Armendariz and Roome 2008; Ashraf 2009; Banerjee and others 2009; Bruhn and Love 2011; Fafchamps and Quisumbing 2002; Kabeer 2001; Kantor 2005; Klapper and Parker 2010).

Fourth, the reforms that businesses want most are not necessarily those in the public interest, and so need to be interpreted with some caution. Businesses will, for example, almost always want lower taxes and cheaper credit (World Bank 2004).

Constraints Facing Entrepreneurs

Both subjective and quantitative information shed light on the extent to which women and men face different constraints.

Subjective Information

The detailed gender module in the five countries and the survey of new entrepreneurs in four countries (see box 1.3) asked respondents, regardless of the overall severity of the constraint, whether women and men would face different degrees of constraint. Interestingly, both men and women identified areas where they thought women face greater challenges—and similar proportions agreed on the same areas, though women reported interactions with the police and court systems as greater (figure 6.1).

That these areas pose greater constraints for women makes sense in that they are areas where characteristics of the individual entrepreneur could make a difference. For areas like access to electricity or macroeconomic instability, the surveys found no gender differences.

The responses do not, however, take into account gender patterns in the types of enterprises women and men run, and how these could affect constraints. It turns out that controlling for enterprise characteristics is again important in explaining much of the gender gap in constraints to improved performance.

Figures 6.2 and 6.3 show the responses to the subjective questions in the enterprise surveys, looking at four issues: access to finance, access to land, corruption, and labor regulations. So that many more countries can be covered, the data are based on the broader definition of female participation in ownership, rather than the definition that takes into account decision-making control. Figure 6.2 compares small and large formal firms, and includes small informal enterprises to facilitate comparison between informal and small formal firms. The exercise is repeated in figure 6.3 using only sole proprietors, to ensure that the designated gender of the enterprise captures decision-making power too.

Figure 6.1 Do Women Face Greater Constraints? Many Women—and Men—Think So

How would women fare compared to men?

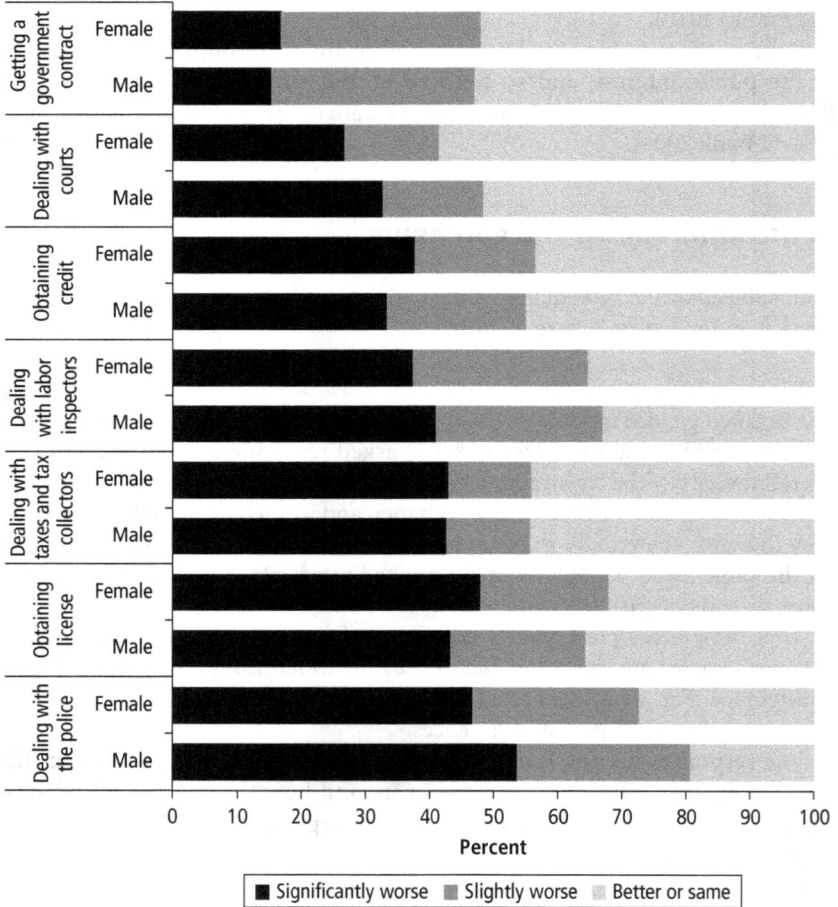

Source: Aterido and Hallward-Driemeier 2010.

For three of these issues the differences are more significant by formality and size than by gender. For access to finance, small formal firms perceive themselves as having a harder time than large formal firms. Small informal enterprises do not share this view, however, no doubt precisely because they often operate at a very small scale where expectations of better bank loans are minimal. Small, particularly informal, firms report access to land as a bigger constraint. Large formal firms regard labor regulations as constraining, presumably reflecting

Figure 6.2 Obstacles Vary More by Formality and Size of Firm Than by Gender (subjective responses)

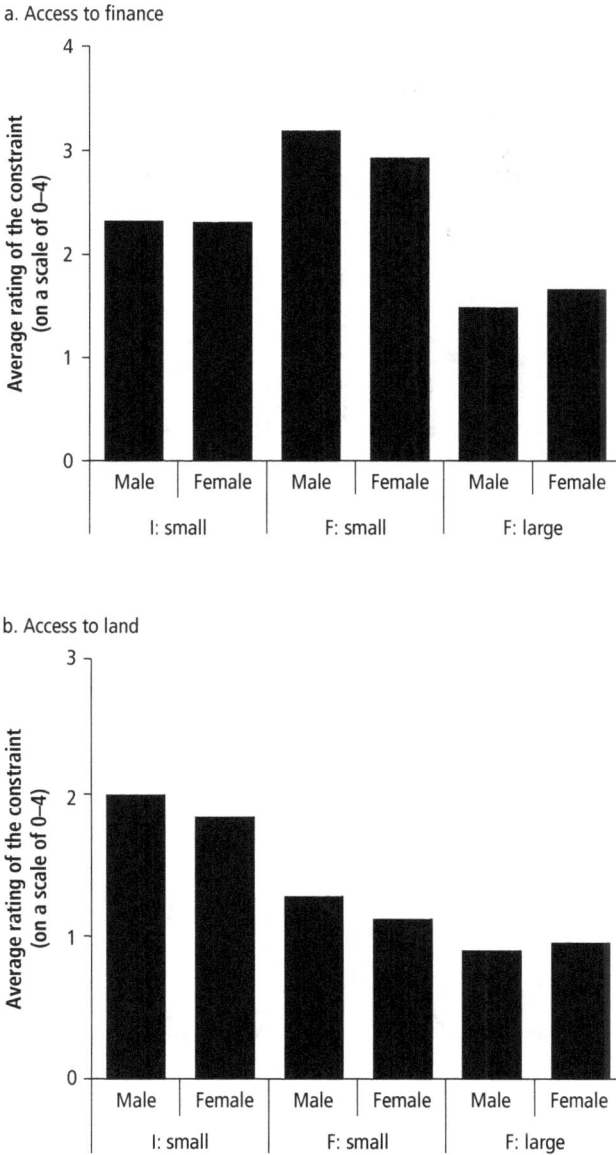

a. Access to finance

b. Access to land

—Continued

Figure 6.2 *(continued)*

c. Corruption

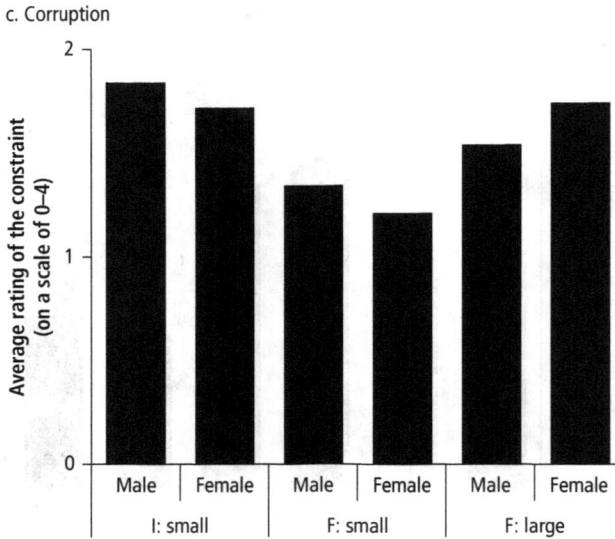

d. Labor regulations

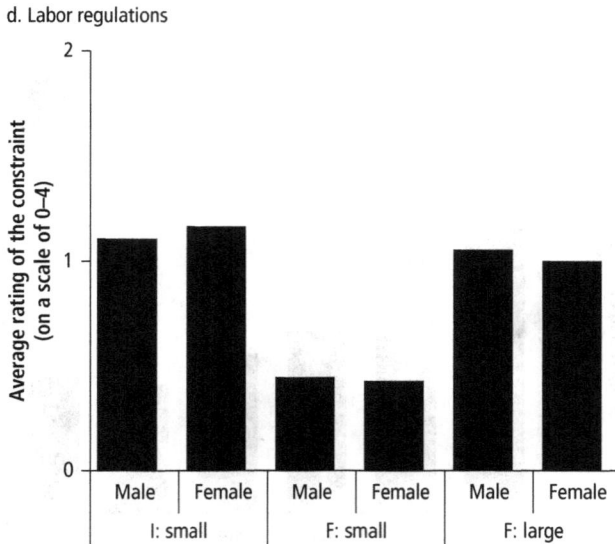

Source: Enterprise Surveys, World Bank, http://www.enterprisesurveys.org.
Note: I = informal; F = formal. A small firm is defined as one with less than 20 employees; a large firm has 20 or more employees. Respondents rated severity of obstacles on a scale of 0 to 4.

Figure 6.3 Obstacles Facing Sole Proprietors Show Somewhat Larger Differences by Gender (subjective responses)

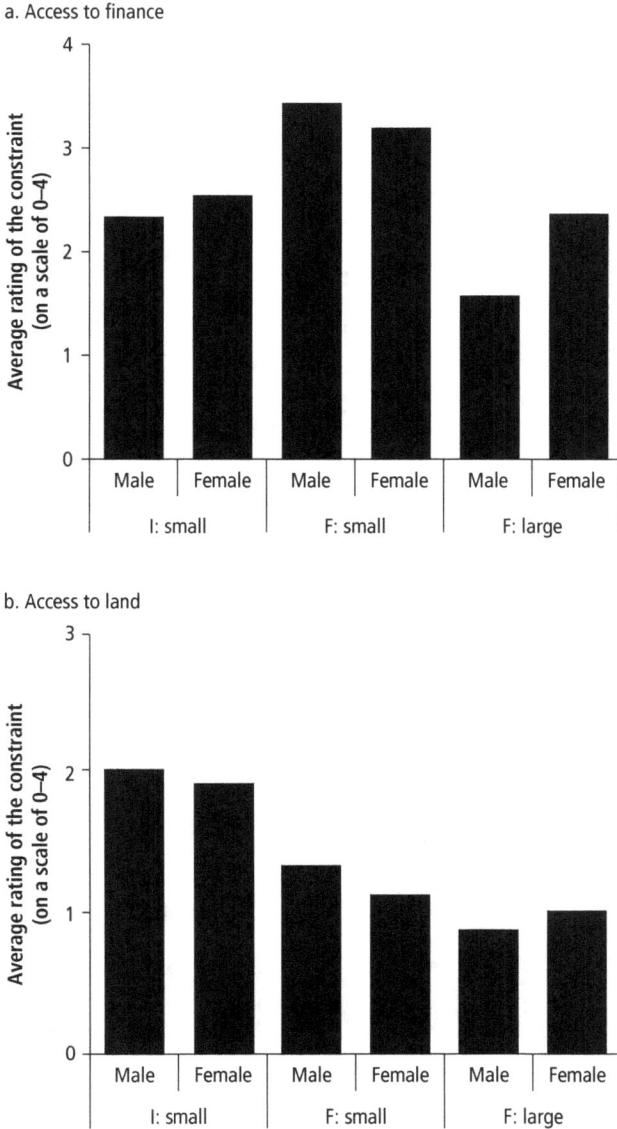

a. Access to finance

b. Access to land

—Continued

Figure 6.3 *(continued)*

c. Corruption

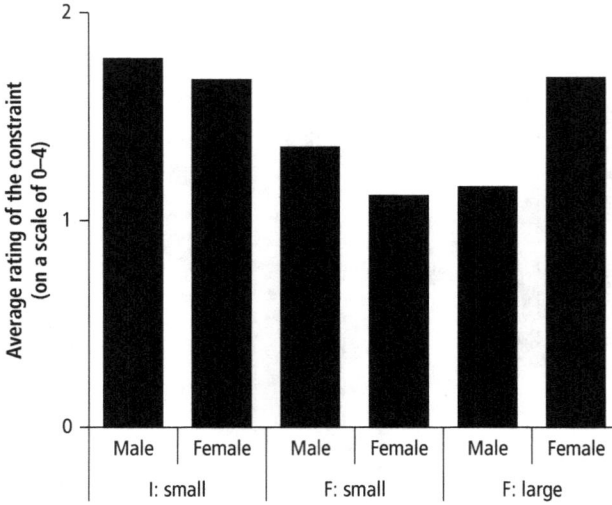

d. Labor regulations

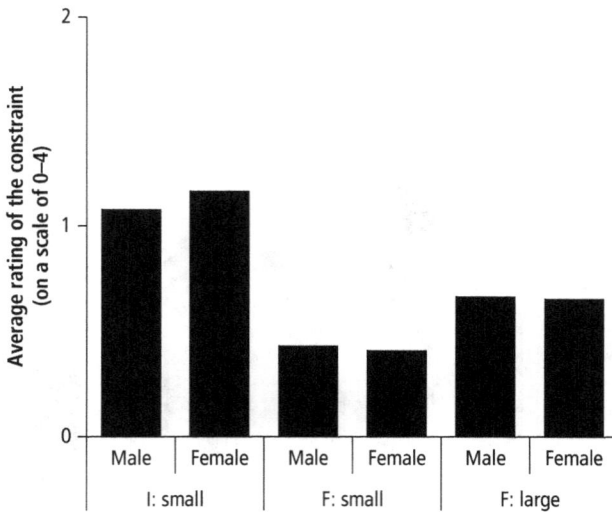

Source: Enterprise Surveys, World Bank, http://www.enterprisesurveys.org.
Note: I = informal; F = formal. A small firm is defined as one with less than 20 employees; a large firm has 20 or more employees. Respondents rated severity of obstacles on a scale of 0 to 4.

the greater red tape that comes with having more employees. Informal firms also see them as a constraint, possibly reflecting the fact that labor regulations are one of the main reasons some firms stay informal (McKenzie and Sakho 2010; McKenzie and Woodruff 2006). Large female formal firms report corruption as a significant constraint.

Objective Information

Respondents answered objective questions on four issues: frequency of payments needed to "get things done," access to specific financial services, the amount of managers' time spent with officials, and losses due to electricity outages. Unfortunately, there is no corresponding indicator for access to land. We use these more objective measures to see if we can confirm that differences vary less by gender and more by enterprise size and sector.

The survey results do confirm the pattern: differences are generally more significant by size than gender (figure 6.4). For access to finance, small firms complained more than large firms—consistent with fewer small firms having a loan or even a bank account. The time managers spend with officials is also dramatically different by size, but only slightly by gender. Large firms' managers spend much more time dealing with officials, partly because their firms try to comply with regulations (rather than trying to operate under the radar).

For corruption, the quantitative measure is of the share of firms that report "firms like theirs" making payments to "get things done." The subjective rankings show less variation by size or gender; the objective data also show less variation by size and only mild variation by gender. But informal microfirms seem less likely to pay (informality as a strategy of staying below the radar can succeed). Losses due to electricity outages were greater for smaller firms than larger firms. Part of the explanation is that larger firms have the scale and resources to pay for generators. As expected, there is no difference in this measure by gender within size categories of enterprises.

Similar patterns are also found when dividing the sample by industry and gender rather than by size (figure 6.5). Thus enterprise characteristics (rather than gender) help account for the obstacles to operating and expanding a business.

Influence of Constraints on Employment Category

The discussion of the microdata on constraints has focused on enterprise performance, and has looked specifically at whether these obstacles could affect women's relative performance within an employment category. But there is a second way these constraints could have a gender impact. They could affect the employment category men and women are more likely to enter. Thus constraints, particularly gender gaps in constraints, could be what underlie

Figure 6.4 Obstacles to Doing Business Vary More by Size Than Gender (quantitative responses)

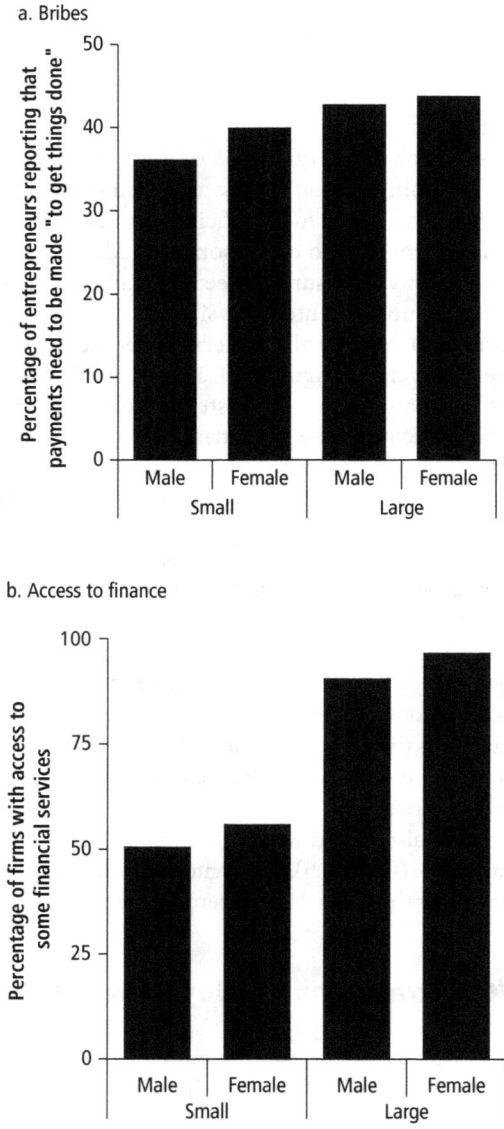

a. Bribes

b. Access to finance

Figure 6.4 *(continued)*

c. Manager time with officials

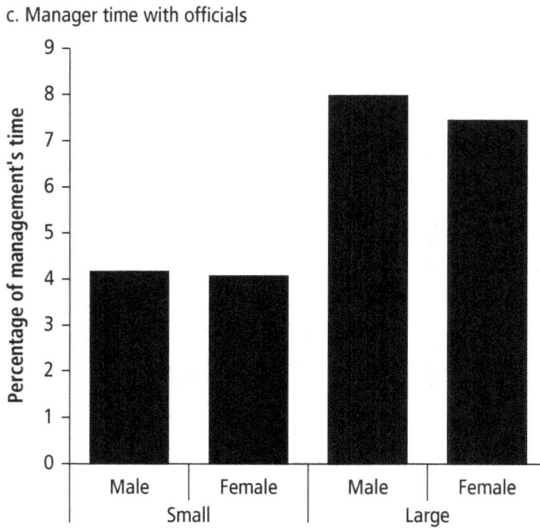

d. Losses due to outages

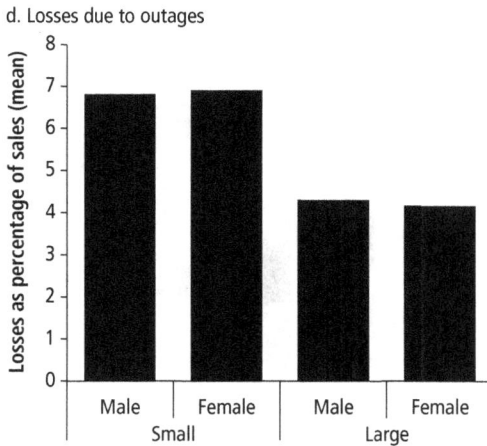

Source: Enterprise Surveys, World Bank, http://www.enterprisesurveys.org.
Note: A small firm is defined as one with less than 20 employees; a large firm has 20 or more employees.
"Access to finance" (figure 6.4b) is defined as having a bank account, overdraft, or loan.

Figure 6.5 Obstacles Vary More by Industry Than Gender (quantitative responses)

a. Bribes

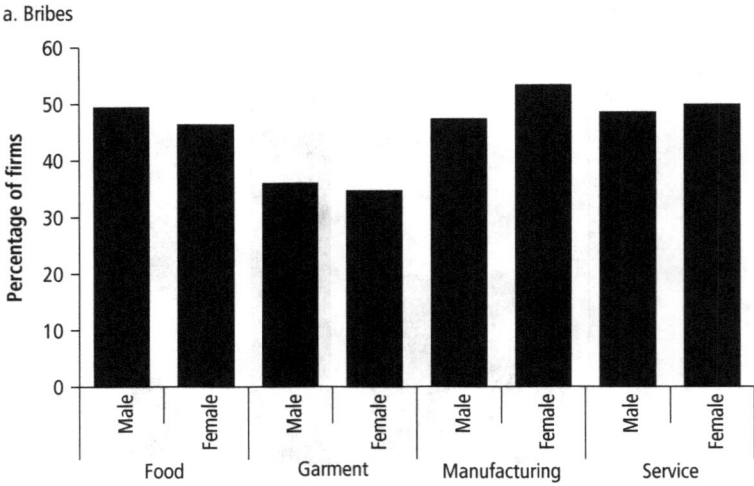

b. Access to finance

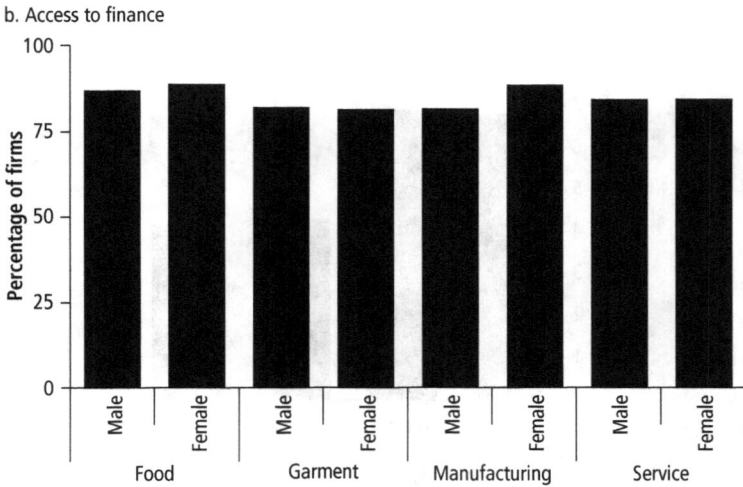

Figure 6.5 *(continued)*

c. Management time with officials

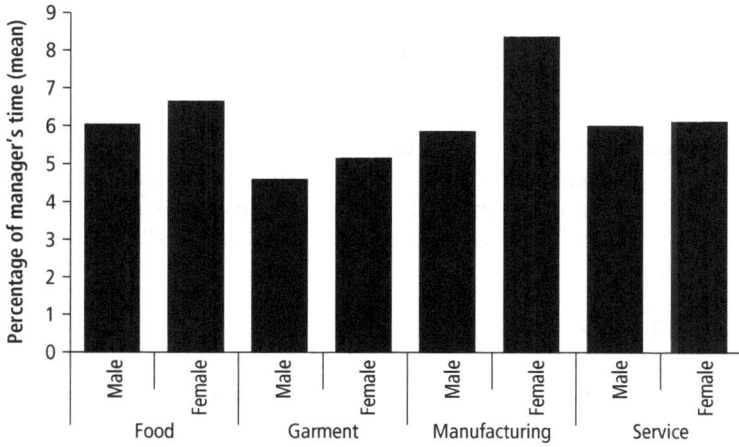

d. Losses due to outages

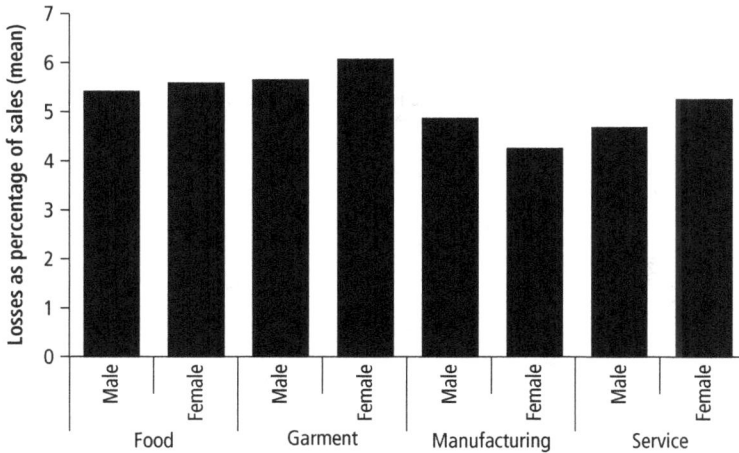

Source: Enterprise Surveys, World Bank, http://www.enterprisesurveys.org.

the differential entry into activities to begin with. Both directions of causality are of interest. Again, data limitations restrict the extent to which this second channel can be examined because there are few or no gender-disaggregated data on constraints faced by those who do not become entrepreneurs. Thus one cannot examine how the presence of constraints affected the entry decision. (Chapter 8 addresses this potential channel when looking deeper into issues of access to finance.)

Among established enterprises, the surveys of new entrepreneurs in Côte d'Ivoire, Kenya, Nigeria, and Senegal are as close as we can get to understanding the role of the constraints to entry. The data show four areas where gender could have a role: access to finance, interactions with government officials, corruption, and harassment.

Access to Finance

The surveys show that access to finance varies greatly by formality, but gender matters as well. Men in the formal sector are far more likely to have a loan than either men in the informal sector or women in the formal sector (figure 6.6). Indeed, men in the informal sector make up a somewhat larger share (albeit very low) of firms with a loan than women in the formal sector.

Similar patterns pertain for the start-up capital that entrepreneurs had when launching their business: it is higher in the formal than informal sector, and in both, higher for men than women (figure 6.7).

Figure 6.6 Male Formal Entrepreneurs Are Far More Likely to Have Loans Than Other Groups

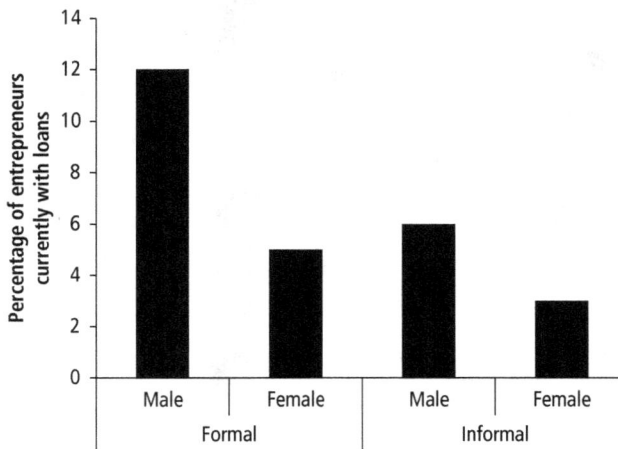

Source: Gajigo and Hallward-Driemeier 2010.
Note: Data are for newly established enterprises in Côte d'Ivoire, Kenya, Nigeria, and Senegal.

Figure 6.7 Male Formal Entrepreneurs Had More Start-Up Capital Than Other Groups

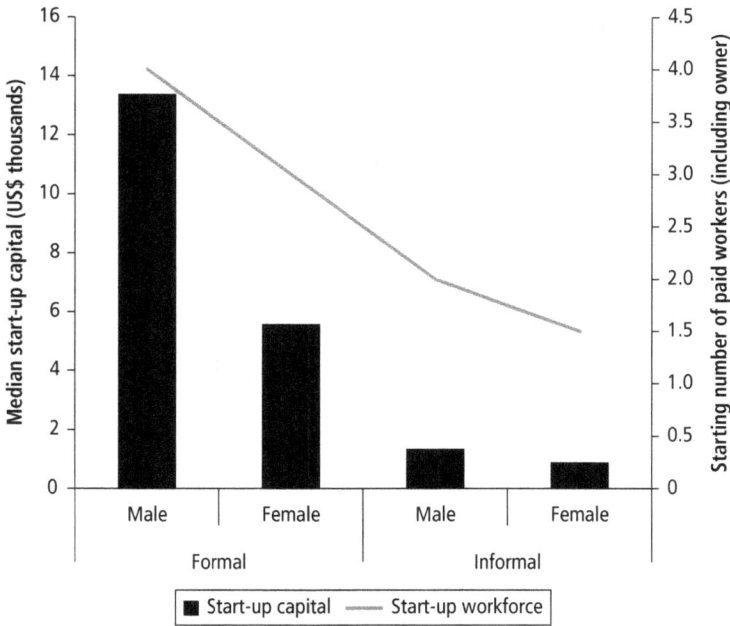

Source: Gajigo and Hallward-Driemeier 2010.
Note: Data are for newly established enterprises in Côte d'Ivoire, Kenya, Nigeria, and Senegal.

Some sources of start-up capital are also correlated with enterprise productivity (Gajigo and Hallward-Driemeier 2010). Entrepreneurs whose largest source of start-up capital is commercial banks or friends and relatives have significantly higher profitability than those who tapped other sources. Getting the bulk of one's start-up capital from friends and relatives has no gender gradient on productivity, unlike relying on commercial banks. This pattern is consistent with female entrepreneurs being more constrained than their male counterparts.

These results are consistent with those of studies looking at gender gaps in access to credit across different sources of finance. Fafchamps (2000, 2001) found that women did not face gaps in getting credit from banks once firm size was taken into account. However, with more informal, relationship-based lending, women were less likely to receive credit. Fafchamps's work on the importance of networks primarily focuses on issues of ethnicity, but it has important implications for gender too—particularly if women have not traditionally been part of these networks (see discussion in chapter 8).

Interactions with Government Officials

For the time that management spends dealing with government officials, both formality and gender again appear important (figure 6.8). Entrepreneurs in the formal sector spend much more time dealing with officials than those in the informal sector—and in both sectors, men spend more time than women. This last difference may reflect the tendency of men's businesses to be larger and perhaps need more licenses, or the lesser ability of larger firms to ignore regulatory requirements.

Corruption

One concern with interactions with officials is that women may be softer targets for bribes than men, or less able to negotiate lower informal payments to "get things done."

Information on the frequency of bribes paid shows that formal firms are much more likely to make "gifts" than those in the informal sector (figure 6.9). The gender difference is small, except that women in the

Figure 6.8 Formality and Gender Affect the Time Managers Spend with Officials

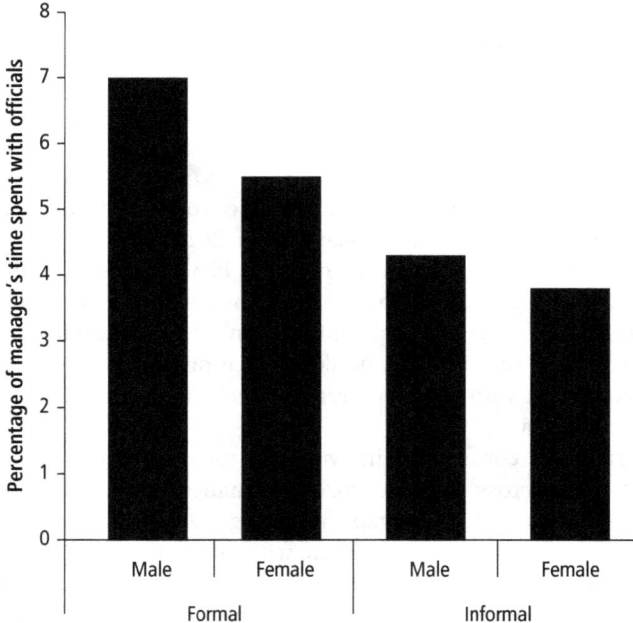

Source: Gajigo and Hallward-Driemeier 2010.
Note: Data are for newly established enterprises in Côte d'Ivoire, Kenya, Nigeria, and Senegal.

Figure 6.9 Formal Firms Are Much More Likely to Make "Gifts" Than Informal Firms

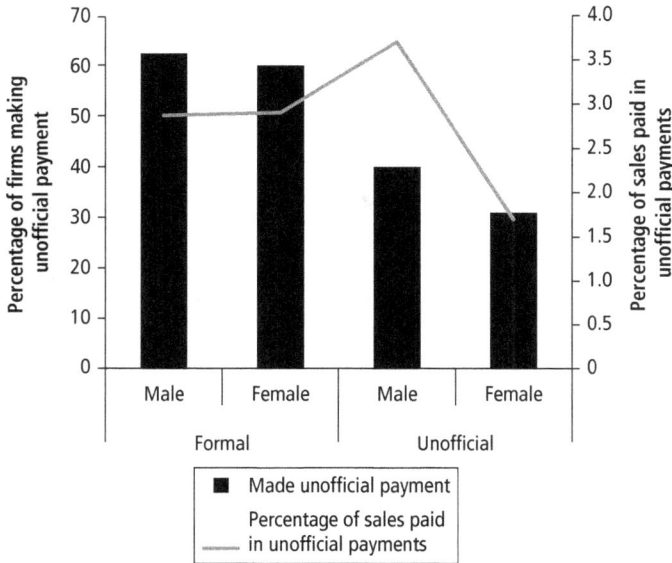

Source: Gajigo and Hallward-Driemeier 2010.
Note: Data are for newly established enterprises in Côte d'Ivoire, Kenya, Nigeria, and Senegal.

informal sector appear less likely to pay than men, and their payments are lower than men's.

What is also interesting is that formal entrepreneurs report having a better sense of the amount of money that is needed "to get things done" (figure 6.10) and greater confidence that the payment will achieve its aim (figure 6.11).

The view that informality allows the entrepreneur to remain under the radar and not subject to harassment from officials may be true in some cases. But in many others the very fact that a business is not registered and may face larger sanctions is what gives officials the ability to demand gifts.

The survey also inquired about payments made to other firms in the private sector for "protection" (figure 6.12). Like bribes, they are more common in the formal sector, but payments are larger in the informal sector. The gender bias is attenuated, though women in the formal sector were somewhat less likely to make such payments.

As with getting things done, the formal sector entrepreneurs again reported having a better sense of what the payments were likely to be (figure 6.13) and were slightly more confident that they would receive the benefits of such payments (figure 6.14).

Figure 6.10 Formal Entrepreneurs Believe They Know How Big Their "Gifts" Should Be

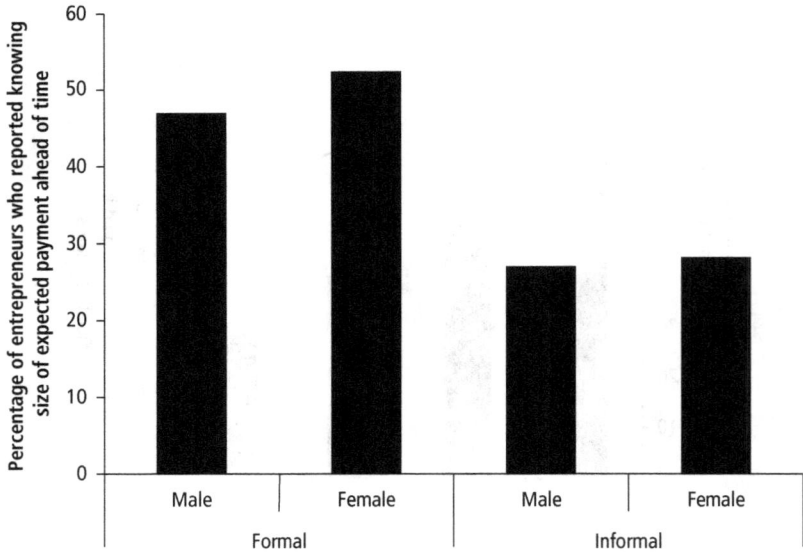

Source: Gajigo and Hallward-Driemeier 2010.
Note: Data are for newly established enterprises in Côte d'Ivoire, Kenya, Nigeria, and Senegal.

Figure 6.11 Many Formal Entrepreneurs Believe That Their "Gifts" Will Achieve Their Purpose

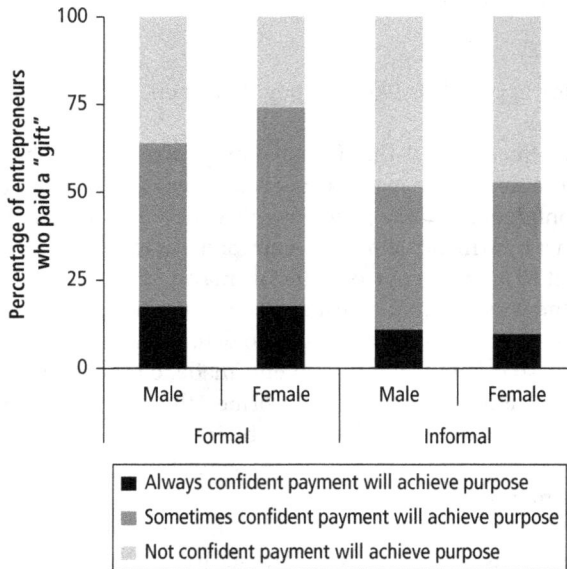

Source: Gajigo and Hallward-Driemeier 2010.
Note: Data are for newly established enterprises in Côte d'Ivoire, Kenya, Nigeria, and Senegal.

150

Figure 6.12 Formal Firms Are More Likely to Pay for Protection Than Informal Firms—but Pay Less for It

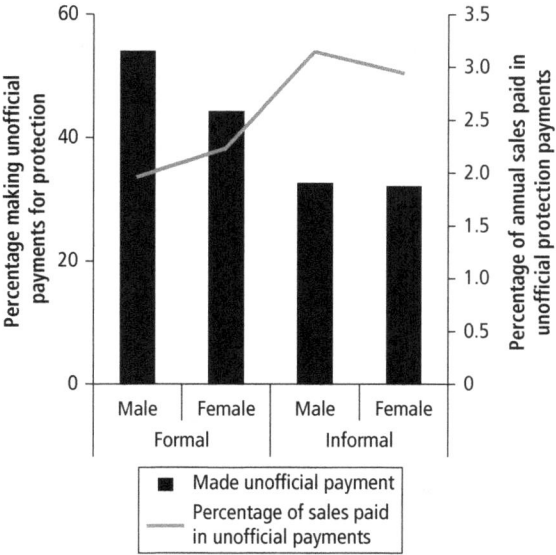

Source: Gajigo and Hallward-Driemeier 2010.
Note: Data are for newly established enterprises in Côte d'Ivoire, Kenya, Nigeria, and Senegal.

Figure 6.13 Formal Entrepreneurs Believe They Know How Big Their Payments for Protection Should Be

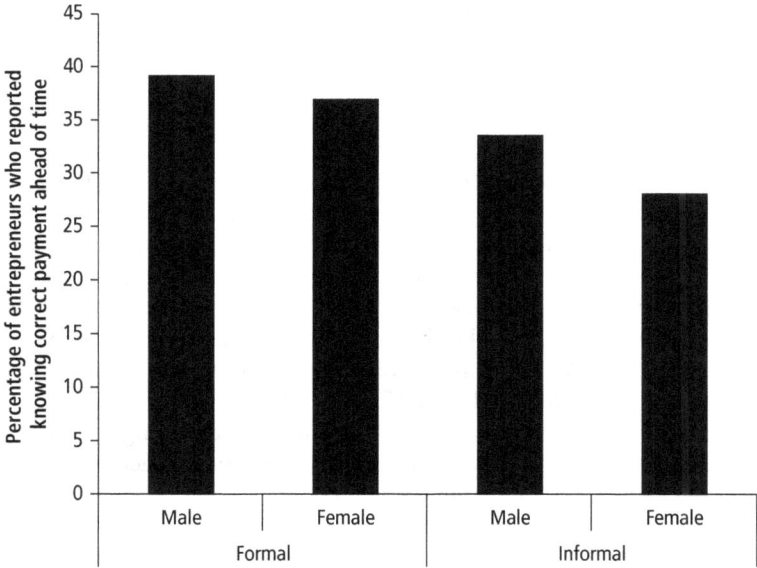

Source: Gajigo and Hallward-Driemeier 2010.
Note: Data are for newly established enterprises in Côte d'Ivoire, Kenya, Nigeria, and Senegal.

Figure 6.14 Many Formal Entrepreneurs Believe That Their Payments for Protection Will Achieve Their Purpose

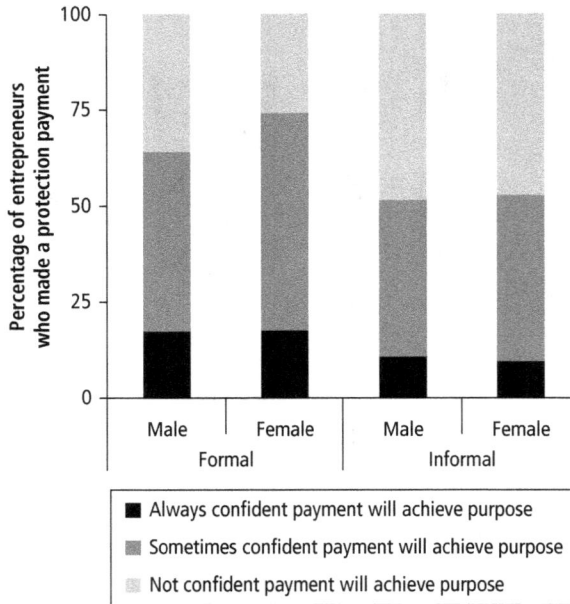

Source: Gajigo and Hallward-Driemeier 2010.
Note: Data are for newly established enterprises in Côte d'Ivoire, Kenya, Nigeria, and Senegal.

Harassment

Some challenges for female entrepreneurs may vary only in degree from men's, but some are different in kind. One of the concerns raised by women in a series of focus groups held with entrepreneurs from 15 countries was that the "gifts" sought were not always monetary. When asked whether they knew of cases where sexual favors had been asked for, the majority replied "yes" (with almost equal shares reporting they heard of such harassment "occasionally" and "frequently") (figure 6.15). Formal sector entrepreneurs, male and female, were more likely to report having heard of such activities. The transactions most susceptible to harassment varied: borrowing money and dealing with suppliers were deemed more susceptible, dealing with government officials (inspectors or those granting licenses) marginally less so.

What is particularly troubling is that women also fear harassment from those who should be protecting them. In discussions with several women's groups in preparing this work, we heard repeatedly about women's inability to go to a police station for fear of encountering further harassment. This fear makes it very difficult for women to have their complaints investigated by the authorities,

Figure 6.15 When Women Borrow Money or Engage in Other Business Transactions, They May Be Asked for Sexual Favors

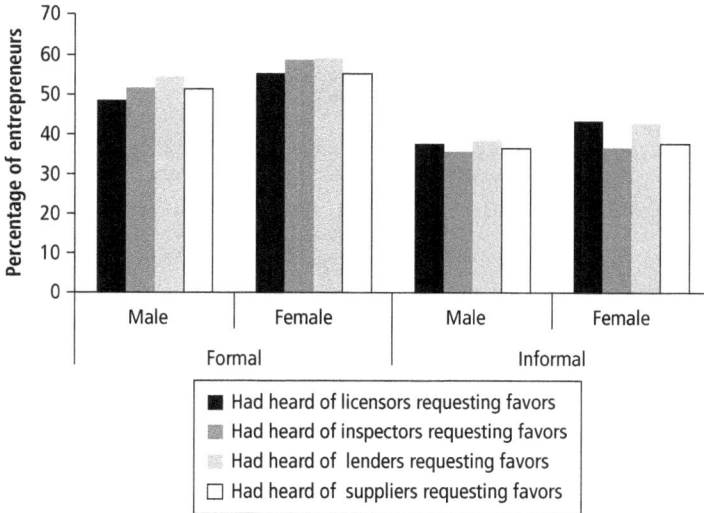

Source: Gajigo and Hallward-Driemeier 2010.
Note: Data are for new entrepreneurs in Côte d'Ivoire, Kenya, Nigeria, and Senegal. Figure indicates percentages of entrepreneurs who indicated they had "sometimes" or "frequently" heard of sexual favors being asked for.

let alone have much confidence that the formal system would provide assistance or enforce their rights if property was stolen or disputes arose in the course of running their businesses.

Clearly this is not to say that sexual harassment is something all women face—nor are women's successes to be attributed to their providing sexual favors. That many have heard of harassment may reflect a few examples that were widely discussed in the media or among the respondents. But concerns about potential sexual harassment need to be addressed in their own right—and harassment could have additional indirect costs too. It could keep women from undertaking certain economic activities that would otherwise be viable.

Thus, overall, women may face some constraints as women—and these need to be addressed. However, for most issues, the type of enterprise rather than the gender of the entrepreneur determines which constraints matter relatively more.

Notes

1. A similar finding, that gender becomes insignificant once firm size is controlled for, is found for access to finance in the analysis of access to banking credit in Fafchamps (2000). However, it does not hold for access to trade finance, where gender (and ethnic) ties remain important predictors of who receives trade credit.

2. Similarly, the surveys do not capture those enterprises that exited. Panel surveys can capture the conditions enterprises faced prior to exit, although they may fail to capture shocks or deteriorating conditions that pushed the enterprise into going out of business. Frazer (2005) and Harding, Söderbom, and Teal (2006) did find reported constraints were often higher for firms that subsequently exited.

References

Armendariz, B., and N. Roome. 2008. "Gender Empowerment in Microfinance." Working paper, Department of Economics, Harvard University, Cambridge, MA.

Ashraf, N. 2009. "Spousal Control and Intra-household Decision Making: An Experimental Study in the Philippines." *American Economic Review* 99 (4): 1245–77.

Aterido, R., and M. Hallward-Driemeier. 2010. "The Impact of the Investment Climate on Employment Growth: Does Sub-Saharan Africa Mirror Other Low-Income Regions?" Policy Research Working Paper 5218, World Bank, Washington, DC.

Aterido, R., M. Hallward-Driemeier, and C. Pages. 2011. "Big Constraints to Small Firms' Growth? Business Environment and Employment Growth across Firms." *Economic Development and Cultural Change* 59 (3): 609–47.

Banerjee, A., E. Duflo, R. Glennerster, and C. Kinnan. 2009. "The Miracle of Microfinance? Evidence from a Randomized Evaluation." Working paper, Massachusetts Institute of Technology, Cambridge, MA.

Bardasi, E., M. Blackden, and J. C. Guzman. 2007. "Gender, Entrepreneurship, and Competitiveness." In *Africa Competitiveness Report 2007*, edited by World Economic Forum, African Development Bank, and World Bank, 69–86. Geneva: World Economic Forum, African Development Bank, and World Bank.

Batra, G., D. Kaufmann, and A. Stone. 2003. *Investment Climate around the World: Voices of the Firms from the World Environment Survey*. Washington, DC: World Bank.

Bigsten, A., P. Collier, S. Dercon, M. Fafchamps, B. Gauthier, J. Gunning, A. Oduro, R. Oostendorp, C. Pattillo, M. Söderbom, F. Teal, and A. Zeufack. 2003. "Credit Constraints in Manufacturing Enterprises in Africa." *Journal of African Economies* 12 (1): 104–25.

Bruhn, M., and I. Love. 2011. "Gender Differences in the Impact of Banking Services: Evidence from Mexico." *Small Business Economics* 37 (4): 493–512.

Dollar, D., M. Hallward-Driemeier, and T. Mengistae. 2005. "Investment Climate and Firm Performance in Developing Economies." *Economic Development and Cultural Change* 54 (1): 1–31.

Fafchamps, M. 2000. "Ethnicity and Credit in African Manufacturing." *Journal of Development Economics* 61 (1): 205–35.

_____. 2001."Networks, Communities, and Markets in Sub-Saharan Africa: Implications for Firm Growth and Investment." *Journal of African Economies* 10 (Suppl. 2): 109–42.

Fafchamps, M., and A. R. Quisumbing. 2002. "Control and Ownership of Assets within Rural Ethiopian Households." *Journal of Development Studies* 38 (2): 47–82.

Frazer, G. 2005. "Which Firms Die? A Look at Exit from Manufacturing in Ghana." *Economic Development and Cultural Change* 53 (3): 585–617.

Gajigo, O., and M. Hallward-Driemeier. 2010. "Entrepreneurship among New Entrepreneurs." Working paper, World Bank, Washington, DC.

Harding, A., M. Söderbom, and F. Teal 2006."The Determinants of Survival among African Manufacturing Firms." *Economic Development and Cultural Change* 54 (3): 533–56.

Kabeer, N. 2001. "Conflicts over Credit: Re-Evaluating the Empowerment Potential of Loans to Women in Rural Bangladesh." *World Development* 29 (1): 63–84.

Kantor, P. 2005. "Determinants of Women's Microenterprise Success in Ahmadabad, India: Empowerment and Economics." *Feminist Economics* 11 (3): 63–83.

Klapper, L., and S. Parker. 2010. "Gender and the Business Environment for New Firm Creation." *World Bank Research Observer* 26 (2): 237–57.

McCormick, D., M. N. Kinyanjui, and G. Ongile. 1997. "Growth and Barriers to Growth among Nairobi's Small and Medium-Sized Garment Producers." *World Development* 25 (7): 1095–110.

McKenzie, D., and Y. S. Sakho. 2010. "Does It Pay Firms to Register for Taxes? The Impact of Formality on Firm Profitability." *Journal of Development Economics* 91: 15–25.

McKenzie, D., and C. Woodruff. 2006. "Do Entry Costs Provide an Empirical Basis for Poverty Traps? Evidence from Mexican Microenterprises." *Economic Development and Cultural Change* 55: 3–42.

Ramachandran, V., A. Gelb, and M. K. Shah. 2009. *Africa's Private Sector: What's Wrong with the Business Environment and What to Do About It.* Washington, DC: Center for Global Development.

World Bank. 2004. *World Development Report 2005: A Better Investment Climate for Everyone.* Washington, DC: World Bank.

Part IV

Shifting Women to More Productive Work

Where individuals work shapes their opportunities. Thus the agenda moving forward is to address the factors that account for gender sorting across types of entrepreneurial activities. Four issues are highlighted: strengthening the economic right to own and control assets, increasing access to finance, improving access to education and business skills, and strengthening women's voice in the reform process. Part IV draws on examples of the impact of reforms and explores variations across countries to show the importance of this agenda in expanding economic opportunities for women in Africa.

Chapter **7**

Increasing the Right to Own and Control Assets

Can you reap the rewards of your investments of time and resources? Are you restricted in your legal ability to make decisions that affect your economic activities? These are central questions for people in business everywhere, and both relate to property rights and the ability to make economic decisions in one's own name.[1] The strength of these rights determines the incentives to invest and put time and energy into a business venture. It also determines the ability to control collateral to obtain credit, and the types of risks that will be taken.

This chapter provides evidence confirming earlier research (see box 7.1) that a woman's ability to engage in economic activity is affected by what property and economic rights she enjoys and what legal capacity she possesses. The new database of indicators relating to women's formal property rights and legal capacity, Women–LEED–Africa, shows the extent of discriminatory family, marital property, and inheritance laws. Along with legal restrictions on women's mobility, employment outside the home, and administration of personal assets, those laws present barriers to women's economic opportunity.[2]

The chapter will describe the three main findings of Women–LEED–Africa, summarized briefly here. First, all 47 Sub-Saharan African countries recognize the principle of nondiscrimination in their constitutions or in treaties— but allow many legal exceptions. Second, the treatment of women's economic rights is not closely related to a country's level of income or development, so active measures are needed to close gender gaps in these rights; closing income gaps is not sufficient. (These measures can work, as the case of Ethiopia shows; see box 3.1 and Hallward-Driemeier and Gajigo 2011). Third, many discriminatory provisions that women face apply not to women as women, but to women as married women. Marital status, and the capacities and limitations associated with it, determine women's effective property rights and economic autonomy, in ways often markedly different from men's.

The customary and social norms from which many laws derive are deep challenges to reform, because customary law is extremely important both as a

BOX 7.1

Earlier Research on the Impact of Property Rights on Economic Opportunities

An extensive literature shows the importance of property rights for growth, investment, and government effectiveness.[a] Aggregate cross-country data show a positive association between growth and the quality of institutions or property rights, though the exact causal mechanism can be hard to establish.[b]

Much recent literature focuses on microeconomic analyses, generally within a single country that has changed legal rights or that grants different rights to different groups. This box highlights examples of such changes to property rights or family law.

Strong Land Rights Can Promote Investment

Empirical work suggests that a greater share of resources controlled by women promotes agricultural productivity (Besley and Ghatak 2009; Quisumbing 1996; Saito, Mekonnen, and Spurling 1994; Udry and others 1995) and helps reduce poverty (World Bank 2001). Insecure property rights to land have multiple ramifications for agriculture and for how rural economic activity is organized. For one, the risk that land will be expropriated deters investment. Insecure property rights also reduce borrowers' ability to pledge land as collateral, and thus tighten credit constraints. Finally, ill-defined property rights to land can inhibit land transactions—rentals or sales—thereby costing owners the potential gains from trade (Aryeetey and Udry 2010).

Udry and Goldstein (2008) examine the effect of contested land rights on investment and productivity in agriculture in Akwapim, Ghana. They show that individuals who hold powerful positions in a local political hierarchy have more-secure tenure rights, and therefore invest more in land fertility, leading to much higher output. The intensity of investments on different plots cultivated by a given individual corresponds to that individual's security of tenure over those specific plots.

Besley (1995), also in Ghana, shows that individuals vary their investment across plots depending on the security of their rights—and that property rights need to be understood as embedded in a broader social context.

Many countries have formal titling programs. Some evaluations have shown an associated increase in agricultural productivity and a (weak) increase in access to credit (for example, Pande and Udry [2005]). The weak increase in access to credit has been attributed to two factors. First, creditors often have only weak rights to foreclose on land (Field and Torero 2008). Second, collateral is not the only constraint to accessing finance: a profitable idea and the ability to work in a reasonably hospitable investment climate are also needed (Besley and Ghatak 2009).

One of the challenges for women is that titling has too often been done under a single name, that of the male head of household.

Strong Land Rights Can Increase Labor Supply

Field (2007) evaluates the impact of a titling program in the slums of Peru. She finds little impact of a title on decisions to invest in the home or plot of land, but does find an impact on labor supply, particularly for women. The title freed members of the household from having to remain on the plot to ensure a claim over it.

Changes in Inheritance Laws Alter the Incentive of Families to Invest in Daughters

Deininger, Goyal, and Nagarajan (2010) analyze the effect in some southern states of changes to the Hindu Succession Act, which gave equal rights to females in inheriting property. The effect of the new law was to raise the likelihood of women inheriting land (without fully eliminating the gender difference), increase the age at marriage for girls, raise their educational attainment, and increase household investments in daughters. Roy (2008) found that the law increased women's autonomy.

Changes in Family Law Can Strengthen Women's Economic Empowerment

As family law determines issues of legal capacity or who controls assets in the family, changes in legislation can affect economic opportunities. Part of the effect may come from shifts in intrahousehold bargaining power, as illustrated by Stevenson and Wolfers (2006) and Gray (1997), who looked at the changes in divorce laws in the United States. For an account of progress in Ethiopia, see box 3.1.

Source: Hallward-Driemeier and Hasan 2012.

a. Pande and Udry (2005) provide a review of the literature, focusing on microeconomic analyses. Besley and Ghatak (2009) provide a synthesizing theoretical framework of the relationship of property rights and economic outcomes (particularly investment), and also discuss the existing evidence on the importance of property rights.

b. See, for example, Acemoglu and Johnson (2005); Acemoglu, Johnson, and Robinson (2001); Glaeser and others (2004); Johnson, McMillan, and Woodruff (2002); Rodrik, Subramanian, and Trebbi (2004).

formal source of law and as informal practice. It touches the lives of the majority of the population in much of Africa.

Moreover, the diversity of legal systems and sources of law complicates the task of determining women's legal status and effective rights, and adds to uncertainty in the business environment. Family law, seldom addressed in programs to improve the business environment, shapes the business environment for women.

Such diversity is mirrored by a corresponding diversity in case law and interpretations, examined in greater detail in the companion report (Hallward-Driemeier and Hasan 2012). Even where women's rights are enshrined in law, contradictions among formal sources of law undermine the equality of these rights for women, and the gulf is often wide between paper and practice. Contradictory provisions within laws, and a high degree of variability in the interpretations given to these laws, especially concerning marital property, circumscribe women's legal rights and act as a brake on their ability to seize economic opportunities.

The chapter ends with recommendations for improving the substance of laws, strengthening the process of the formal and informal legal systems, and strengthening the administration of laws and access to justice. Where possible, the formal and informal sectors should be linked, so that decision makers can be cognizant of their impact on peoples' daily lives—with the goal of identifying strategies to improve the economic rights of women within their sphere of influence.

Regulations, Formal Law, and Practice

Regulations on business stipulate the procedures for registering property and businesses, enforcing contracts, and safeguarding investor and creditor rights. They rarely have gender-differentiated provisions. Almost all, with the exception of some labor laws (discussed below), are gender blind. (The few areas where they treat men and women differently are usually specific situations, such as pregnancy or night work.) The impact in practice, of course, may not be gender neutral if women face greater time constraints, have more-limited mobility, or face cultural restrictions on the transactions they can engage in—or if officials see them as softer targets for harassment. Gender-blind regulations also presuppose that the parties can enter contracts, have freedom of movement and access to economic exchange, and can own property or control assets in their own name. This is not always the case for women, so gender-blind regulations do not guarantee gender equality in economic rights.

Other areas of the law, rarely addressed in analyses of the business environment, play a determining role in framing these rights—notably family law for marriage, divorce, and inheritance, as well as laws for land rights and labor markets. These laws, more than business regulations, determine whether women and men can make economic decisions in their own name, or whether there are restrictions on their ability to enter contracts or to own, administer, transfer, or inherit assets and property. It is in these areas that gender differences, including outright discrimination, are most apparent.

Two other factors are important. First is the frequency with which laws within a country are subject to overlapping legal systems, such as when constitutions and statutes explicitly recognize marriage, inheritance, and property as domains where formal customary or personal law applies. Second is the tendency to grant these domains formal exemption from nondiscrimination provisions.[3]

Formal law defines formal economic rights, articulated in international law, in constitutions, and in specific statutes. The formal rules reflect what should happen if the legal system functions well, and they thus are worth examining for their incentives and protections. The strength of de jure rights provides a measure of the potential to use the law to address discriminatory practices.

If formal laws do not provide safeguards against discrimination, that closes a critical avenue for redress.

But the strength of formal economic rights is determined not only by the content of formal laws but also by how effectively the formal legal system safeguards these rights. Ambiguity in defining or enforcing any of these rights, coupled with multiple sources of law and legal systems in many African countries, limits the use of property, raises transaction costs, and increases uncertainty and unpredictability in exercising economic rights.

Practical constraints—including distance, cost, and language—can further shape people's ability to exercise formal economic rights, with important gender-differentiated effects. So, the de jure indicators in the next few sections do not fully reflect de facto, or actual, practices. Nor do many people engage with the formal legal system, or have much knowledge of the protections it affords. Particularly in areas with low incomes, low education, and strong customary traditions, as well as in areas that are more rural, people rarely turn to the formal system to secure economic rights. They turn instead to local elders or chiefs and follow customary practices.

Constitutional and statutory provisions do not treat women as a homogeneous group. Some treat men and women differently, based purely on gender. Others recognize a gender difference on marriage, and women's legal capacity and the strength of their property rights most often weaken then. Any assessment of the equality of de jure economic rights must therefore consider both gender and marital status.

The law is not of course the only factor that influences a person's decision to become an entrepreneur or that affects an enterprise's performance. Many other factors—including individuals' skills as well as their access to assets, technology, and infrastructure—also matter. Men and women can have different preferences for how they spend their time, and different interests and abilities in their economic activities. Changing the laws to ensure equality of economic rights for women and men will likely be insufficient to bring about equality of participation and performance for women and men. But unequal legal protection will make achieving such a goal all but impossible.

Focus of Women–LEED–Africa

The first step in assessing women's legal rights is to look at the rights on the books according to official sources of law in each country, and to determine how these (de jure) rights differ from men's. The Women–LEED–Africa database gives the dimensions for which differential treatment between women and men is legally allowed in different countries. The subject coverage is not exhaustive; the focus is on areas that have first-order effects on existing and potential businesspeople: legal capacity, property rights (land and assets), and restrictions in labor laws.

The database covers the five sources of law:

- *International treaties and conventions on women's rights.* They provide legal protections that are binding on their signatories. Their direct application domestically can vary by monist or dualist state system (they are directly applicable in the former, but need to be incorporated into domestic laws in the latter).

- *Constitutions.* They are the highest source of law in a country and lay out the guiding principles for legal rights. The focus is on provisions for nondiscrimination on the basis of sex and, as appropriate, for explicitly promoting gender equality.

- *Statutes.* Family and civil codes, marital property laws, land laws, and labor laws—rather than generic business regulations—determine who has legal capacity, who can own property, and what the restrictions are on equal labor opportunities.

- *Customary law.* Many African countries' constitutions or statutes (or both) recognize customary law as a separate—often equal—source. Some countries recognize only certain areas of customary law. The interest here is in its applicability to legal capacity, property, and inheritance.

- *Religious law.* Many regional countries recognize religious law as a separate—often equal—source. Some recognize it as the primary source of law, others as the applicable source of law for members of a particular religion or for certain issues (or both). Again, the interest is in its applicability to issues of legal capacity, property, and inheritance.

Using seven indicators of where women's economic and legal rights differ from men's, Women–LEED–Africa looks at each of these five sources of law in all 47 Sub-Saharan African countries. The database does not try to assess how extensive the male-female differences are; it categorizes countries as "yes" or "no" on each indicator. (The country indicators are listed in appendix C.)

The first three indicators measure the recognition of different sources of law that could affect the protection of nondiscrimination on the basis of gender:

- *International agreements and conventions.* At issue is the status of signature/ratification of the Convention on the Elimination of All Forms of Discrimination against Women; the Protocol to the African Charter of Human and Peoples' Rights on the Rights of Women in Africa; and key International Labour Organization (ILO) Conventions, notably Convention 100 on equal remuneration for men and women workers for work of equal value, Convention 111 on equality of opportunity and treatment in respect of employment and occupation, and Conventions 171 and 183 on the labor rights of women with respect to night work and the labor rights of women who are pregnant or breastfeeding.

- *Nondiscrimination provisions.* At issue are protections for nondiscrimination on the basis of gender and for gender equality within constitutions. Specific provisions addressed include recognition of nondiscrimination on the basis of sex, provisions explicitly promoting gender equality, guarantees of property ownership, guarantees of women's property ownership, and equal rights to work and to equal pay.

- *Recognition of customary and/or religious law.* At issue is whether countries recognize customary and/or religious law, whether this recognition stems from provisions within the constitution or statutes, and whether customary and/or religious law is explicitly exempt from constitutional provisions for gender nondiscrimination.

The four remaining indicators measure topical issues, showing where the economic rights of men and women differ:

- *Legal capacity.* This mainly involves "head-of-household" laws, which give husbands power to choose the marital domicile, or which require the husband's permission for the wife to enter a trade or profession, to work outside the home, to enter into contracts, or to open a bank account.

- *Property rights related to marriage and inheritance.* These concern the provisions of different marital property regimes, including within marriage, and on divorce or death of the spouse, including treatment of nonmonetary contributions.

- *Land laws.* The focus is on key provisions relating to the protection of women's land rights in land laws, statutory recognition of customary law on land ownership and inheritance, exemption of customary ownership from statutory succession laws, and availability of co-ownership options in marriage for women.

- *Labor laws.* The focus is on statutory provisions relating to equal pay for equal work, restrictions of women's work (sectors or hours worked), application to pregnant women, and maternity leave (duration and funding).

These indicators largely relate to statutes, but also record customary or religious laws when they are recognized as the prevailing source of law.

Database compilation benefited from several concurrent initiatives, including the Gender Law Library of the World Bank and its accompanying publication *Women, Business, and the Law* (World Bank 2010; see appendix C), and the work by the International Finance Corporation's Women in Business Program (Simavi, Manuel, and Blackden 2010).

Main Findings from Women–LEED–Africa

Three key messages emerge from the database. First, all 47 Sub-Saharan countries recognize the *principle* of nondiscrimination—in their constitutions or in treaties (or both). Many countries, however, grant various legal exceptions to nondiscrimination, including many in the constitution itself. A common exception is the recognition of customary law, which often is not bound to respect nondiscrimination as a principle. Moreover, the multiplicity of sources of law adds uncertainty to defining women's economic rights: despite recognizing nondiscrimination as a guiding principle of law, many countries' statutes discriminate.

Second, the treatment of women's economic rights is not closely related to a country's level of income or development. One implication is that simply raising national income is not likely to be sufficient to improve women's legal and economic rights; to meet this goal more active reforms will likely be needed. Some countries have expanded overall income even with gaps in women's economic rights—while others, with strong protections for nondiscrimination, have not. The legal framework is not the only factor, but the strength of legal protections affects women's economic opportunities, particularly their ability to run and expand larger enterprises and to move out of self-employment. The share of women entrepreneurs who are employers is significantly higher where women's economic rights are stronger—across the income spectrum.

Third, many of the discriminatory provisions apply not to women as women, but to women as married women. From a legal standpoint, marriage changes the legal status and rights of women, sometimes radically, often conferring legal capacities and responsibilities on husbands, and removing them from wives. As discussed below, this type of change applies particularly to property regimes, to rights in and after marriage, and to rules affecting women's economic capacity and decision making within marriage.

Nondiscrimination

The principle of nondiscrimination is recognized in all Sub-Saharan countries, either in constitutions or in the international conventions to which countries are signatories (figures 7.1 and 7.2).

The constitutional recognition of customary law is pervasive—it applies in all common law countries and in almost half the civil law countries. Where customary law is not recognized in constitutions, this recognition is implicitly provided in statutes, particularly those for marriage or inheritance. What varies across countries is the extent to which constraints are placed on customary law in upholding the principle of nondiscrimination (figure 7.3).

Figure 7.1 All Sub-Saharan Constitutions Enshrine the Principle of Nondiscrimination, and Most Enshrine Gender Equality

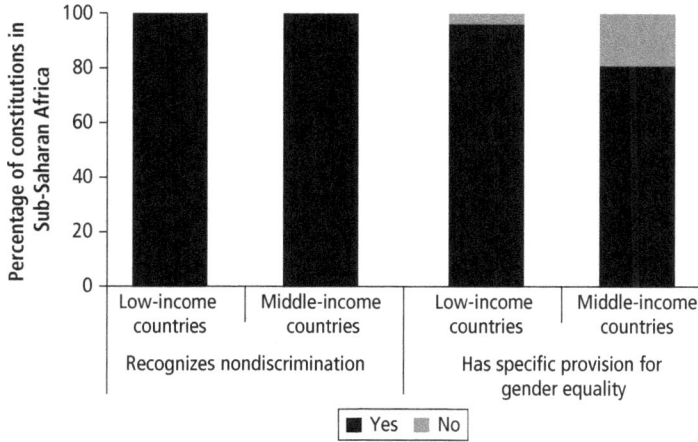

Source: M. Hallward-Driemeier, T. Hasan, M. Blackden, J. Kamangu, and E. Lobti, Women's Legal and Economic Empowerment Database.

Figure 7.2 Almost All Sub-Saharan Countries Are Signatories to at Least Some International Conventions on Nondiscrimination

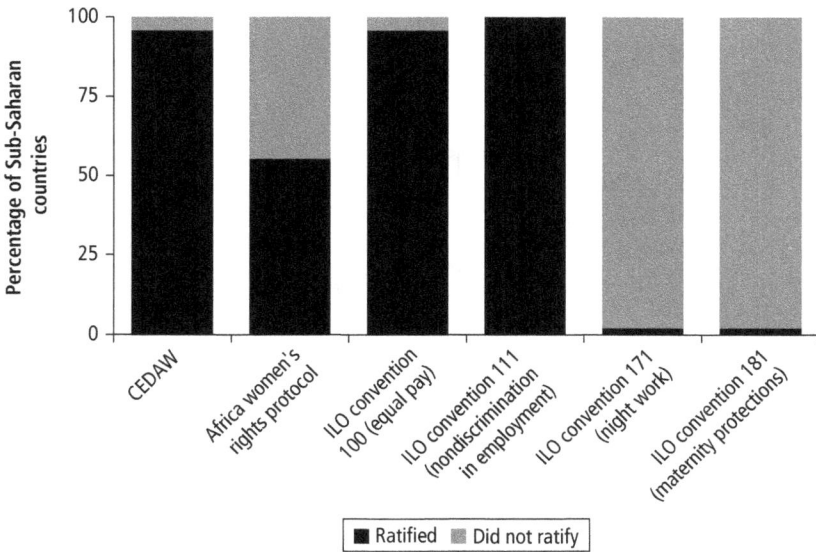

Source: M. Hallward-Driemeier, T. Hasan, M. Blackden, J. Kamangu, and E. Lobti, Women's Legal and Economic Empowerment Database.
Note: CEDAW = Convention on the Elimination of All Forms of Discrimination against Women; ILO = International Labour Organization.

Figure 7.3 The Constraints Placed on Customary Law in Upholding Nondiscrimination Vary across Countries

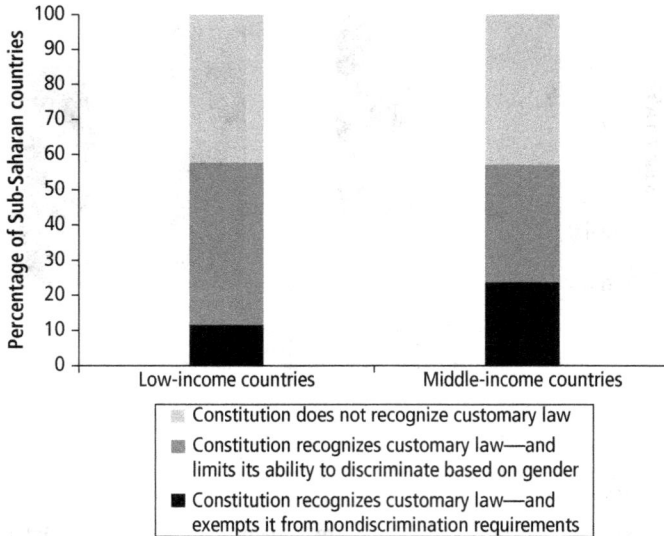

Source: M. Hallward-Driemeier, T. Hasan, M. Blackden, J. Kamangu, and E. Lobti, Women's Legal and Economic Empowerment Database.

Income

Restrictions on women's legal capacity do not differ much by country income, but they are found largely in civil law countries, where various laws stipulating the man as "head of household" apply. (The two common law countries that restrict women's legal capacity are Sudan and Swaziland.) While one indicator measures the countries that have a "head-of-household" provision, its implications can mislead—for two reasons. First, some countries without such a provision still have statutes that provide for the same powers of husbands over their wives. Second, some countries deem the man as head of household to be a *social* distinction, and they have explicit provisions indicating that husbands do not have power over the *economic* decisions of their wives. In short, a "head-of-household" provision is not an infallible indicator of who makes the economic decisions.

Husbands have power over their wives' economic activities in three main ways. The right of the husband to choose the matrimonial home is the most common, followed by his ability to deny his wife permission to pursue a job or profession. The need to get his signature to open a bank account is less

Figure 7.4 Head-of-Household Rules Provide Several Ways Husbands Can Control Their Wife's Assets

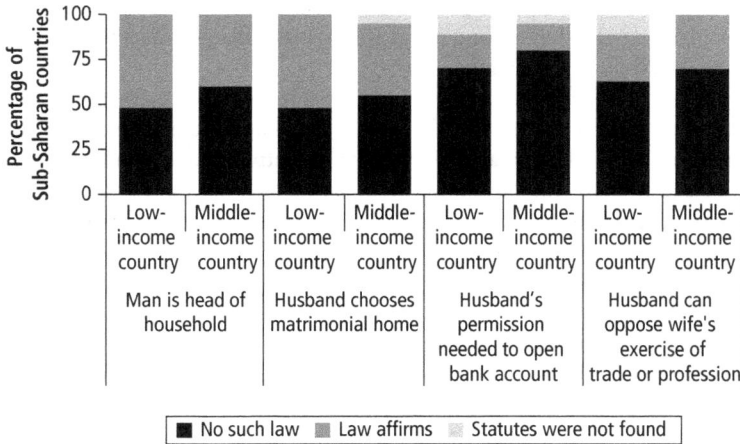

Source: M. Hallward-Driemeier, T. Hasan, M. Blackden, J. Kamangu, and E. Lobti, Women's Legal and Economic Empowerment Database.

common, at least in laws governing marriage (though many countries allow banks to require this as part of their business practice) (figure 7.4).

Property Regime for Marriage

The type of property regime in marriage determines the ability of both spouses to own property during marriage and after its dissolution through death or divorce. These property rights in turn determine spouses' access to and control of assets and other productive resources that can be used as collateral for loans or for other business purposes. Statutory, customary, and religious marriages are subject to various property regimes. The most common are community of property (including universal community of property), separate ownership of property, dowry, and customary law. The default marital regime that applies is regulated by the relevant family statute or code, which in turn depends on the type of marriage contract that the parties enter.

The community of property regime offers women a better chance of maintaining their property rights on dissolution of marriage than separate ownership regimes, because it entitles them to a portion of the property, generally half, without having to make proof of contribution. Not having to prove contribution is vital, because millions of women in Africa contribute to marital property through nonmonetized activities, such as performing household chores and working in subsistence agriculture.

Even when community of property is the default regime, it may not always apply, particularly in polygamous marriages, where the default is separate ownership. Separate property in a polygamous marriage protects a wife from having her property divided among other wives, but it also limits a wife's access to assets acquired during marriage.

The nature of the marital property regime is important as it determines married women's control over assets that can be used as collateral in applying for a loan or used in a business, as well as their incentive to accumulate additional assets or expand a business. The share of assets a woman is entitled to when a marriage ends can be critical in determining whether she can run a business and if so what type of business.

Inheritance Regime

Inheritance remains one of the main ways for women to acquire and control property (figure 7.5) and one of the main areas where women find themselves involved in property disputes. The legal framework for succession laws in Sub-Saharan Africa falls under constitutions as well as family, customary, and religious laws. Judicial precedence also plays a large role. All these factors affect whether women, married and unmarried, can own and control property and thus have the ability to use such assets in their business. Figure 7.5 focuses on inheritance of marital property on the death of the husband intestate.[4] Under a separate property regime, married women do not automatically inherit from their husband's estate. Some countries provide for some inheritance, but the share is usually far less than half.

Land

Land is central to getting finance, especially in Africa's collateral-based banking systems, and is a key resource for enterprise development. Land issues bring to the fore many of the problems associated with multiple legal systems, specifically involving customary law and practices for land ownership and access rights as well as deep-rooted gender biases (Quisumbing and others 2001). Some land laws are gender neutral, some explicitly favor men, and others recognize the rights of women to own land (figure 7.6).

Gender differences in access to and control over land remain a key problem in Sub-Saharan Africa. The avenues available to women in access to land include purchase, allocation in case of customary land tenure, inheritance, and distribution in the event of divorce. The challenges arising in inheritance and divorce have been examined extensively elsewhere.[5] Many studies have shown clearly that women's rights over land are inferior to those of men. For example, while the majority of males reported unfettered rights to give land to family members, fewer than 5 percent of women could do so across

Figure 7.5 Inheritance Is One of the Main Ways Women Can Acquire and Control Property—But Such Rights Vary

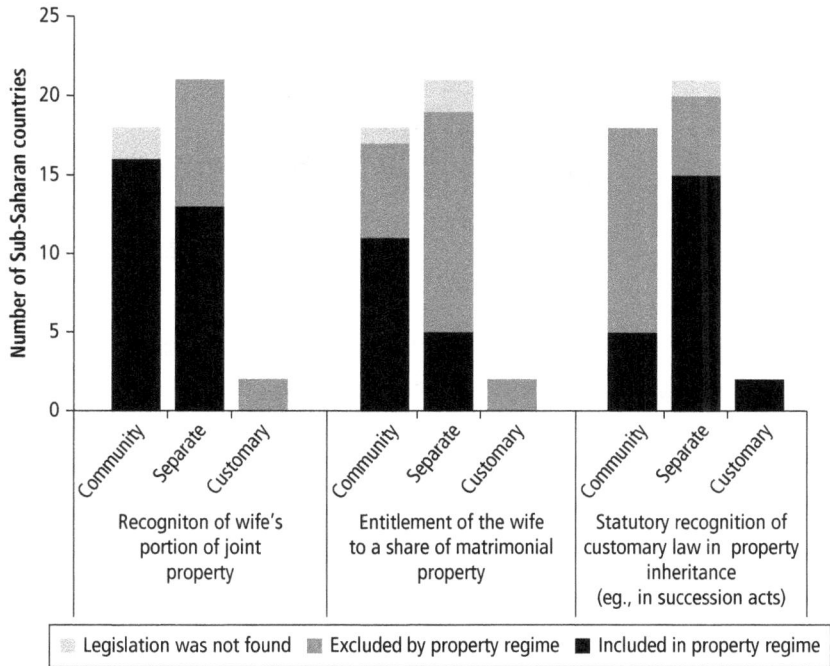

Source: M. Hallward-Driemeier, T. Hasan, M. Blackden, J. Kamangu, and E. Lobti, Women's Legal and Economic Empowerment Database.
Note: Data are for wife's right to inherit matrimonial property if husband dies intestate under three property regimes (community, separate, and customary).

sites in Burundi, Uganda, and Zambia (Place 1995). There are, however, a few exceptions, such as in cocoa-growing areas of Ghana, where women are granted rights to land and trees through gifts. Yet women are rarely allowed to inherit land, even in matrilineal systems. As for acquisition of short-duration rights to land through renting or sharecropping, women appear to fare better.

Intestate succession laws in several countries, including Ghana and Zambia, exclude customary or lineage land from property that a wife can inherit on the death of her husband. Instead, the land follows customary rules of inheritance, usually going to a male heir. Customary land comprises 72 percent of all land in Malawi, 80 percent in Mozambique, 60 percent in Swaziland, and 81 percent in Zambia (UNECA 2003), so this rule is a major impediment to women's land rights.

Figure 7.6 Not All Land Laws Recognize Women's Right to Own Land

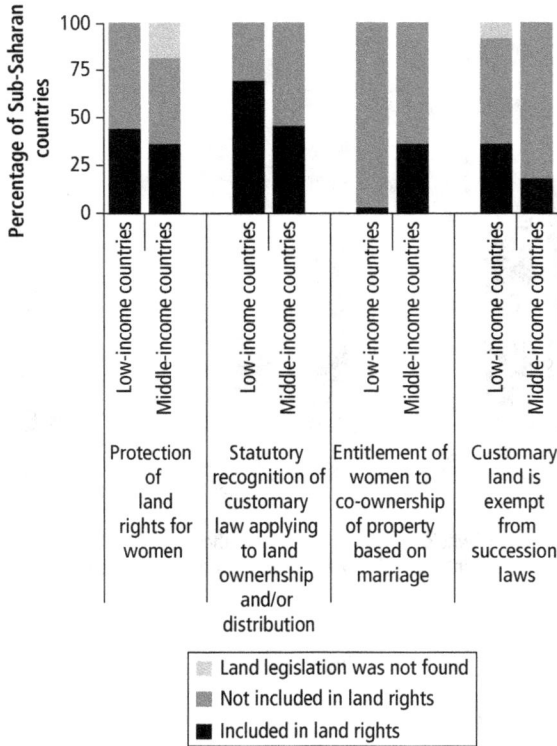

Source: M. Hallward-Driemeier, T. Hasan, M. Blackden, J. Kamangu, and E. Lobti, Women's Legal and Economic Empowerment Database.

Labor

Legal safeguards for women's labor rights in Sub-Saharan Africa are in the ILO conventions that countries sign and in the constitutions and labor laws of countries. Because men's and women's economic activities outside agriculture are mainly as self-employed entrepreneurs, as employers, or as wage earners, their options are affected by laws, regulations, and practices governing labor and employment. Thus while labor laws directly affect employees, they can also affect entrepreneurs by raising or lowering the availability and attractiveness of wage employment. Constitutions in 30 countries in the region go beyond a general clause on nondiscrimination to provide equal rights to work or equal pay (or both). Effectively implementing the principle of nondiscrimination is critical in enforcing labor rights for women to ensure equal pay for equal work.

Restrictions on women's labor hours, or on the nature of the work they may undertake, still apply in many countries. Women's ability to participate fully in the labor force, unlike men's, is therefore constrained, limiting access to some opportunities.

Some restrictions apply to all women, some only to pregnant women, ostensibly aimed at protecting them. Fifteen countries restrict the nature of the work any woman may engage in, and 20 more apply such restrictions only to pregnant women (figure 7.7). Twenty-three countries restrict the hours that any woman may work, and a further 12 restrict only pregnant women. These restrictions, combined with other limitations resulting from head-of-household provisions, are a severe obstacle to women becoming wage earners. They may be contributing to the tendency of women who are not agricultural workers to be self-employed in informal and small enterprises.

Figure 7.7 Restrictions on Women's Hours and Type of Work Vary

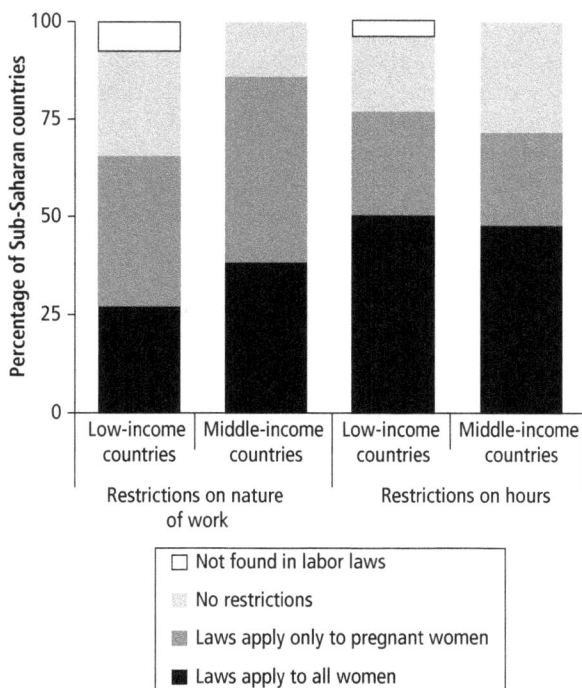

Source: Hallward-Driemeier, T. Hasan, M. Blackden, J. Kamangu, and E. Lobti, Women's Legal and Economic Empowerment Database.

Gaps between Principle and Practice

According to the Women–LEED–Africa database, governments have made much progress in enshrining rights for women in law, even if, in some critical areas, such rights still remain precarious or poorly defined. The gap between what is in law in principle and what can be realized in practice is, however, very wide.

Formal legal pluralism limits women's economic rights in three main ways. First, the very existence of customary law exemplifies the multiple systems and sources of law, and raises questions about which systems prevail in which circumstances. Second, legal systems have conflicting, sometimes contradictory, provisions for where women's property rights are addressed—inconsistently— across different areas of law and through different legal instruments. Third, customary law has discriminatory provisions that are allowed under statutory law.

But other factors keep the principle-practice gap wide as well. Barriers in administrative law include physical access to the justice system (distance to courts and legal services, and costs in time and money); gender-based differences in representation in the justice system; complex legal proceedings (including language and procedures); cultural obstacles in the way communities address disputes; hierarchies of legal systems, where formal/statutory and infor- mal/customary legal systems coexist, raising questions of jurisdiction (which system prevails?); and "forum shopping" by those with the power and resources to obtain the most favorable results.

Customary law also presents women with multiple constraints in access- ing justice. Even though it may be physically and culturally more accessible, women's experience within customary institutions can differ significantly from men's. Most of the customary courts are adjudicated by men and tend to favor men in their decisions. Women are traditionally excluded from adjudi- cating matters of customary law and so cannot influence the law's evolution. Women may not be able to voice their grievances directly, and it is up to the male head of the family to bring a grievance to the attention of elders.

Before presenting recommendations for the way forward, we show how easily case law can reverse earlier gains (box 7.2).

The Way Forward

Case law can be a progressive instrument for change when statutes are inter- preted equitably or legal ambiguities are creatively filled in to advance women's rights.

To reduce the potential for discrimination, efforts should be directed toward drafting clear legislation, in harmony with constitutional principles of gender

BOX 7.2

A Step Back: A Kenyan Court's Ruling on Dividing Marital Property

In the Kenyan case of *Echaria v. Echaria*, the spouses had been married for 23 years. The wife was university educated and had worked outside the home for some time, but she had spent much of her married life looking after their four children and supporting her husband, who had risen in the diplomatic service to become an ambassador. The family had lived abroad and, on her return to Kenya, Mrs. Echaria worked as a senior education officer. In the divorce proceedings, Mrs. Echaria claimed a 50 percent share of the matrimonial property.

The Court of Appeal decided the case and overturned an earlier decision of the High Court recognizing nonmonetary contributions. It held that the division of property in marriage would be determined under the general laws of contract in Kenya and that a woman would have to show her monetary contribution.

The Court of Appeal awarded her only a quarter share of the property. It concluded that the only contribution toward the acquisition of the property that Mrs. Echaria could have made was by payment of monthly installments for a loan. The court further stated that the mere status of marriage does not entitle a spouse to a beneficial interest in the property registered in the name of the other. Nor did the performance of domestic duties qualify as a contribution to the acquisition of marital property.

Source: Hallward-Driemeier and Hasan 2012.

---

equality and nondiscrimination. In family law and inheritance, women's rights to marital and inheritance property should be unequivocally equal to men's.

Based on the more in-depth analysis in the companion report, *Empowering Women: Expanding Economic Opportunities in Africa* (Hallward-Driemeier and Hasan 2012), we propose recommendations in three areas to address gaps in legal and economic rights for women—as they exist on the books as well as in the form of practical constraints to accessing justice (box 7.3).

Despite the obvious benefits of reform, success is more likely if governments proceed with caution, and with respect for existing systems. For reforms to be effective, buy-in from all stakeholders is essential; this is the only way to ensure that the change is enacted—and enforced.

To unify and strengthen women's rights, all sources of law should be subject to the principle of nondiscrimination. If protections are important enough to be included as a guiding constitutional principle, they should apply equally to all people. They should cover all sources of law, including customary and religious law. And they should specifically cover, rather than

BOX 7.3

Recommendations for Closing Gaps in Legal and Economic Rights

The following recommendations for closing gaps in legal and economic rights summarize those made in the companion report.
Improve the substance of laws by

- Reforming family law, including measures to strengthen the legal recognition of nonmonetary contributions to marriage in division of property after divorce or death, and removal of head-of-household and related provisions in family codes and other statutes that diminish women's legal capacity and economic autonomy
- Reforming land laws, notably to facilitate and encourage joint land titling
- Reforming labor and employment laws, primarily to address restrictions on all women or on married women that limit the type of work women may engage in or the hours they may work
- Strengthening in customary law the application of nondiscrimination principles, especially for marital property and land, and building on the strengths and accessibility of customary dispute-resolution mechanisms, while offsetting areas of gender bias in how customary law is applied

Strengthen the process of formal and informal systems by

- Addressing the political economy, especially in relation to amending family codes or laws
- Taking the sociocultural context into account when drafting new laws that are specifically appropriate to the country situation
- Undertaking a thorough analysis of the legal framework of the country as an integral part of the reform process

Strengthen the administration of laws and access to justice by

- Taking steps to encourage the registration of marriages, including customary marriages
- Encouraging the use of prenuptial agreements and wills, to provide a foundation for articulating and enforcing women's rights in marriage and inheritance—and building capacity in the use of these instruments
- Expanding access to laws and legal decisions in the judiciary
- Improving accountability in the judicial system
- Undertaking gender-sensitivity training for key members in the judicial system, notably judges and magistrates
- Encouraging greater participation of women in judicial decision-making bodies

- Implementing steps to reduce costs and simplify procedures
- Giving thought to institutional reforms to improve access, such as establishing small claims courts to tackle smaller business disputes, and using alternative dispute resolution mechanisms in family law and property disputes, because such mechanisms may be more familiar to communities already accustomed to traditional justice forums

Source: Hallward-Driemeier and Hasan 2012.

exempt, family law and other laws affecting property rights in and outside marriage.

Notes

1. Other rights matter, too, such as civil and political rights. But the focus here is on issues that most directly affect the ability to engage in business, and, specifically, on gender differences in these areas.
2. The database is M. Hallward-Driemeier, T. Hasan, M. Blackden, J. Kamangu, and E. Lobti, Women's Legal and Economic Empowerment Database, http://worldbank.org/gender/womenleedafrica. The companion report, *Empowering Women: Legal Rights and Economic Opportunities in Africa* (Hallward-Driemeier and Hasan 2012), presents the Women–LEED–Africa database and offers a legal analysis of gaps in property rights, including analysis of court decisions, the importance of customary law and practices, and the impact of overlapping legal systems on women's economic rights. It also explores the practical gaps in accessing formal justice and outlines a legal reform agenda for policy makers. This chapter summarizes some of that report's findings.
3. As shown in chapter 3, women are more likely to stream into self-employment in countries with weaker legal rights—and more likely to be employers in countries with stronger legal rights.
4. Collecting information on inheritance rights of daughters compared to sons was beyond the scope of this book.
5. See Quisumbing and others (2001), Lastarria-Cornhiel (1997), Place (1995), and Deininger (2003).

References

Acemoglu, D., and S. Johnson. 2005. "Unbundling Institutions." *Journal of Political Economy* 113 (5): 949–95.

Acemoglu, D., S. Johnson, and J. Robinson. 2001. "The Colonial Origins of Comparative Development: An Empirical Investigation." *American Economic Review* 91 (5): 1369–401.

Aryeetey, E., and C. Udry. 2010. "Creating Property Rights: Land Banks in Ghana." *American Economic Review Papers and Proceedings* 100 (2): 130–34.

Besley, T. 1995. "Property Rights and Investment Incentives: Theory and Evidence from Ghana." *Journal of Political Economy* 103 (5): 903–37.

Besley, T., and M. Ghatak. 2009. "Property Rights and Economic Development." CEPR Discussion Paper 7234, Centre for Economic Policy Research, London.

Deininger, K. 2003. *Land Policies for Growth and Poverty Reduction.* Policy Research Report, World Bank, Washington, DC.

Deininger, K., A. Goyal, and H. Nagarajan. 2010. "Inheritance Law Reform and Women's Access to Capital: Evidence from India's Hindu Succession Act." Policy Research Working Paper 5338, World Bank, Washington, DC.

Field, E. 2007. "Entitled to Work: Urban Property Rights and the Labor Supply in Peru." *Quarterly Journal of Economics* 122: 1561–602.

Field, E., and M. Torero. 2008. "Do Property Titles Increase Credit Access among the Urban Poor? Evidence from a Nationwide Titling Program." Working paper, Harvard University, Cambridge, MA.

Glaeser, E. L., R. La Porta, F. Lopez-de-Silanes, and A. Shleifer. 2004. "Do Institutions Cause Growth?" *Journal of Economic Growth* 9 (3): 271–303.

Gray, J. 1997. "The Fall in Men's Return to Marriage: Declining Productivity Effects or Changing Selection." *Journal of Human Resources* 32 (3): 481–504.

Hallward-Driemeier, M., and O. Gajigo. 2011. "Strengthening Economic Rights and Women's Occupational Choice: The Impact of Reforming Ethiopia's Family Law." Paper presented at Centre for the Study of African Economics annual conference, St. Catherine's College, Oxford, March 20–22.

Hallward-Driemeier, M., and T. Hasan. 2012. *Empowering Women: Legal Rights and Economic Opportunities in Africa.* Washington, DC: World Bank and Agence Française de Développement.

Johnson, S., J. McMillan, and C. Woodruff. 2002. "Property Rights and Finance." *American Economic Review* 92 (5): 1335–56.

Lastarria-Cornhiel, S. 1997. "Impact of Privatization on Gender and Property Rights in Africa." *World Development* 25 (8): 1317–33.

Pande, R., and C. Udry. 2005. "Institutions and Development: A View from Below." Economic Growth Center Discussion Paper 928, Yale University, New Haven, CT.

Place, F. 1995. *The Role of Land and Tree Tenure on the Adoption of Agroforestry Technologies in Zambia, Burundi, Uganda, and Malawi: A Summary and Synthesis.* Madison, WI: Land Tenure Center, University of Wisconsin–Madison.

Quisumbing, A. E. 1996. "Male-Female Differences in Agricultural Productivity: Methodological Issues and Empirical Evidence." World Development 24 (10): 1579–95.

Quisumbing, A. E., Payongayong, J. B. Aidoo, and K. Otsuka. 2001. "Women's Land Rights in the Transition to Individualized Ownership: Implications for Tree-Resource Management in Western Ghana." *Economic Development and Cultural Change* 50 (1): 157–82.

Rodrik, D., A. Subramanian, and F. Trebbi. 2004. "Institutions Rule: The Primacy of Institutions over Geography and Integration in Economic Development." *Journal of Economic Growth* 9 (2): 1381–438.

Roy, S. 2008. "Female Empowerment through Inheritance Rights: Evidence from India." STICERD working paper, London School of Economics, London.

Saito, K. A., H. Mekonnen, and D. Spurling. 1994. "Raising Productivity of Women Farmers in Sub-Saharan Africa." Discussion Paper 230, World Bank, Washington, DC.

Simavi, S., C. Manuel, and M. Blackden. 2010. *Gender Dimensions of Investment Climate Reform: A Guide for Policy Makers and Practitioners.* Washington, DC: World Bank.

Stevenson, B., and J. Wolfers. 2006. "Bargaining in the Shadow of the Law: Divorce Laws and Family Distress." *Quarterly Journal of Economics* 121 (1): 267–88.

Udry, C., and M. Goldstein. 2008. "The Profits of Power: Land Rights and Agricultural Investment in Ghana." *Journal of Political Economy* 116 (6): 981–1022.

Udry, C., J. Hoddinott, H. Alderman, and L. Haddad. 1995. "Gender Differentials in Farm Productivity: Implications for Household Efficiency and Agricultural Policy." *Food Policy* 20 (5): 407–23.

UNECA (United Nations Economic Commission for Africa). 2003. *Land Tenure Systems and Sustainable Development in Southern Africa.* ECA/SA/EGM.Land/2003/2. Lusaka, Zambia: UNECA.

World Bank. 2001. "Engendering Development: Through Gender Equality in Rights, Resources and Voice." Policy Research Report, World Bank, Washington, DC.

———. 2010. *Women, Business, and the Law 2010.* Washington, DC: World Bank.

Chapter 8

Expanding Women's Access to Finance

Starting a business requires assets. Once a business is started, internal resources are not always adequate, particularly for expansion. And if business and household finances are not fully independent, it can be a challenge to keep resources from being diverted from the business. Financial services provide solutions to these challenges by securing access to productive resources, smoothing cash flow, and providing savings instruments (box 8.1). They can be provided by the informal sector too, but the focus here is largely on formal financial services provided by microcredit institutions and banks.

Limited access to finance is cited as a top constraint facing entrepreneurs, and indeed, few firms, particularly in lower-income and weak rule of law countries, report having formal loans from banks (Banerjee and Duflo 2008; Beck, Demirgüç-Kunt, and Maksimovic 2008). In Sub-Saharan Africa fewer than one in five households has access to formal financial services. It is a systemic issue for businesses (male or female), which are 40 percent less likely to have any formal financial access than their peers in other regions.[1] But larger companies do have an advantage in accessing financial institutions.

More men than women have access to formal financial services. However, it is not necessarily due to discrimination within the financial sector. Education and experience are associated with using credit more productively, and thus both are highly correlated with the ability to secure access to finance. An analysis of individuals strongly suggests that gender differences in income, education, and employment status explain women's lower access to formal financing. Education, which is lower for women on average, rather than gender per se, is a better predictor of whether someone is likely to get credit. This finding makes clear that strengthening women's human capital and managerial skills (the subject of chapter 9) is an integral part of the agenda to expand access to finance.

At the same time, the Enterprise Surveys show that established enterprises run by women in the formal sector do not seem more financially constrained than those run by men.[2] Access to financial resources depends more on the size and registration status of the firm than on the gender of the manager. But what is striking is that women own and run such a small proportion of these large formal firms. This raises two points. The few women who run large formal firms have strong educational backgrounds and prior work experience and are thus able to qualify for credit (Aterido, Beck, and Iacovone, forthcoming). But precisely because there are disproportionately fewer women in this tier, gender dynamics may be at work in accessing finance at entry.

Does access to finance act as a barrier to entry that is particularly difficult for women to surmount? Certainly among new entrepreneurs, women's businesses have less access than men, and this difference is strongly associated with the nature of their business. Data suggest that prior to entry, women have more-limited access, consistent with their starting smaller and less capital-intensive firms, which are then less likely to access external finance once they are running. The earlier analysis showing that fewer women are employers where gaps in legal and economic rights persist is consistent with women facing barriers at entry. However, more data are needed to conclusively examine the barriers to entry.[3]

The concern over limited access to finance stems from the belief that if credit were available, entrepreneurs would be able to exploit additional opportunities that are otherwise cut off from them.[4] Certainly the data show a positive association of access to credit and profitability, not just in the data used here but in most of the literature (for example, Bardasi and Sabarwal 2009; Karlan and Morduch 2010; World Bank 2007).[5] But if creditors are doing their job in allocating capital, it should go to those with higher potential, so selection is clearly contributing to the relationship. A better way to measure causation is to look at studies that randomize access to credit. These studies indeed show very high rates of return to credit (de Mel, McKenzie, and Woodruff 2008; McKenzie and Woodruff 2008). However, in some cases women have not benefited as much as men (de Mel, McKenzie, and Woodruff 2009). Gender sorting into less capital-intensive sectors could be part of the explanation; less control within the household over how profits are used is another. Box 8.1 reviews the literature on women's access to finance; the rest of this chapter examines the extent to which women have differential access to different sources of finance.

Sub-Saharan Africa in a Global Context

Many entrepreneurs, worldwide, fail to secure the finance they want, but the problem is worse in Sub-Saharan Africa than in other regions. Data from 112 countries, including 37 from Sub-Saharan Africa, show a smaller proportion of formal businesses in the region have access to formal external finance, whether for investment or working capital, than elsewhere in the world (figure 8.1). The share of firms with some type of formal access to finance (bank account, credit line, or loan) is also lower (figure 8.2). This result is consistent with other

BOX 8.1

A Review of the Literature on Women's Access to Finance

As documented by an extensive and still growing literature, access to credit is important for firm growth, especially that of small firms (Beck, Demirgüç-Kunt, and Maksimovic 2005), and for new business creation (Klapper, Laeven, and Rajan 2006). Randomized field experiments confirm that access to capital can be critical (de Mel, McKenzie, and Woodruff 2008) for both women and men. Dupas and Robinson (2009) found that in Kenya opening a bank account increased the investments of female traders but not male.

As chapter 2 discussed, the inability to access external finance is reported as a top constraint by entrepreneurs in the region. Both men and women report that women are likely to face greater obstacles in accessing external credit. There is increasing research on the gender gap in access to credit (see Klapper and Parker 2010 for a survey). Cross-country studies have shown that women are less likely to get financing from a formal financial institution, are charged higher interest rates than men (Muravyev, Schäfer, and Talavera 2007), and generally raise less formal and informal venture capital than men (Brush and others 2004).

The literature has also explored the reasons behind such a gender gap. Buvinic and Berger (1990) find that female entrepreneurs struggle more with loan applications, while Lusardi and Tufano (2009) find lower overall financial literacy among women. Fafchamps and others (2010) studied microenterprises in urban Ghana and found that capital alone is not sufficient to enhance growth of subsistence businesses run by women; human capital measures and behavioral characteristics can matter too. According to Karlan and Valdivia (2011), women trained in financial literacy can apply their new knowledge and pass it on in their communities.

Legal restrictions or property requirements for formal financing could lead women to have recourse to informal, though more expensive financing. Such restrictions might include requirements for married women to obtain their husband's signature to open a bank account, a provision in the laws of eight Sub-Saharan countries (see chapter 7). Richardson, Howarth, and Finnegan (2004) find for Sub-Saharan Africa that women entrepreneurs are more likely than men to rely on internal or informal financing. Evidence from Sub-Saharan Africa shows that in many instances, only male heads of households can receive formal credit (Johnson 2004; Narain 2009). Women can also be affected by a husband's adverse credit history and (as in South Africa) be required to repay the debt or be denied credit (Blanchard, Zhao, and Yinger 2005; Naidoo and Hilton 2006).

Behavioral differences between men and women could suggest that gender gaps in credit are due to cultural preferences rather than statistical discrimination (Beck, Behr, and Madestam 2011). Fafchamps and others (2010) find that microenterprises' returns to positive shocks in urban Ghana yield positive outcomes only for in-kind grants. Cash grants, by contrast, do not increase profits and tend to be spent in the house,

—Continued

BOX 8.1 *continued*

especially when given to women. This differential effect seems to be due to behavioral—not external—causes. However, other studies find few statistical differences in liquidity, risk aversion, and entrepreneurial ability in explaining gaps in returns and investment rates (Falco 2012).

The differences in sectors chosen or activities undertaken by women and men could partly explain the gender gap in finance. Indeed, the gender gaps found by de Mel, McKenzie, and Woodruff (2008) close significantly when taking sector into account—but not entirely (and this still raises the question of whether differential access to finance underlies differences in choice of activity).

Not all studies find a gender gap. In a study of eight Latin American countries, Bruhn (2009) does not find evidence of access to finance explaining the gender difference in size of existing enterprises. Looking at Kenya, Akoten, Sawada, and Otsuka (2006) find that while there are some gender differences in credit sources, the only statistically significant gender difference in average loan size occurs when the loan is from friends and relatives (female loans on average are higher). De Mel, McKenzie, and Woodruff (2008) find that female entrepreneurs experienced lower returns to capital; they also find differences in the kinds of investment by gender.

The question explored here is whether women do indeed have greater trouble getting finance—and if so, the extent to which this difficulty is due to gender biases or to the concentration of women in enterprises that are less attractive to lenders. While not conclusive because of data limitations, the discussion here also explores whether differential access to finance underlies differences in the initial choice of enterprise by women and men.

---

findings based on earlier rounds of firm surveys in the region (Bigsten and Söderbom 2006).

Female-owned enterprises in Sub-Saharan Africa seem to have slightly more access to finance than those owned by men only, though access also depends on formality and other enterprise characteristics. (For example, formality is a significant predictor of the financial sources—internal, microfinance institutions, moneylenders, commercial banks, or friends and relatives.) This finding may mask the fact that firms with at least one woman among owners are typically larger, more likely to innovate, and as a consequence more likely to have more access to external finance. For sole proprietors, the gender gap disappears (figures 8.1 and 8.2), though for financing investments, female-owned businesses have slightly more access.

Data from the gender module of the Enterprise Surveys show, however, that female-run firms (rather than female-owned firms) have somewhat less access to finance. This discrepancy once again shows the problem of defining a firm with any female owner as a female business.

Figure 8.1 Sub-Saharan Africa Lags in Access to Formal Finance, Including Bank Accounts, Credit Lines, and Loans

a. All formal firms

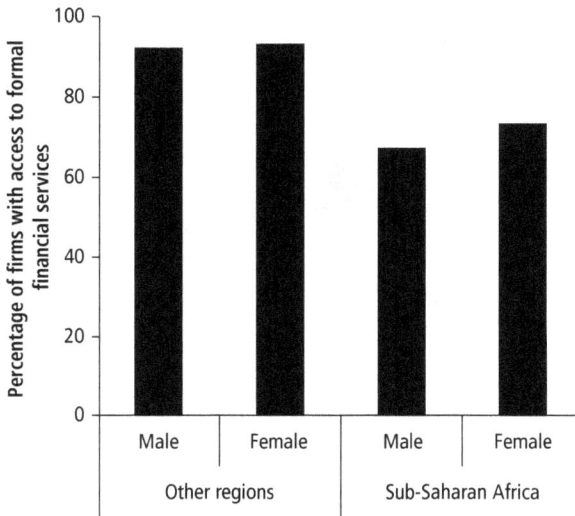

b. Formal sole proprietorships

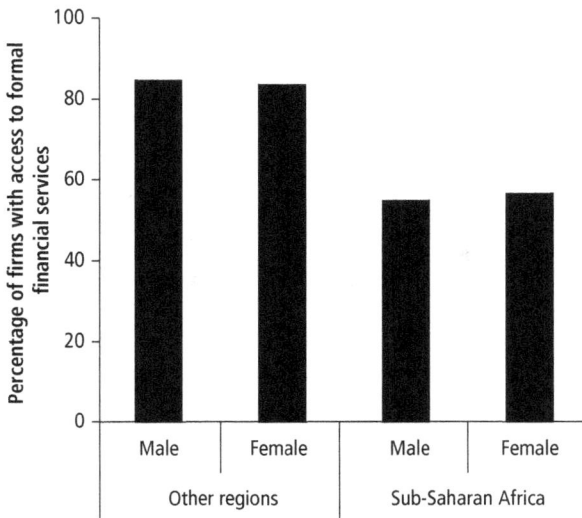

Source: Enterprise Surveys, World Bank, http://www.enterprisesurveys.org.

Figure 8.2 Sub-Saharan Africa Lags in Access to Formal External Finance

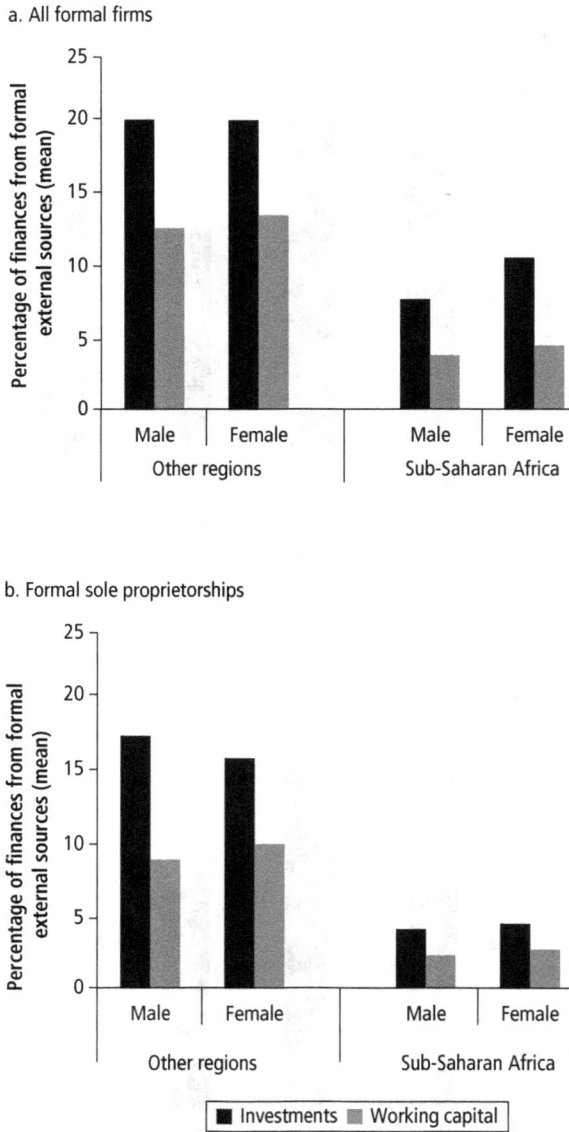

a. All formal firms

b. Formal sole proprietorships

■ Investments ■ Working capital

Source: Enterprise Surveys, World Bank, http://www.enterprisesurveys.org.

The patterns shown in figures 8.1 and 8.2 are robust to controlling for other characteristics in a multivariate regression analysis. The result that Sub-Saharan businesses are less able to access formal financial services is extremely robust. Regional businesses receive 9–14 percentage points less in external financing from formal institutions for both their investments and working capital, and are 40 percent less likely to access any formal financial services at all, including a bank account. The results also show that larger companies have a significant advantage in getting financial institutions to finance both their investments and working capital: an increase in firm size of 10 percent is associated with a 12–18 percentage point increase in the share of investment or working capital financed by financial institutions (Aterido, Beck, and Iacovone, forthcoming).

Whereas size is strongly correlated with access to formal financial services, gender is not. One exception is that larger enterprises of female sole proprietors tend to have *greater* access to finance in Sub-Saharan Africa compared to other regions. Analyzing only Sub-Saharan Africa in separate subsamples for formal and informal enterprises confirms the absence of statistically significant difference by gender in access to finance. Female enterprises in the region have the same access to finance as male-owned firms. These results apply to formal and informal companies, and are robust in the subsample of companies with a sole proprietor (Aterido, Beck, and Iacovone, forthcoming).

Part of this explanation comes from the expansion of alternative forms of finance that in many cases explicitly target women (see box 8.2). Four examples of International Finance Corporation (IFC) initiatives provide additional practical insights into how women entrepreneurs' access to finance could be expanded (box 8.3).

Individuals' Access to Finance

To what extent does access to finance itself drive the selection of the type of firm that an entrepreneur runs? Unfortunately, the data are too scarce to address this question directly. Panel data on individuals and their access to assets and finance would be needed, along with information on individuals' employment history and entrepreneurial activities. If the analysis controlled for individual characteristics, these data could capture the factors shaping entry decisions.

Lacking such data, we look in this section and the next at two sets of evidence. This section looks at data at the individual level on who has access to financial services. Individual rather than household data are important for gender analysis. The data cover individuals with various employment histories—so, one caveat is that not all individuals are entrepreneurs. Correlations between access to finance and loans do not determine causation, of course, but they do allow one to see if those who are entrepreneurs are more (or less) likely to have

BOX 8.2

Alternative Finance for Women in Sub-Saharan Africa

Many microfinance institutions (MFIs) have targeted women, helping to shrink gender gaps in access to credit. In some cases, the focus of MFIs on women has actually led to more women than men having access to finance (Armendariz and Roome 2008; Pitt, Khandker, and Cartwright 2003). The Women's World Banking (2009) report on microfinance in Africa finds that in Kenya, Nigeria, and South Africa, MFIs' clientele is more than 50 percent women. Some MFIs offer services almost exclusively to female clientele (GAWFA in The Gambia, KWFT in Kenya, Microloan Foundation MWI in Malawi, MECREF in Niger, LAPO in Nigeria, and SEF in South Africa[a]). According to the Consultative Group to Assist the Poor (CGAP 2010), some West African countries' MFIs have extended their activities such that deposit-taking microfinance institutions have more depositors than commercial banks.

Beyond microcredit, many individuals and enterprises across the developing world use informal financial services, ranging from moneylenders to Rotating Savings and Credit Associations. This type of financing is very expensive but requires less collateral and has fewer legal requirements. In countries where women face gender-specific legal constraints, women may have recourse more frequently to this type of informal financing. Given the limitations of microcredit and informal lending, both in volume and in outreach, it is still important to understand gender differences in the use of formal banking services (Honohan 2004).

a. GAWFA = Gambia Women's Finance Association; KWFT = Kenya Women Finance Trust (KWFT); MECREF = Mutuelle d'Epargne et de Credit des Femmes; LAPO = Lift Above Poverty Microfinance Bank Ltd.; SEF = Small Enterprise Foundation.

BOX 8.3

Expanding Access to Finance for Female Entrepreneurs— Insights from the Supply Side

Financial institutions are recognizing that, with women as half of all entrepreneurs, there is a large and underserved market opportunity in developing a larger female clientele. Since 2006 the IFC has partnered with 14 financial institutions to increase access to finance for women entrepreneurs. It has also helped enact reforms to support women's participation in the private sector in more than a dozen countries.

Case 1. Expanding a Bank's Financial Outreach to Female Clients in Nigeria
IFC research in Nigeria showed that women had different attitudes than men toward finance, that women poorly understood what banks required of their clients, and that

banks did not understand how best to serve their women clientele. One of the key structural issues was the paucity of historical credit information from independent sources like credit bureaus.

The IFC provided a US$15 million credit line along with a US$400,000 Advisory Services Program to Access Bank Nigeria, which in turn contributed US$500,000 toward developing and running the program. One objective was to improve Access Bank's financial service delivery to the women's market in Nigeria, including staff training, strategic planning, market positioning, and segmentation. A second was to assist Access Bank in improving the quality of its female client base by providing women entrepreneurs with financial literacy and business skills. Several new women-friendly products and services were developed, such as flexible collateral, including the pledging of equipment and cash flow–based lending.

Between 2006 and 2009 more than US$35 million in loans was disbursed to women entrepreneurs, while maintaining a nonperforming loan ratio of less than 1 percent (1,300 new deposit accounts and 1,700 checking accounts were opened; 650 women were trained). Its success led Access Bank to replicate the program in The Gambia and Rwanda. Other banks in Nigeria have followed suit, and a new private equity fund and an asset management fund targeting women have entered the Nigerian market.

Case 2. Building Credit Histories and Expanding Loan Guarantees for Female Entrepreneurs in Uganda

The Women In Business program of the Development Finance Company of Uganda (DFCU) shows how access to finance and skill development can drive the growth of female-owned enterprises. The DFCU has built a portfolio of business loans, leases, mortgages, and other products targeting women entrepreneurs. The effort began in 2007 after IFC research showed that Ugandan women owned nearly 40 percent of registered businesses but received less than 10 percent of commercial credit.

A lack of information on these businesses was a key barrier. Working with the IFC, DFCU emphasized equipment leases over traditional loans to help women build a credit history. DFCU introduced group borrowing as well as land loans to enable women to acquire collateral. Financial training and business support completed the picture.

Since 2007, more than 368 women have been trained in entrepreneurship and business and management best practices. As of December 2009, DFCU had disbursed close to US$16.1 million in term loans, working capital loans, mortgages, leases, and land loans to 300 female entrepreneurs in the small and medium enterprise (SME) sector. The default rate for the women's SME portfolio (1.5 percent) is lower than that for male borrowers (2.5 percent). IFC supports similar projects in Benin, Burundi, Côte d'Ivoire, the Democratic Republic of Congo, Kenya, Malawi, Mozambique, Niger, Nigeria, and Tanzania.

—Continued

BOX 8.3 *continued*

Case 3. Providing Finance Where Laws Limit Women's Access to Traditional Sources of Collateral: Sero Lease and Finance Ltd. in Tanzania

Tanzania's customary law largely excludes women from owning land, and with a predominantly collateral-based banking system, women were effectively excluded from loans, including business loans. Sero Lease and Finance Ltd. (Selfina) is a women's leasing and finance company that went into microleasing in 1997 to enable women to acquire equipment for immediate use with a down payment and financial lease. It targeted 3,000 SMEs and had a zero default rate and 99 percent payback rate, with an average loan size of $500.

A further objective was to help women use their good credit history in microfinance to gain access to commercial banking. The IFC helped broker a $1 million loan from the Exim Bank facility to Selfina. As of October 2007, 150 Selfina clients had already opened "Tumaini" savings accounts at Exim Bank. IFC training for the women enhanced their knowledge of the application process and also included courses on business planning and management.

Case 4. Global Banking Alliance for Women: Recognizing Best Practices in the Delivery of Financial Services to Women

Originally founded by four banks from developed countries, the Global Banking Alliance for Women (GBA) has grown into a truly global organization. The GBA mission is to accelerate the growth of women in business and aid in women's wealth creation, while generating superior business outcomes for member financial institutions. Members share best practices and research and collaborate with financial institutions to provide women with vital access to capital, markets, education, and training. The GBA chapter in Uganda, for example, allows GBA member banks like DFCU to provide their customers with a streamlined exchange of information, research, and resources, giving women a chance to spur their business growth.

Source: IFC, Sustainable Finance Department, "Banking on Women Pays Off: Creating Opportunities for Women Entrepreneurs," http://www.intracen.org/uploadedFiles/intracenorg/Content/About_ITC/Where_are_we_working/Multi-country_programmes/Women_and_trade/Banking%20on%20Women%20pays%20off.pdf.

access to finance. Another caveat is that the financial services included can be for personal use. Still, the benefit of this approach is that these types of loans are often those available to prospective entrepreneurs.

This section focuses more on savings and payments (formal and informal) than credit. It uses data on nine Sub-Saharan countries from household surveys, called FinScope or FinAccess surveys, which gather information on individuals rather than households.[6] While this approach might reduce representativeness (and hence overall accuracy) because the individual has indirect access to financial services through other household members, it has the advantage of being able to focus on gender. All surveys used in this section were undertaken between 2004 and 2009; the analysis is done in the nonagriculture sector.

The analyses focus on three segments: formal banking services; informal financial services, including unregulated SACCOs, ASCAs, and ROSCAs;[7] and exclusion from any service. Revealing large cross-country variation in use (figure 8.3), the surveys also indicate the high degree of financial exclusion across eastern and southern Africa.

All nine surveys showed that compared to men, women were less likely to use formal financial services, were generally more likely to use informal services, and were generally as likely or more likely to be excluded from access to any financial service.

These results are consistent with the hypothesis of a gender gap in the use of formal banking services, but because they do not control for other individual characteristics, we used a multivariate regression analysis to explore whether these unconditional differences still hold with controls (table 8.1).

For access to formal financial services, unconditional gender gaps lose significance once education and experience are controlled for. Women on average are no more (or less) likely to use them. (South Africa is a notable exception—women are 12.2 percentage points less likely to use them.)

The use of formal financial services is correlated with an array of other individual factors, which seem to explain why women are less likely to have access to such services, and why once those characteristics are controlled for the gender difference disappears. In work conducted for this project, Aterido,

Figure 8.3 A High Degree of Financial Exclusion Exists across Eastern and Southern Africa

a. Banking

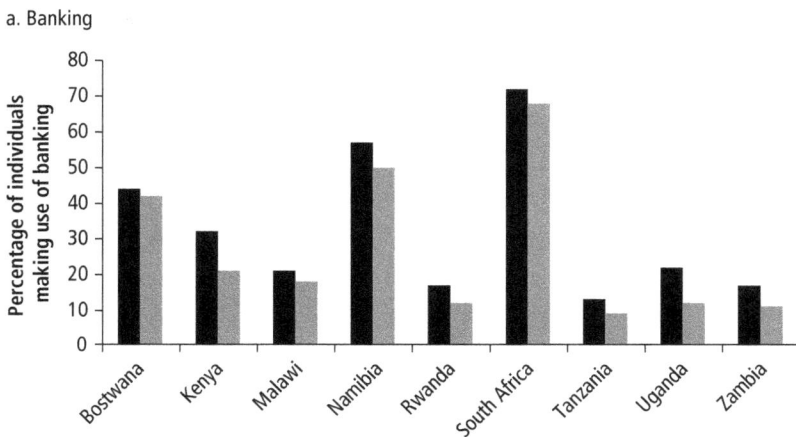

—Continued

Figure 8.3 *(continued)*

b. Informal

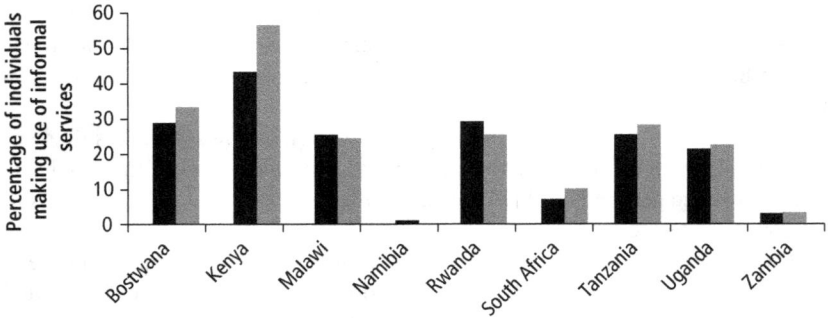

c. Excluded

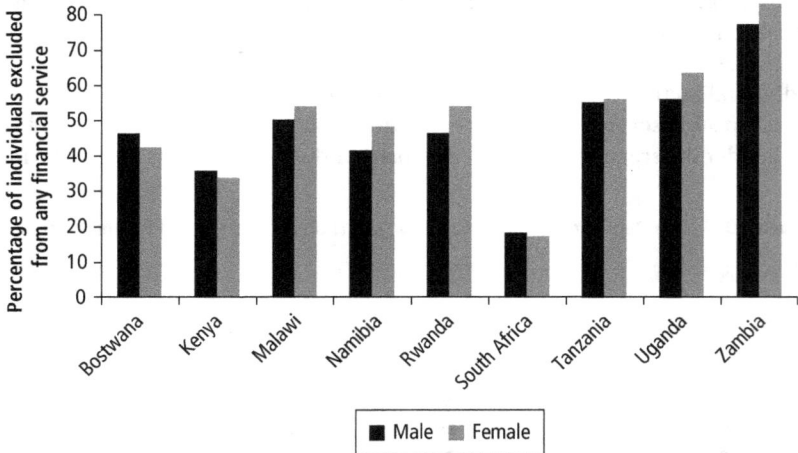

■ Male   ■ Female

Source: Aterido, Beck, and Iacovone, forthcoming.
Note: Data are for the nonagricultural sector and are drawn from the FinScope surveys, http://www.finscope.co.za.

Beck, and Iacovone (forthcoming) show that the biggest effect seems to come from income differences between men and women, which explain up to half of the gender difference. This explanation is particularly significant in Rwanda. Another big effect stems from women's lower level of education. Adding the economic effect of lower education across primary, secondary, and tertiary

Table 8.1 Once Education and Experience Are Controlled for, Women Are No More Likely Than Men to Use Formal Financial Services

Sample	All	Botswana	Kenya	Malawi	Namibia	Rwanda	South Africa	Tanzania	Uganda	Zambia
Female	0.017	0.027	−0.018	0.024	−0.019	−0.008	−0.118	−0.002	−0.029	0.005
	[0.019]	[0.041]	[0.030]	[0.018]	[0.040]	[0.018]	[0.050]**	[0.008]	[0.025]	[0.006]
Individual characteristics	Yes	Yes	Yes	Yes	Yes	Yes	Yes	Yes	Yes	Yes
Regional effects	Yes	Yes	Yes	Yes	Yes	Yes	Yes	Yes	Yes	Yes
Observations	33,872	974	6,589	4,712	1,065	1,894	3,345	5,864	1,674	3,990
Pseudo R²	0.43	0.37	0.46	0.36	0.47	0.32	0.27	0.40	0.41	0.53
Use of informal financial services										
Female	0.058	0.105	0.147	−0.013	−0.000	−0.086	0.011	0.063	0.041	−0.000
	[0.010]***	[0.034]***	[0.029]***	[0.018]	[0.000]	[0.032]***	[0.011]	[0.019]***	[0.029]	[0.002]
Individual characteristics	Yes	Yes	Yes	Yes	Yes	Yes	Yes	Yes	Yes	Yes
Regional effects	Yes	Yes	Yes	Yes	Yes	Yes	Yes	Yes	Yes	Yes
Observations	33,173	974	6,589	4,712	228	1,869	3,345	5,864	1,674	3,990
Pseudo R²	0.33	0.29	0.10	0.07	0.33	0.05	0.19	0.05	0.08	0.25
Excluded from using financial services										
Female	−0.068	−0.127	−0.076	0.017	0.019	0.090	0.055	−0.076	−0.067	−0.004
	[0.020]***	[0.040]***	[0.021]***	[0.025]	[0.040]	[0.035]***	[0.032]*	[0.023]***	[0.037]*	[0.011]
Individual characteristics	Yes	Yes	Yes	Yes	Yes	Yes	Yes	Yes	Yes	Yes
Regional effects	Yes	Yes	Yes	Yes	Yes	Yes	Yes	Yes	Yes	Yes
Observations	33,872	974	6,589	4,712	1,065	1,894	3,345	5,864	1,674	3,990
Pseudo R²	0.43	0.35	0.31	0.11	0.48	0.10	0.31	0.18	0.19	0.44

Source: Aterido, Beck, and Iacovone, forthcoming.
Note: Dprobit regressions. Robust standard errors in brackets. Individual characteristics include education, income level, employment status, whether individual uses a mobile phone, whether individual is household head, marital status, numerical literacy, measure of risk aversion, and region.
Significance level: * = 10 percent, ** = 5 percent, *** = 1 percent.

education in the pooled regression gives a total effect of four percentage points.

Another large effect comes from women's lower likelihood of heading the household; this accounts for three percentage points of difference in the pooled regression. Employment also counts: women are less likely to be formally employed than men, a difference with an economic effect of 5.5 percentage points in the pooled regression. Finally, the ownership of mobile phones, a significant factor in explaining the univariate gender gap in use of formal financial services, adds another two percentage points (Aterido, Beck, and Iacovone, forthcoming).

The individual characteristics that explain the use of formal services also largely explain the use of informal services, but they do not explain them entirely. Gender gaps remain once other individual characteristics are included. The effect is also economically large in some countries, with women on average 3.3 percentage points more likely than men to use informal financial services, a figure driven by Botswana, Kenya, Tanzania, and Uganda.

Looking at exclusion from all financial services (formal and informal) unconditionally, women are excluded more than men. However, when one controls for individual characteristics, the gap flips, as the characteristics help explain the gap in women's access to formal but not to informal services. The relatively large reliance of women on informal finance means that overall, they are not more excluded than men at the same level of education and work experience.

These results are consistent with other work that looks at access to finance and differentiates between formal and informal sources. Fafchamps (2000) looks at access to bank loans among entrepreneurs in Kenya and Zimbabwe and finds that the gender gap disappears once firm size is controlled for. However, he finds that the effect on gender (and ethnicity) remains significant for trade credit and other forms that rely on more relationship-based lending.

These findings suggest that women's lower use of formal banking services is not due to discrimination in the banking system or lower inherent demand by women—it is due to disadvantages in other areas, namely women's lower levels of education and income. They also suggest that some of the findings might be driven by the survey methodology of interviewing individuals rather than households: women may have indirect access to formal financial services through their formally employed husbands, the household heads.

Access to Finance: A Barrier to Entry?

The second set of evidence looks at data from the surveys of new entrepreneurs in Côte d'Ivoire, Kenya, Nigeria, and Senegal, in the formal and informal sectors. Looking at the amount and sources of start-up capital sheds light on gender gaps in access to finance and how they vary across activities and types of enterprises. The data suggest that women are indeed more constrained in their access to finance.

Finance is crucial for prospective entrepreneurs and, according to them, the biggest obstacle when they set up a business. This is especially true for female entrepreneurs in the informal sector, of whom almost 60 percent report finance as the largest stumbling block. Although male entrepreneurs in the formal sector are the least likely (among men and women in the formal and informal sectors) to report lack of access to finance as the biggest obstacle, 40 percent of them report that it is.

New entrepreneurs depend primarily on their own resources or those of their friends and relatives when starting an enterprise (figure 8.4). Those with limited savings or wealth face serious difficulties in starting a business; and even when they do set up one, their capacity to invest to optimal levels is constrained.

Figure 8.4 New Entrepreneurs Depend Primarily on Their Own, or on Friends' and Relatives', Resources

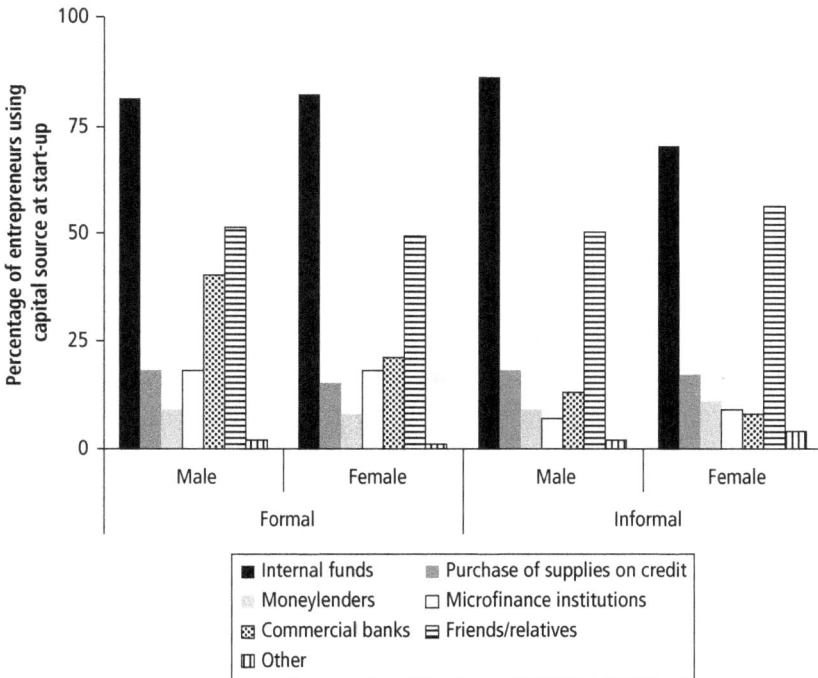

Source: Gajigo and Hallward-Driemeier 2010.
Note: Data are for newly established enterprises in Côte d'Ivoire, Kenya, Nigeria, and Senegal.

Individual or household wealth is therefore likely to be an important predictor not only of investment but also of profitability, because poorer entrepreneurs are less able to meet their optimal financing needs.

As figure 8.4 shows, in sources of external finance accessed at start-up, strong sector and gender components reveal themselves. Both male and female entrepreneurs in the formal sector use banks more often than those in the informal sector, but in the formal sector men use them significantly more than women. However, when entrepreneurs cite the single largest source of financing at start-up, the sectoral differences dominate the gender ones (figure 8.5).

Difference in access to microfinance institutions is present only along sector lines: male and female entrepreneurs in the formal sector have significantly more access to them than their informal counterparts. Formality, rather than gender, also explains differences in patterns of financing sources. Male and female formal entrepreneurs are remarkably similar in depending on the various sources of finance. And while for the informal sector we detect a gender

Figure 8.5 Sector Matters More Than Gender in Start-Ups' Access to Formal Finance—Although Some Gender Gaps Appear in the Informal Sector

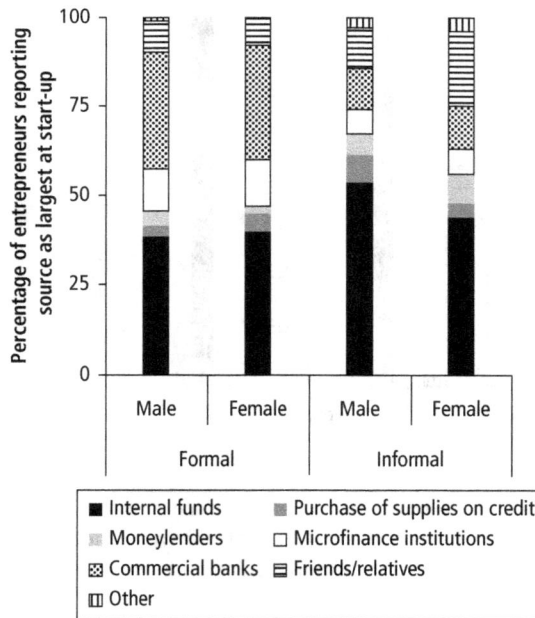

Source: Gajigo and Hallward-Driemeier 2010.
Note: Data are for newly established enterprises in Côte d'Ivoire, Kenya, Nigeria, and Senegal.

difference in the importance of moneylenders and friends and relatives, little or no such difference appears in the importance of other sources of finance.

As we indicated in chapter 4, patterns in the way new businesses are created also have gender dimensions. First, men are more likely to create a business from an existing one than from scratch, while women show no difference. Second, women start with less than half the initial capital of men (figure 4.8a).

Many new entrepreneurs lack access to finance. When the surveys asked them why they did not apply for a loan, at least 55 percent of respondents who had been in business for at least 12 months said they would like credit but could not access it; they were intimidated by the complexity of the application process, thought the interest was too high, did not have a guarantee, or did not think that they would be approved. The 55 percent figure is likely an underestimate; as discussed below, a much higher proportion would have made different investment decisions if they had had twice as much money at start-up.

Conditional results for the determinants of various sources of start-up capital yield a significant positive female effect for dependence on internal funds (that is, the entrepreneur's own funds) and funds from friends or relatives. The gender difference is negligible within the formal sector, but not within the informal sector. Female entrepreneurs in the informal sector are significantly less likely to depend on internal funds relative to males, while formal sector female entrepreneurs have no significantly different effect. Female entrepreneurs are significantly more likely to depend heavily on friends or family, but the likelihood is lower for female entrepreneurs in the formal sector once we control for industry and other variables. In other words, the unconditional high female dependence on this source of finance is driven mainly by those in the informal sector.

Overall, the dependence on various sources of finance to start up a new business is driven more by firm characteristics, particularly formality, than by gender—but women in the informal sector do rely more on informal sources of finance, which would be consistent with finance as a significant barrier to operating in the formal sector.

Financing New Businesses: Access to Loans after Start-Up

Access to finance is limited after start-up: only about 9 percent of new entrepreneurs had a loan at the time of the survey, a rate similar to estimates from other studies. That proportion contains strong gender and sector differences (figure 8.6). In the formal and informal sectors, at least twice as many male as female entrepreneurs had loans. Given their legal status, it is unsurprising that formal entrepreneurs had more loans. But a gender difference within sectors points to women facing greater constraints in accessing loans.

Figure 8.6 Strong Gender and Formality Differences Come through for the Few New Entrepreneurs with Loans

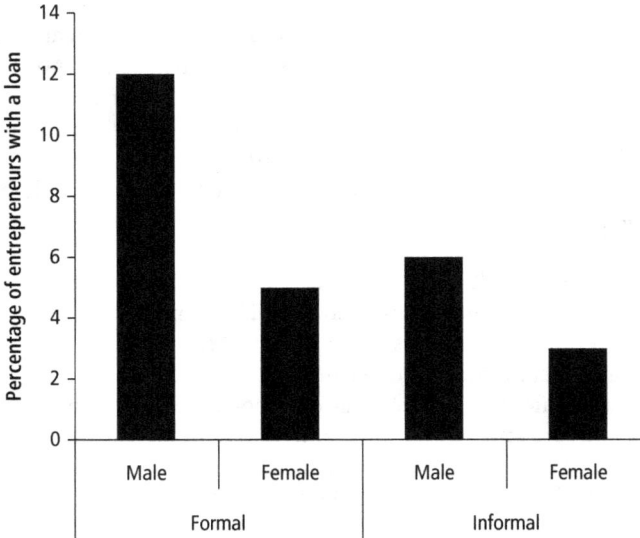

Source: Gajigo and Hallward-Driemeier 2010.
Note: Data are for new entrepreneurs in Côte d'Ivoire, Kenya, Nigeria, and Senegal.

Despite being informal, some entrepreneurs secured loans from commercial banks through various means (figure 8.7). Because of the small number of entrepreneurs with loans, the analysis had to be limited to sectors and not gender. Formal sector entrepreneurs depend more on land and buildings as guarantees. Informal entrepreneurs are significantly more likely to use the owner's assets and to find someone to cosign the loan.

Among those with loans, most formal sector entrepreneurs secured their loans from commercial banks (figure 8.8). Informal entrepreneurs' single-biggest source was microcredit institutions, most likely due to specific targeting by them. Nearly one-third of informal entrepreneurs managed to get loans from banks, and one-fifth borrowed from moneylenders. Only a very small minority in both sectors borrowed from suppliers or customers.

Entrepreneurial Choice Limited by Access to Finance

One concern about the impact of limited access to finance is that it constrains which opportunities can be pursued. This section looks at how choices might have been different if more capital was available: what would entrepreneurs have

Figure 8.7 Sources of Loan Guarantees Vary by Sector Formality

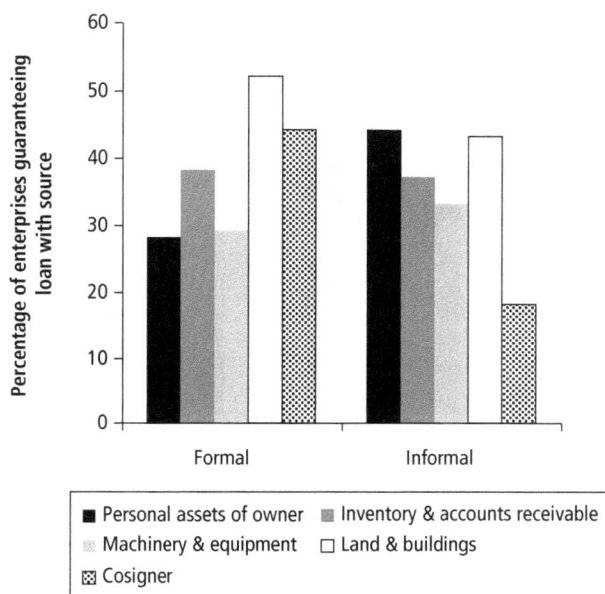

Source: Gajigo and Hallward-Driemeier 2010.
Note: Data are for newly established enterprises in Côte d'Ivoire, Kenya, Nigeria, and Senegal. Sample size is too small to disaggregate by gender.

done with twice as much money at start-up? And if the choices would have been different, what are the reasons given as to why a loan was not taken out?

Changing location and hiring more workers are the two most common responses to the "what if?" question (figure 8.9). The desire to increase capital investment is particularly strong among male formal entrepreneurs. Even though male entrepreneurs tend to have much more start-up capital than female entrepreneurs, it is still possible that men may be more capital constrained, given that gender sorting across industries and formal-informal activities is not uniform. For example, male entrepreneurs are overrepresented relative to women in manufacturing.

More men than women reported that they would have used additional money to hire more workers. As with capital, this difference may well stem from unequal concentrations across industries with greater scale economies and formal-informal activities.

With twice the money at start-up, more informal than formal entrepreneurs would have chosen a different line of business (admittedly the sample is small).

Figure 8.8 Of Firms with External Start-Up Financing, Commercial Banks Are the Main Source of Capital for Formal Firms

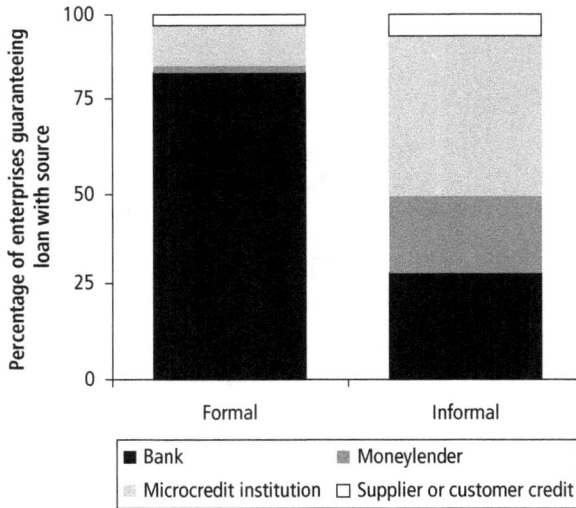

Source: Gajigo and Hallward-Driemeier 2010.
Note: Data are for newly established enterprises in Côte d'Ivoire, Kenya, Nigeria, and Senegal and show the source of the loan for the 9 percent of entrepreneurs who currently have loans.

Limited access to finance may therefore alter the distribution of firms across industries and formal-informal activities, because high investment needs close off certain business lines.

The gender pattern that shows more male entrepreneurs wanting to invest in machinery is robust when controlling for more variables. This finding is positively correlated with start-up capital, suggesting that even those with higher start-up capital in this sample are likely to be operating below their investment needs. The initial gender difference in the preference for hiring workers is not, however, robust to controls for other variables.

Are entrepreneurs actually constrained? The number of entrepreneurs who applied for a loan in the previous 12 months—only 17 percent—initially suggests not. But the reasons for not applying are important (figure 8.10).

The frequency with which specific reasons for nonapplication were reported does not significantly differ from that found in other studies. The biggest reason (45 percent, combining men and women, formal and informal) was a claim of no need (the same proportion among women in both sectors, but 10 percentage points higher among male formal than male informal entrepreneurs). But this response may need to be interpreted

Figure 8.9 With Twice the Money at Start-Up, Nearly All Entrepreneurs Would Have Done Things Differently

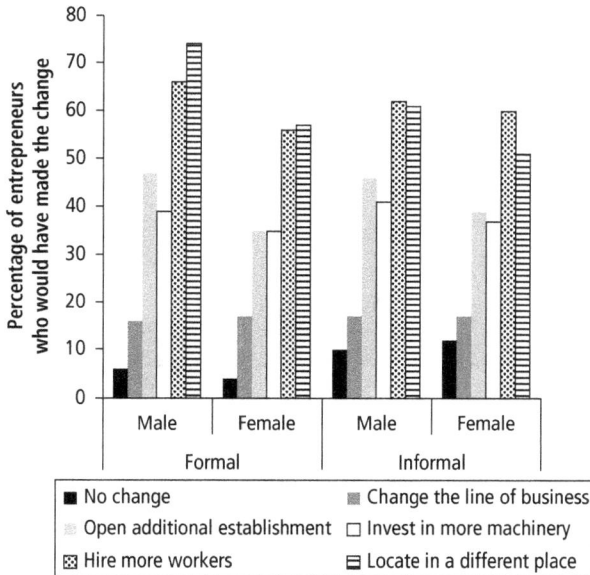

Source: Gajigo and Hallward-Driemeier 2010.
Note: Data are for newly established enterprises in Côte d'Ivoire, Kenya, Nigeria, and Senegal and show what entrepreneurs report they would have done differently if their money at start-up had been twice what it actually was.

with caution. Some individuals who assert they have no need may believe that, perhaps because of existing debt, assuming further debt is not a good course of action.

About 18 percent of all those not applying point to the complexity of loan applications. Although the proportion is slightly higher in the informal sector, the gender difference points in different directions in the two sectors, with women in the formal sector and men in the informal sector more likely to raise this concern. The fact that perceived transaction cost is preventing a significant proportion from even applying suggests that there is room for public or other nongovernment initiatives to increase access to finance through sensitization programs that reduce this cost.

One of the two areas with a significant sector difference is a perceived high interest rate: around 24 percent of formal, but only around 15 percent of informal, entrepreneurs report this reason. This area also has a significant gender difference in the formal sector, with men more likely to report this as

Figure 8.10 Credit Constraints Appear to Be Common Among Sub-Saharan Entrepreneurs

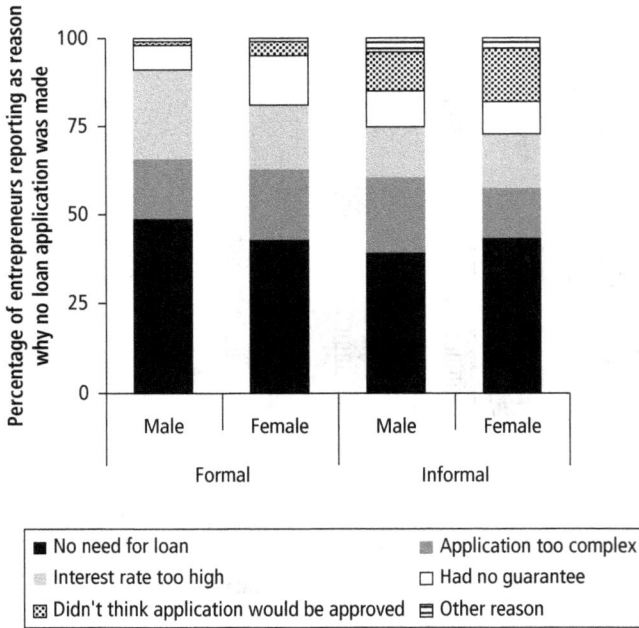

Source: Gajigo and Hallward-Driemeier 2010.
Note: Data are for enterprises that have been in operation for at least 12 months, based on surveys in Côte d'Ivoire, Kenya, Nigeria, and Senegal.

their top concern. Women report more concerns about the application procedures themselves, or believe that an application would be futile because it would not be approved. In short, almost half of the respondents express a need for credit, but the large majority of them do not have it. A higher percentage of respondents indicate they would have made different investment decisions in establishing their business had they had twice as much capital. The goal should not be to extend credit to everyone who wants it; the point of a well-functioning financial system is precisely to allocate resources to their most productive uses. But when entrepreneurs are discouraged by application procedures, transaction costs of applying, and perceptions that they will not be given due consideration, it raises questions about how well the financial system is functioning, particularly for the smaller and less traditional borrower and for those without an established track record, that is, for entrants. Further work on understanding the financial barriers to entry should be a priority going forward.

Notes

1. Data on access to formal finance are from Finscope surveys for nine countries in Sub-Saharan Africa, http://www.finscope.co.za.
2. Enterprise Surveys, World Bank, http://www.enterprisesurveys.org.
3. Bruhn and Love (2011) examine how expanding access to finance in Mexico was associated with more men becoming entrepreneurs, but women were more likely to increase their involvement with wage work. Some of the discrepancy could be that couples worked in family enterprises, with the husband reported as the entrepreneur and the wife a wage employee of the enterprise.
4. Economic opportunities are the focus here, but the literature also looks at the effect of access to credit and of income earnings on women's empowerment within the home, and specifically on whether women's bargaining positions are strengthened. Much of the literature finds an effect, but Armendariz and Roome (2008) caution that there can also be unintended consequences (see also Ashraf 2009; Ashraf, Karlan, and Yin 2009; Banerjee and others 2009).
5. It should also be noted that simply not having access to credit is not equivalent to being credit constrained. As discussed below, many firms report not wanting credit, as there is insufficient demand for their product. One measure of credit constraints is to examine if firms' investment decisions are correlated with cash flow. The evidence from Africa shows this pattern is greater for smaller firms, but the effect is not very large (Bigsten and others 2003; Bigsten and Söderbom 2006). These studies did not look at the issue of gender.
6. The discussion draws on Aterido, Beck, and Iacovone (forthcoming), who analyzed FinScope data from nationally representative samples of individuals on their perceptions and experiences accessing financial services in nine Sub-Saharan countries. For more information, see also http://www.finscope.co.za.
7. SACCO = Savings and Credit Cooperative Organization; ASCA = Accumulating Savings and Credit Association; ROSCA = Rotational Savings and Credit Association.

References

Akoten, J. E., Y. Sawada, and K. Otsuka. 2006. "The Determinants of Credit Access and Its Impacts on Micro and Small Enterprises: The Case of Garment Producers in Kenya." *Economic Development and Cultural Change* 54 (4): 927–44.

Armendariz, B., and N. Roome. 2008. "Gender Empowerment in Microfinance." Working paper, Department of Economics, Harvard University, Cambridge, MA.

Ashraf, N. 2009. "Spousal Control and Intra-household Decision Making: An Experimental Study in the Philippines." *American Economic Review* 99 (4): 1245–77.

Ashraf, N., D. Karlan, and W. Yin. 2009. "Female Empowerment: Impact of a Commitment Savings Product in the Philippines. *World Development* 38 (3): 333–34.

Aterido, R., T. Beck, and L. Iacovone. Forthcoming. "Gender and Finance in Sub-Saharan Africa: Are Women Disadvantaged?" *World Development.*

Banerjee, A., and E. Duflo. 2008. "Do Firms Want to Borrow More? Testing Credit Constraints Using a Directed Lending Program." MIT Working Paper 02–25, Massachusetts Institute of Technology, Cambridge, MA.

Banerjee, A., E. Duflo, R. Glennerster, and C. Kinnan. 2009. "The Miracle of Microfinance? Evidence from a Randomized Evaluation." Working paper, Massachusetts Institute of Technology, Cambridge, MA.

Bardasi, E., and S. Sabarwal. 2009. "Gender, Access to Finance, and Entrepreneurial Performance in Sub-Saharan Africa." Working paper, World Bank, Washington, DC.

Beck, T., P. Behr, and A. Madestam. 2011. "Sex and Credit: Is There a Gender Bias in Microfinance?" European Banking Center Discussion Paper 2011-027, Tilburg University, the Netherlands.

Beck, T., A. Demirgüç-Kunt, and V. Maksimovic. 2005. "Financial and Legal Constraints to Firm Growth: Does Firm Size Matter?" *Journal of Finance* 60: 137–77.

————. 2008. "Financing Patterns around the World: Are Small Firms Different?" *Journal of Financial Economics* 89: 467–87.

Bigsten, A., P. Collier, S. Dercon, M. Fafchamps, B. Gauthier, J. Gunning, A. Oduro, R. Oostendorp, C. Pattillo, M. Söderbom, F. Teal, and A. Zeufack. 2003. "Credit Constraints in Manufacturing Enterprises in Africa." *Journal of African Economies* 12 (1): 104–25.

Bigsten, A., and M. Söderbom. 2006. "What Have We Learned from a Decade of Manufacturing Enterprise Surveys in Africa?" *World Bank Research Observer* 21 (2): 241–65.

Blanchard, L., B. Zhao, and J. Yinger. 2005. "Do Credit Market Barriers Exist for Minority and Women Entrepreneurs?" Working Paper 74, Syracuse University Maxwell School Center for Policy Research, Syracuse, NY.

Bruhn, M. 2009. "Female-Owned Firms in Latin America: Characteristics, Performance, and Obstacles to Growth." Policy Research Working Paper 5122, World Bank, Washington, DC.

Bruhn, M., and I. Love. 2011. "Gender Differences in the Impact of Banking Services: Evidence from Mexico." *Small Business Economics* 37 (4): 493–512.

Brush, C., N. Carter, E. Gatewood, P. Greene, and M. Hart. 2004. "Gatekeepers of Venture Growth: A Diana Project Report on the Role and Participation of Women in the Venture Capital Industry." Kansas City, MO: Kauffman Foundation.

Buvinic, M., and M. Berger. 1990. "Sex Differences in Access to a Small Enterprise Development Fund in Peru." *World Development* 18: 695–705.

CGAP (Consultative Group to Assist the Poor). 2010. *Financial Access 2010: The State of Financial Inclusion through Crisis.* Washington, DC: CGAP.

de Mel, S., D. McKenzie, and C. Woodruff. 2008. "Returns to Capital in Microenterprises: Evidence from a Field Experiment." *Quarterly Journal of Economics* 123 (4): 1329–72.

————. 2009. "Are Women More Credit Constrained? Experimental Evidence on Gender and Microenterprise Returns." *American Economic Journal: Applied Economics* 1 (3): 1–32.

Dupas, P., and J. Robinson. 2009. "Savings Constraints and Microenterprise Development: Evidence from a Field Experiment in Kenya." NBER Working Paper 14693, National Bureau of Economic Research, Cambridge, MA.

Fafchamps, M. 2000. "Ethnicity and Credit in African Manufacturing." *Journal of Development Economics* 61(1): 205–35.

Fafchamps, M., D. McKenzie, S. Quinn, and C. Woodruff. 2010. "When Is Capital Enough to Get Female Microenterprises Growing? Evidence from a Randomized Experiment in Ghana." NBER Working Paper 17207, National Bureau of Economic Research, Cambridge, MA.

Falco, P. 2012. "Does Risk Matter for Occupational Choices? Experimental Evidence from an African Labour Market." Working paper, Oxford University, Oxford, U.K.

Gajigo, O., and M. Hallward-Driemeier. 2010. "Entrepreneurship among New Entrepreneurs." Working paper, World Bank, Washington, DC.

Hallward-Driemeier, M., and O. Gajigo. 2010. "Where Women Work: Empowerment and Occupational Choice." Working paper, World Bank, Washington, DC.

Honohan, P. 2004. "Financial Sector Policy and the Poor." Working Paper 43, World Bank, Washington, DC.

Johnson, S. 2004. "Gender Norms in Financial Markets: Evidence from Kenya." *World Development* 32: 1355–74.

Karlan, D., and J. Morduch. 2010. "Access to Finance." In *Handbook of Development Economics*, vol. 5, edited by D. Rodrik and M. Rosenzweig, 4703–84. Amsterdam: North-Holland.

Karlan, D., and M. Valdivia. 2011. "Teaching Entrepreneurship: Impact of Business Training on Microfinance Clients and Institutions." *Review of Economics and Statistics* 93 (2): 510–27.

Klapper, L., L. Laeven, and R. Rajan, 2006. "Entry Regulation as a Barrier to Entrepreneurship." *Journal of Financial Economics* 82 (3): 591–629.

Klapper, L., and S. Parker. 2010. "Gender and the Business Environment for New Firm Creation." *World Bank Research Observer*, doi: 10.1093/wbro/lkp032.

Lusardi, A., and P. Tufano. 2009. "Debt Literacy, Financial Experiences, and Overindebtedness." NBER Working Paper 14808, National Bureau of Economic Research, Cambridge, MA.

McKenzie, D., and C. Woodruff. 2008. "Experimental Evidence on Returns to Capital and Access to Finance in Mexico." *World Bank Economic Review* 22 (3): 457–82.

Muravyev, A., D. Schäfer, and O. Talavera. 2007. "Entrepreneurs' Gender and Financial Constraints: Evidence from International Data." Discussion Papers of DIW Berlin 706, German Institute for Economic Research, Berlin.

Naidoo, S., and A. Hilton. 2006. *Access to Finance for Women Entrepreneurs in South Africa*. Washington, DC: International Finance Corporation.

Narain, S. 2009. "Access to Finance for Women SME Entrepreneurs in Bangladesh." Working paper, World Bank, Washington, DC.

Pitt, M., S. Khandker, and J. Cartwright. 2003. "Does Micro-Credit Empower Women? Evidence from Bangladesh." Policy Research Working Paper 2998, World Bank, Washington, DC.

Richardson, P., R. Howarth, and G. Finnegan. 2004. "The Challenges of Growing Small Businesses: Insights from Women Entrepreneurs in Africa." SEED Working Paper 47, International Labour Organization, Geneva.

Women's World Banking. 2009. "Microfinance in Africa: The Challenges, Realities and Success Stories." *MicroBanking Bulletin* 17: 5–11.

World Bank. 2007. *Finance for All? Policies and Pitfalls in Expanding Access.* Washington, DC: World Bank.

Chapter 9

Enriching Managerial and Financial Skills

In their provocatively titled article "What Capital Is Missing in Developing Countries?," Bruhn, Karlan, and Schoar (2010b) answer "human capital," particularly managerial skills.

The importance of human capital has long been recognized. The dimension that has received the lion's share of attention is schooling or formal education. However, when it comes to entrepreneurship, there are other dimensions that can matter, too—as well as specific types of knowledge that may be important, such as management skills, financial literacy, and an aptitude for assessing risks and making deals.

When looking at specific types of skills that are included in business training programs, two questions stand out: Are such skills important in improving performance? Are they skills that can be taught or acquired? Beyond that, it is worthwhile to understand any nuances in the results: For example, are there groups for which the skills are more important? Does one need a certain level of education to benefit from the training? Which types of outcomes are affected by business or management training—does training encourage new entrepreneurs to start a business or improve the performance of those already running a business?

This chapter cannot provide answers to all these questions. However, it looks at results from the gender module and survey of new entrepreneurs to qualitatively assess the prevalence of a broader set of human capital measures and their association with performance outcomes. It finds that women have lower levels of a broad range of measures of human capital on average (consistent with gender gaps in education, discussed in chapters 3 and 4). But education and managerial skills seem to have important effects for both women and men—and the marginal returns to women of the underlying skills are no different from those for men.

It is not just that women benefit as much as men from managerial and financial skills. Both groups also benefit from experience, through having had former employment in the formal sector, exposure to running a business, or a parent who was an entrepreneur. That there is a gender gap in this last effect shows that some teaching needs to be targeted to ensure that women are included. It also implies that as more women become successful entrepreneurs, a more virtuous cycle may be created for their daughters, too.

The chapter shows that four management techniques had a significant effect on productivity among firms sampled in Ghana, Mali, Mozambique, Senegal, and Zambia. Gender differences were not apparent for two techniques (establishing formal objectives and monitoring employee performance), but they were seen in the other two (process innovation and participatory decision making). Male entrepreneurs scored significantly higher than female entrepreneurs in process innovation, but the reverse was true in participatory decision making (Gajigo and Hallward-Driemeier 2010).

The motivation for being an entrepreneur, as discussed in chapter 4, does not have striking gender patterns. As many women as men identify opportunity-related reasons for being an entrepreneur. What does stand out, however, is how little correlation motivation has with actual performance. Self-reporting after the event is a poor measure of potentially higher-growth businesses; being an employer rather than self-employed and being in the formal sector are better predictors of performance. Skills, not motivation, seem to be the most important dimension of human capital.

Evidence from randomized impact evaluations regarding programs that aim to teach specific business and financial skills indicates that the skills to increase business knowledge can be taught, but fails to show unambiguously that these skills improve business outcomes. The method of teaching itself matters, as does participants' initial level of business knowledge (see for example Bruhn, Karlan, and Schoar 2010a; Karlan and Valdivia 2011; Mansuri and Giné 2011).

The literature examining the efficacy of providing business training, credit, or a combination of the two finds the combination is more often significant than either one alone. Simply having more knowledge of how to use credit wisely is not very effective at improving business outcomes where there are few financial resources available. And credit without financial management skills is a risky bet for both the borrower and the lender. Clearly there is a symbiosis between strengthening the human capital of women entrepreneurs and expanding their access to financial services. Better human capital can improve business performance directly, and can improve it indirectly by making the entrepreneur more creditworthy, thus expanding the opportunities available. But there is still a question of whether women can benefit from this symbiosis as much as men can (Coleman 2007).

Managerial Skills

Economic growth models have long recognized the importance of human capital, taking the contribution of labor into account as a key input (Solow 1956, for example). The endogenous growth literature incorporated the quality of that labor, including managerial quality as a factor of production (Aghion and Howitt 1992; Baumol 1968; Lucas 1978; Romer 1990). The empirical work on capturing the quality of human capital lagged in moving beyond measures of formal education, but it has recently made progress in two directions.

First, it has produced better measures of human capital, particularly of managerial skills, which are then related to firm performance (see, for example, Bloom and Van Reenen 2007, 2010). Second, drawing on some of the insights of the first approach, the empirical work has gone beyond correlations to test the importance of specific skills through randomized interventions (see, for example, Bloom and others 2010; Drexler, Fischer, and Schoar 2010).

Education as a Key Driver of Performance
The positive effect of education on enterprise productivity is one of the most robust findings in the literature (Bates 1990; Burki and Terrell 1998; Cohen and House 1996; McPherson 1995). This is unsurprising, given education's enhancement of the quality of services by the entrepreneur, and given that worker productivity also benefits from it. Education can also signal other qualities among entrepreneurs, such as discipline, motivation, versatility in dealing with new challenges, and other attributes that could lower transaction costs for numerous entrepreneurship-relevant activities.

In Sub-Saharan Africa, analyses of surveys of both new and incumbent entrepreneurs find education to be a significant determinant of revenue per worker (Aterido and Hallward-Driemeier 2010). Entrepreneurs with at least secondary education and some vocational training have significantly higher revenue per worker than those with no education. Primary education has no more effect than no schooling (see figure 9.1).

Controlling for other characteristics of the enterprise, women entrepreneurs do not have fewer years of education than men. Nor are the differences in productivity that are associated with higher education statistically different for women and men in the same sector and with enterprises of the same size. Women may have less education overall, but those who receive it get as much benefit from it as their male colleagues by running more productive firms.

These findings are consistent with other findings in the literature on the effect of education on enterprise productivity in developing countries

Figure 9.1 The Effect of Education on Productivity Is the Same for Women as for Men

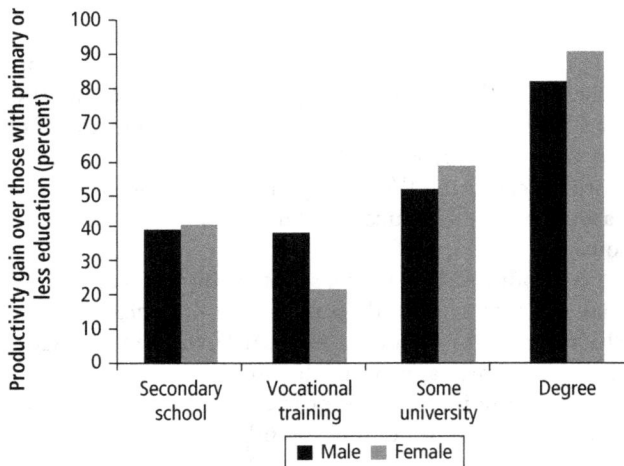

Source: Hallward-Driemeier and Rasteletti 2010.
Note: The figure is based on regression of the log of revenue per worker and controls for firm age, formality, industry, and country effects using the database of national household and labor force surveys for 101 low- and middle-income economies, most recent years (2000–10). The reference school category is those with primary or no schooling. The differences across men and women within the same educational category are not statistically different.

(Bigsten and Söderbom 2006; Mead 1991). In a study of small enterprises in southern Africa, McPherson (1995) found that education is one of the most significant determinants of growth in several countries. Bigsten and others (2000) found significant and increasing returns to human capital, both for education and experience, in large samples of enterprises in five countries in the region.

As seen in earlier chapters, more-educated entrepreneurs tend to run larger, older, and exporting enterprises. Education is also associated with having registered at start-up and being affiliated with other enterprises. On the motivation for being an entrepreneur, education is associated with opportunity rather than necessity. As discussed below, education is also associated with greater use of some management techniques.

Measuring Managerial Skills

Bloom and Van Reenen (2010) set out to quantify a set of particular managerial capabilities, based on interviews with senior managers. They found their indexes varied substantially across firms in ways associated with outcomes, and that the average of the indicators varied across countries—management quality, particularly, was lower in developing countries.

Building on that work and using a smaller set of indicators, Aterido and Hallward-Driemeier (2011) found that management techniques have a significant productivity effect on firms in Ghana, Mali, Mozambique, Senegal, and Zambia. That study considered the following four management techniques:

- Establishing formal objectives: consistently making and following through on formal goals

- Monitoring employee performance: systematically keeping track of employee performance and ensuring the aligning of incentives with firm performance

- Engaging in process innovation: consistently trying to improve enterprise product

- Engaging in participatory decision making:[1] including staff in the decision-making process

The effects of each of these components on productivity were assessed separately and jointly through a composite index.

Aterido and Hallward-Driemeier (2011) found no gender differences in establishing formal objectives and monitoring employee performance, but saw significant differences in process innovation and participatory decision making. Male entrepreneurs score significantly higher than female entrepreneurs in process innovation, though the situation reverses for participatory decision making. The effect of management practice on productivity is robust to numerous individual and enterprise characteristics, with no significantly different gradient by gender. Thus all the management techniques were found to be significantly correlated with productivity—and women entrepreneurs benefited from them as much as their male colleagues.

The study also found that the use of better management techniques is significantly correlated with higher productivity. Women are slightly less likely to use them, but as with education more broadly, those who did use them benefited as much as men. These results are robust to including the entrepreneur's age, education, and prior work experience. Thus management skills provide additional benefits beyond more general education and work experience, with returns similar for women and men.

The surveys of new entrepreneurs also gathered information on management techniques, specifically whether business objectives are recorded in writing, and whether formal records are kept (figures 9.2 and 9.3). Gajigo and Hallward-Driemeier (2010) found that differences due to gender are small relative to those due to sector. They depend largely on education, particularly for the use of formal written records.

Figure 9.2 Whether Business Objectives Are Recorded in Writing Varies Primarily by Sector and Only Secondarily by Gender

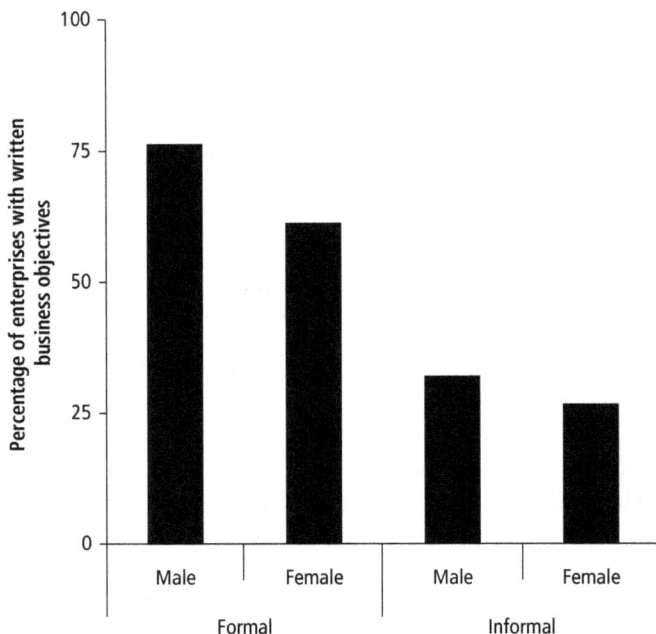

Source: Gajigo and Hallward-Driemeier 2010.
Note: Data are for newly established enterprises in Côte d'Ivoire, Kenya, Nigeria, and Senegal.

Financial Skills

To properly evaluate risk and opportunities among competing options, entrepreneurs need to understand certain key financial concepts. Financial literacy is obviously indispensable for activities directly relevant to business operations, such as keeping track of expenses and revenues, appreciating the advantages and disadvantages of loan contracts, and deciding whether to make an investment or hire another employee. And it is important even in areas not directly related to entrepreneurship.[2] Given that entrepreneurs need to plan in many ways, including saving before starting an enterprise, financial literacy is crucial for them.

Financial literacy can encompass many variables, but it should certainly include some conception of interest rates and inflation. Without such an understanding, the ability to evaluate values over time would be limited.

Figure 9.3 Formal Records Are More Likely to Be Kept among Formal Enterprises, with Little Gender Gap

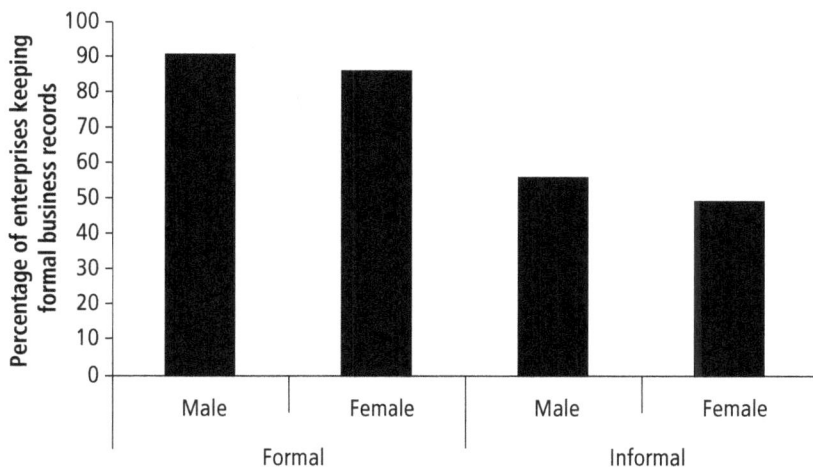

Source: Gajigo and Hallward-Driemeier 2010.
Note: Data are for newly established enterprises in Côte d'Ivoire, Kenya, Nigeria, and Senegal.

The surveys of new entrepreneurs asked two questions to assess financial literacy:[3]

> Let's assume that you deposited K Sh 1,000 in a bank account for five years at 10 percent interest. The interest rate will be earned at the end of each year and will be added to the principal. How much money will you have in your account in five years if you do not withdraw either the principal or the interest [*more than K Sh 1,500, exactly K Sh 1,500,* or *less than K Sh 1,500*]?

> Let's imagine that the interest rate on your savings account in a bank was 1 percent per year and prices were rising at 2 percent per year. After one year, would you be able to buy [*more than today, exactly the same,* or *less than today*] with the money in this bank account?

About 35 percent answered the first question correctly, 23 percent answered the second correctly, and only 7 percent answered both correctly. Gender was not significant, once education was controlled for. Education was the biggest predictor of whether the respondent answered correctly, more than enterprise formality or size.

These findings make clear that significant work is still needed to expand even rudimentary knowledge of financial concepts to those who could benefit from them in running a business. They also caution against simply expanding access to financial products without giving people more information to assess the true costs and benefits of these products, including the risks associated with assuming credit.

Does an entrepreneur's greater understanding of financial concepts make a difference to a firm's performance? Yes. Financially literate entrepreneurs have 10–15 percent higher labor productivity on average (Gajigo and Hallward-Driemeier 2010), though once the analysis controls for education, this difference becomes insignificant. So financial literacy is important for enterprise productivity largely to the extent that it is correlated with other variables that enhance productivity.

Entrepreneurial Skills: Experience and Motivation

The surveys of new entrepreneurs show that years served as a formal-firm employee and as an apprentice are significantly associated with current enterprise productivity (controlling for size, industry, and registration status). The impact of prior experience is not significantly different for female and male entrepreneurs. Years served as a nonenterprise employee (for example, as a teacher or nurse) is, however, significantly associated with lower productivity among female but not male entrepreneurs (Gajigo and Hallward-Driemeier 2010).

Can a Family Background in Entrepreneurship Provide Useful Experience?

A related question is whether entrepreneurs have gained some experience (in a wider sense) from having grown up in a family where a parent was an entrepreneur. Studies from other countries point to this as an important predictor of who becomes an entrepreneur, particularly among those with other employment options available (Djankov and others 2005, 2006). While those studies found a particular role for having a mother who was an entrepreneur, the surveys from Sub-Saharan African countries include too few mothers in the sample, so the analysis focuses on the impact of a father who was an entrepreneur. Indeed, a positive association with current productivity is evident—but only for sons, not daughters. The sons report having received mentoring and introductions to networks of business contacts from their entrepreneur fathers; fewer daughters report having received them (Aterido and Hallward-Driemeier 2011).

Policy levers to address this gender difference seem limited. Still, measures that could expand female entrepreneurship today might well provide the role models and business networks for even more women to be entrepreneurs in the future.

Another potential impact of family background involves the effect of acquiring a business that has been in one's family. The literature has focused on this issue in the context of families with extensive holdings, where "dynastic" ownership and management can be inefficient if later generations do not have the same business skills as earlier (Bennedsen and others 2007; Bertrand and Schoar 2006; Bertrand and others 2008; Caselli and Gennaioli 2005). We made two comparisons. First, for those who became an entrepreneur by acquiring an existing business, we looked at whether it matters if the acquired business was a family business connected to the entrepreneur or a business with no prior ownership links to the entrepreneur or his or her family. Indeed, we find the former are more productive. Second, we compared the productivity of newly acquired family businesses with enterprises that were started from scratch. Here we find the new businesses are more productive than acquired family businesses. The same pattern is found among the larger population of enterprises (Gajigo and Hallward-Driemeier 2010).

The mode of acquisition has greater implications for men's productivity; women show no difference based on how the business was acquired or whether it was a new venture. The new start-ups owned by men appear to be the most productive category. It is true that fewer women acquire existing family businesses, but to the extent such businesses bring with them an established network of suppliers and customers, this advantage does not seem to be passed on to the women in the family. This finding provides a similar message to that of an entrepreneur father benefiting sons rather than daughters.

One alternative family connection that appears to benefit women is having a husband who is also an entrepreneur. This may be because many businesses are jointly run by husbands and wives, and such family businesses may operate more efficiently than one run by either spouse alone.

Productivity and Motivation Differences in Opportunity and Necessity Entrepreneurs

One would expect opportunity entrepreneurs to be more productive than necessity entrepreneurs because their motivation for starting a business was exploiting a market opportunity. Surprisingly, this is not the case. Among the entrepreneurs in the surveys of new entrepreneurs in Côte d'Ivoire, Kenya, Nigeria, and Senegal, those who cited motivations—such as spotting high profit potential, recognizing some form of market opportunity, witnessing an inspiring case, possessing business skills, or claiming special knowledge of their product line—are no more productive when one controls for other individual and enterprise variables. This finding is similar to the finding in Aterido and Hallward-Driemeier (2011) that those who claimed to pursue market opportunities did not have significantly higher productivity than others. Those who say they chose entrepreneurship out of a desire to have greater time flexibility show significantly lower profitability, and this effect is stronger among female entrepreneurs.

If characteristics of the entrepreneur are not controlled for, the analysis reveals a 16 percent labor productivity deficit for necessity entrepreneurs relative to opportunity entrepreneurs (Gajigo and Hallward-Driemeier 2010). (The deficit has no gender dimension.) When variables such as education, sector, and country fixed effects are controlled for, the productivity gap is no longer significant.

An alternative approach to looking at productivity is to divide entrepreneurs by their aspirations—to explore whether those who set more ambitious targets might also exert greater effort and achieve better results. The results show that only those entrepreneurs who claim "being in business for the next 10 years" as a criterion for success show significantly higher labor productivity. And there is no significant gender difference in the importance of this criterion, controlling for other enterprise characteristics; women and men both report being committed to having their enterprise be a longer-run venture.

This finding, which suggests that self-reported assessments of the motivation or goal for the business are a poor indicator of the true potential of a business, may simply reflect weaknesses in the survey approach. For example, respondents may not wish to give answers indicating that they did not choose a certain pathway for themselves. Equally, those who would otherwise be unemployed are likely to be motivated to make the most of the opportunity that they have.

The desire to separate necessity from opportunity entrepreneurs is understandable, since it would help programs targeting high-potential businesses to become more efficient. But basing the categories on self-reported answers is not very informative. The distinction between the self-employed and employers, though not perfect, may be a better proxy for analyzing the two groups.

What Kind of Entrepreneurial Training Is Effective— And for Whom?

A growing line of research investigates the importance of business and financial skills through randomized interventions. It seeks to better identify the causal links, separating out possible selection effects (more successful entrepreneurs might be more likely to enroll in training in the first place). Studies analyze a variety of training methods and substantive content of the programs. Heterogeneous effects across individuals, particularly by initial level of financial literacy, are examined, highlighting the fact that the effectiveness of programs can vary across the range of entrepreneurs.

The level of missing managerial capital can be evident, even among larger firms. Some studies show large, if somewhat "noisy," impacts of more-tailored knowledge initiatives, including those providing consulting services. Bruhn, Karlan, and Schoar (2010a) did a randomized experiment where entrepreneurs running small firms were given access to consulting services. The effects on sales and productivity were significant. A study in India (Bloom and others 2010), looking at somewhat larger textile firms, also found a large jump in productivity for those receiving consulting services. Given the large returns that far outweighed the market costs of these services, there is something of a puzzle concerning why firms are not seeking them. It may well be that they underestimate the benefits of the services, that they do not have access to finance sufficient to pay for them, or that creditors are unwilling to lend for an investment that cannot be collateralized.

The training does not need to be complex, however, depending on the target audience. Indeed, simple "rules of thumb" can have greater impact on outcomes—for less educated entrepreneurs. Drexler, Fischer, and Schoar (2010) find in the Dominican Republic that a "rules of thumb" approach to training in business skills had a larger impact for less educated entrepreneurs than more traditional training in accounting. The result underscores the importance of tailoring training to the group served—and of clarifying even very basic business management ideas, such as keeping separate the accounts and finances of the business and of the household. It also indicates that more traditional education in the mechanics of record keeping is not particularly effective in this group of entrepreneurs.

Bruhn and Zia (2011) evaluate a program in Bosnia and Herzegovina that provides training to existing bank clients. An entrepreneur's initial level of financial literacy is a strong predictor of initial business performance. The training did raise scores on the tests of financial literacy, particularly for those whose initial scores were low. It also led to greater take-up of financial services. The study shows, however, weak impact in spurring those who did not already have a business to start one, nor did it predict subsequent survival. While these improved financial literacy skills are unlikely to be driving entry and exit decisions, there was an effect on increasing sales and profits—strikingly, particularly for those who began with higher levels of financial literacy.

Karlan and Valdivia (2011) examine classroom training for preexisting microenterprise clients of a microfinance program in Peru. All participants in the particular study were female. As participants in the microfinance program, they had access to small loans. The focus of the training was on basic business skills and record keeping. Although business knowledge was found to increase as a result of receiving the training, the results for business outcomes (revenue, profits, or employment) did not change significantly. Still, there is suggestive evidence that revenues fell by less during "bad months" after the training than they had before it.

However, neither human nor financial capital is a magic bullet, particularly if there are deeper constraints at work. A study in Pakistan finds that business training leads to better business knowledge, and subsequently better business practices and improvements in some household outcomes (Mansuri and Giné 2011). The benefits of the program appear to be restricted to male participants, however. That could be due to the lower education and initial level of business knowledge of the women. Or given the extent of the gender-segregated labor market, more women could likely be necessity entrepreneurs rather than opportunity entrepreneurs, facing greater constraints in operating their business.

Exploiting Synergies between Human and Financial Capital

While Bruhn, Karlan, and Schoar (2010b) maintain that human capital is the critical missing source of capital in developing countries, more often the answer is not either financial or human capital alone; the two types often complement, rather than substitute for, one another. Indeed, while recognizing that neither is a magic bullet, combining business training and access to credit is more often significant than either on its own. It is when credit is extended that knowledge about how to use it—and how not to—can be most valuable. Having knowledge, but not the resources to translate it into practice, will erode its effectiveness.

On a deeper level, the synergies between types of capital hold when creditors are deciding to whom they will provide credit. Candidates with better skill sets are more likely to get credit; having the richer human capital makes them a better risk for creditors. This fact also implies that the agenda for expanding skills is a fundamental part of expanding opportunities, including expanding access to finance, as discussed in the previous chapter.

Human capital expands opportunities. Ensuring women can develop their skills is critical in affecting their choice of enterprise and the extent of gender sorting across activities. But simply providing training is not enough. Neither is just providing finance. Entrepreneurs must know what to do with these resources, have a good business idea, and have access to markets. The services provided need to fit their needs—and their abilities. Not everyone will be a successful entrepreneur, but many fewer will be successful without access to capital, human or financial.

Notes

1. Bloom and others (2010) built into each indicator measures of the frequency of its use and how participatory the practice was. Aterido and Hallward-Driemeier's (2011) measures do give higher scores for more frequent use of the practice. However, in that work, the participatory nature of the practices is separated out and the importance of participatory management is tested for directly.
2. For example, it is hard for entrepreneurs to assess whether the savings from income is enough for longer-run plans (investment or retirement) unless they understand

interest rates and inflation. Lusardi and Mitchell (2007) have shown that certain types of economic and financial literacy have a large effect on saving and investment, in turn affecting retirement outcomes.

3. Amounts and currency were adapted to countries to reflect the currency used and to show a "normal" amount in a round figure that would facilitate the calculations. The questions are not intended to test computational skills as much as the concepts of compounding interest and real purchasing power.

References

Aghion, P., and P. Howitt. 1992. "A Model of Growth through Creative Destruction." *Econometrica* 60 (2): 323–51.

Aterido, R., and M. Hallward-Driemeier. 2010. "The Impact of the Investment Climate on Employment Growth: Does Sub-Saharan Africa Mirror Other Low-Income Regions?" Policy Research Working Paper 5218, World Bank, Washington, DC.

———. 2011. "Whose Business Is It Anyway?" *Small Business Economics* 37 (4): 443–64.

Bates, T. 1990. "Entrepreneur Human Capital Inputs and Small Business Longevity." *Review of Economics and Statistics* 72 (4): 551–59.

Baumol, W. 1968. "Entrepreneurship in Economic Theory." *American Economic Review* 58 (2): 64–71.

Bennedsen, M., F. Perez-Gonzalez, K. Nielsen, and D. Wolfenzon. 2007. "Inside the Family Firm: The Role of Families in Succession Decisions and Performance." *Quarterly Journal of Economics* 122 (2): 647–91.

Bertrand, M., S. H. Johnson, K. Samphantharak, and A. Schoar. 2008. "Mixing Family with Business: A Study of Thai Business Groups and the Families behind Them." *Journal of Financial Economics* 88: 466–98.

Bertrand, M., and A. Schoar. 2006. "The Role of Family in Family Firms." *Journal of Economic Perspectives* 20: 73–96.

Bigsten, A., P. Collier, S. Dercon, M. Fafchamps, B. Gauthier, J. Gunning, A. Oduro, R. Oostendorp, C. Pattillo, M. Söderbom, F. Teal, A. Zeufack, and S. Appleton. 2000. "Rate of Return on Human and Non-Human Capital in Africa's Manufacturing Sector." *Economic Development and Cultural Change* 48 (4): 801–27.

Bigsten, A., and M. Söderbom. 2006. "What Have We Learned from a Decade of Manufacturing Enterprise Surveys in Africa?" *World Bank Research Observer* 21 (2): 241–65.

Bloom, N., B. Eifert, A. Mahajan, D. McKenzie, and J. Roberts. 2010. "Does Management Matter? Evidence from India." NBER Working Paper 16658, National Bureau of Economic Research, Cambridge, MA.

Bloom, N., and J. Van Reenen. 2007. "Measuring and Explaining Management Practices Across Firms and Countries." *Quarterly Journal of Economics* 122 (4): 1351–408.

———. 2010. "Why Do Management Practices Differ Across Firms and Countries?" *Journal of Economic Perspectives* 24 (1): 203–24.

Bruhn, M., D. Karlan, and A. Schoar. 2010a. "The Impact of Offering Consulting Services to Small and Medium Enterprises: Evidence from a Randomized Trial in Mexico." Working paper, World Bank, Washington, DC.

————. 2010b. "What Capital Is Missing in Developing Countries?" *American Economic Review* 100 (2): 629–33.

Bruhn, M., and B. Zia. 2011. "Stimulating Managerial Capital in Emerging Markets: The Impact of Business and Financial Literacy for Young Entrepreneurs." Working paper, World Bank, Washington, DC.

Burki, A. A., and D. Terrell. 1998. "Measuring Production Efficiency of Small Firms in Pakistan." *World Development* 26 (1): 155–69.

Caselli, F., and N. Gennaioli. 2005. "Dynastic Management." *Journal of the European Economic Association* 3 (2–3): 679–89.

Cohen, B., and W. J. House. 1996. "Labor Market Choices, Earning, and Informal Networks in Khartoum, Sudan." *Economic Development and Cultural Change* 44 (3): 589–618.

Coleman, S. 2007. "The Role of Human and Financial Capital in the Profitability and Growth of Women-Owned Small Firms." *Journal of Small Business Management* 45 (3): 303–19.

Djankov, S., E. Miguel, Y. Qian, G. Roland, and E. Zhuravskaya. 2005. "Who Are Russia's Entrepreneurs?" *Journal of the European Economic Association* 3 (2–3): 587–97.

Djankov, S., Y. Qian, G. Roland, and E. Zhuravskaya. 2006. "Who Are China's Entrepreneurs?" *American Economic Review* 96 (2): 348–52.

Drexler, A., G. Fischer, and A. Schoar. 2010. "Keeping It Simple: Financial Literacy and Rules of Thumb." CEPR Discussion Paper 7994, Centre for Economic Policy Research, London.

Gajigo, O., and M. Hallward-Driemeier. 2010. "Entrepreneurship among New Entrepreneurs." Working paper, World Bank, Washington, DC.

Hallward-Driemeier, M., and A. Rasteletti. 2010. "Women's and Men's Entrepreneurship in Africa." Working paper, World Bank, Washington, DC.

Karlan, D., and M. Valdivia. 2011. "Teaching Entrepreneurship: Impact of Business Training on Microfinance Clients and Institutions." *Review of Economics and Statistics* 93 (2): 510–27.

Lucas, R. E. Jr. 1978. "On the Size Distribution of Business Firms." *Bell Journal of Economics* 9 (2): 508–23.

Lusardi, A., and O. S. Mitchell. 2007. "Baby Boomer Retirement Security: The Roles of Planning, Financial Literacy and Housing Wealth." *Journal of Monetary Economics* 54 (1): 205–24.

Mansuri, G., and X. Giné. 2011. "Money or Ideas? A Field Experiment on Constraints to Entrepreneurship in Rural Pakistan." Working paper, World Bank, Washington, DC.

McPherson, M. 1995. "Growth of Micro and Small Enterprises in Southern Africa." *Journal of Development Economics* 48: 253–77.

Mead, D. C. 1991. "Review Article: Small Enterprises and Development." *Economic Development and Cultural Change* 39 (January): 409–20.

Romer, P. 1990. "Endogenous Technical Change." *Journal of Political Economy* 98: 71–102.

Solow, R. M. 1956. "A Contribution to the Theory of Economic Growth." *Quarterly Journal of Economics* 70 (1): 65–94.

Chapter 10

Strengthening Women's Voices in Business-Environment Reforms

As other chapters in this study show, women are important economic actors in Africa's private sector, and their experiences of legal, regulatory, and administrative barriers to business tend to be different from those of their male counterparts. Women's experiences also differ from men's in that women are largely excluded from policy making in the private sector—and even from many of the mechanisms and instruments for promoting public-private dialogue (PPD), which has been developed to facilitate interactions between representatives of the business community and government decision makers. More still needs to be done to promote gender inclusion and to make space for identifying and tackling business-environment issues of interest to women.

Such exclusion and underrepresentation are costly, not just to individual women and their businesses, but to the economy. As this and other studies show, Sub-Saharan Africa has considerable hidden growth potential in its women. Tapping that potential—by removing barriers at entry and empowering women economically through access to and control of resources—can make a huge difference to Africa's growth and poverty reduction. Bringing women's voices into PPD and other dialogue mechanisms is at the core of establishing and sustaining a business environment that is favorable to women and that creates opportunities for all.

Women's business associations provide a platform to advocate women's business interests. But many of them are not involved in mainstream dialogue and advocacy, and many lack the capacity and experience to pursue such work effectively.

What is encouraging, however, is that more attention is gradually being paid to understanding and addressing the gender dimensions of the business environment—and to developing practical guidance to tackle gender issues in business-environment reform (Simavi, Manuel, and Blackden 2010).[1] Some initiatives are amplifying the voices of women entrepreneurs in policy making, such as the Africa Businesswomen's Network and its affiliated country-based networks of women's business associations.

This chapter focuses on the experience of women in making their voices heard in business and looks at how they can participate in, and inform, policy making for business and entrepreneurship. It reviews some PPD mechanisms for private and public actors to define and implement business-environment reforms. It also looks at the representation of men and women in business associations and other forums promoting dialogue and partnership around policy making for business and entrepreneurship.

Why Focus on Women's Voices?

Investment-climate reform that enables women, as well as men, to become more productive businesspeople and to stimulate economic development must address challenges faced by both men and women. It is more likely to do so if women are full participants in policy discussions and reform efforts. The effectiveness of women's voices also depends partly on the extent to which solid, gender-informed, and sex-disaggregated analyses are available to inform policy debates.

Two sets of issues are important for strengthening women's voices in making business policy. The first is women's participation in the policy arena—that is, having women at the table where decisions are made. The second is women's role in setting the agenda discussed at the table, and in framing the policy debate. These two issues are discussed below in the context of business associations and other mechanisms designed to bring the private and public sectors together in reforming the business environment.

Business associations have traditionally been a means to expand business networks, but they can also lobby for particular policies. Of course, other advocacy mechanisms, including those promoting women's legal rights and human rights more generally, can strengthen women's property rights and, by extension, their capacity to engage in economic and entrepreneurial activity. Underlying any efforts to integrate gender considerations into business-environment reform is the need for solid empirical analysis so that a fuller understanding of gender roles and gender-based constraints can inform policy choices.

This chapter reviews a specific PPD model developed by the International Finance Corporation (IFC) to increase the private sector's participation in policy making. In doing so, it illustrates more generally the challenges of, and potential for success in, giving women a greater role in advocacy and policy reforms in areas of importance to business.

Underlying the two sets of issues—bringing more women to the table and having issues important to women on the agenda—is a debate over whether it is better for women to work through parallel structures focused on women, or to seek stronger integration into mainstream mechanisms of policy dialogue and business associations. Should women encourage more *women's* business associations? Or should they promote greater female participation in existing business associations?

Similarly, should the agenda focus on issues specific to women in business (a gender perspective)? Or should women expand the ways they participate in, and contribute to, advocacy on issues that are not gender specific but are of importance to business more generally? The review of experience shows where each can be effective. A dual-track approach—separate women's mechanisms and better integration into the mainstream—is often required.

Grounding Policy Advocacy in Gender-Informed Analysis

Advocacy for policy reforms needs to be grounded in solid, country-specific analysis of the opportunities and constraints in the business environment and, specifically, of the ways these opportunities and constraints differ for men and women.

The lack of sex-disaggregated data on business activity and entrepreneurship and a corresponding absence of gender-informed analysis have until now made it hard to identify the nature and extent of gender-based barriers in the business environment—and to develop ways to address them. This situation is changing. Indeed, one of the objectives of this book is to fill a gap in this area. But much more gender-informed and sex-disaggregated data and analysis are needed.

A gender-informed analysis of investment-climate obstacles provides the essential underpinning needed to identify, and advocate for, specific legal and regulatory reforms. Recent years have seen several gender-focused analyses of those obstacles in several African countries, including Ghana, Kenya, Rwanda, Tanzania, and Uganda (Ellis, Blackden, and others 2007; Ellis, Cutura, and others 2007; Ellis, Manuel, and Blackden 2006; IFC 2007a, 2007b). Similar studies have been carried out in various Pacific island countries (for example, Bowman and others 2009; Hedditch and Manuel 2010).

Drawing on broad analysis of the legal environment and links between gender inequality and economic growth, these assessments focused on regulatory and administrative barriers to business registration, operation, and closing; business licensing and taxation; access to land and finance; access to justice; and issues in particular sectors. The studies identified gender-based differences in the application of business regulations and proposed specific regulatory reforms to address them.

In conjunction with these detailed studies of the legal and regulatory environment affecting women in business, the International Finance Corporation also undertook its "Voices of Women Entrepreneurs" series, with works on

Ghana (IFC 2007a), Kenya (IFC 2006b), Rwanda (IFC 2008), and Tanzania (IFC 2007b).[2] By providing examples of women in business who have experienced the obstacles identified in the technical analyses, the "Voices" studies had an explicit purpose of supporting advocacy efforts around specific reforms.

These reports show how women perceive the business environment and the obstacles they face. They reveal both the importance of networking and the problems women face in seeking to network—problems that make it harder for women to develop new opportunities, build a customer base, and expand markets. Consistent across all countries are problems associated with balancing work and family obligations, the need to deal with complex (and often time-consuming) regulations, the higher probability that women will be subject to harassment and discrimination by public servants and officials overseeing compliance with business regulations, and access to finance. Still, in different ways and to differing degrees, women in some countries have broken down barriers and stereotypes and are working in nontraditional sectors—for example, computer manufacturing in Rwanda, petroleum distribution and transport in Kenya, and the emerging information and communication technology sector in Ghana.

The gender assessments provide a foundation for defining reforms responsive to women's concerns. For people to be effective advocates on gender issues, capacity building may be needed to extend their skills to investment-climate issues. Conversely, organizations representing business interests to government may require capacity building to improve their understanding of gender issues in business. In Uganda, a gender coalition was set up to lobby for the assessment's recommendations, and it achieved some success in carrying out legal and regulatory reform (box 10.1). It needed skills in commercial law to take full part in the policy debate.

Having the knowledge and analysis is an important step toward getting issues on the policy agenda. Women still need a seat at the table, however.

Women and Business Associations

Strengthening women's participation in business associations is important for greater inclusion of women and gender issues in business-related decisions. Strengthening the capacity of women's business associations to advocate and lobby for business-environment reforms—not yet a sharp focus—is also important.

Advantages of Business Associations

The advantages of business associations are clear. They facilitate the networking that helps members share market information, identify business opportunities,

BOX 10.1

Uganda Gender Coalition: Using Gender Analysis to Lobby for Change

Uganda's Ministry of Finance, Planning, and Economic Development asked the IFC to assess the country's investment climate through a gender lens. The resulting analysis and recommendations were published as part of Uganda's Gender and Growth Assessment (GGA) (Ellis, Manuel, and Blackden 2006). A GGA team from the IFC followed up with a two-day workshop on advocacy and public-private dialogue. During the workshop a gender coalition was formed to take the recommendations forward through lobbying and advocacy.

The coalition comprises seven core civil society organizations: the Uganda Investment Authority, Private Sector Foundation Uganda, Council for Economic Empowerment for Women in Africa–Uganda Chapter, Uganda Association of Women Lawyers, Uganda Women Entrepreneurs Limited, Uganda Women's Network, and African Women's Economic Policy Network. Members have focused on thematic areas identified by the GGA, drawing on their area of technical expertise. Legal and regulatory reform is complex and time-consuming, with impacts occurring over several years, but some positive results have already emerged:

- GGA recommendations were incorporated in Uganda's Private Sector Development Strategy 2005–2009, the National Gender Strategy 2005–2014, and the National Development Plan 2010–2020.

- Following lobbying from the coalition, GGA recommendations were incorporated in four labor law bills: the Employment Bill, the Occupational Safety and Health Bill, the Labour Dispute Bill, and the Labour Unions Bill. The bills were passed in March 2006, and the president gave his assent. Uganda is now recognized in the World Bank's (2007) *Doing Business* report as the seventh-best country in the world for "employing workers."[a]

Incorporating these recommendations, the 2006 Employment Act outlines general principles relating to forced labor, discrimination in employment, and sexual harassment in the workplace. It protects the rights of women, though compliance is still very low, and the main enforcement machinery—the Ministry of Gender, Labour, and Social Development—has insufficient funding for its mandate.

Enforcement is therefore weak, particularly relating to prohibition of discrimination based on sex, prohibition of sexual harassment in the workplace, and the right to return to the same job after maternity leave.

Source: Personal communication with Dr. Maggie Kigozi, executive director, Uganda Investment Authority.

a. Uganda's earlier ranking is not comparable due to a change in how this indicator is calculated.

and generate cross-referrals—and supports individual entrepreneurs who might otherwise feel isolated. Business associations also amplify the voices of their members in the public sphere.

Africa has many business-focused organizations, but reliable information on women's participation in them is patchy—for several reasons. First, obtaining membership data is difficult, in part because many associations do not wish to share their client lists out of concerns about confidentiality, or because of fears that researchers might "take" their clients. Second, information disaggregated by sex is largely absent from these data, except for data from women-focused business associations. Third, some associations have individuals as members and others have businesses, and the sex of the business owner can be difficult to establish (as with family businesses, for example, or businesses with multiple owners, particularly if ownership and decision-making authority are separate), or it can be irrelevant (as with many corporate entities).

One analysis of state-business relations inventories almost 450 business organizations in 20 countries (te Velde 2006). An extensive database of Africa's development-focused institutions has listings for all 47 Sub-Saharan countries, including many government, international, and faith-based organizations.[3] But one cannot determine how much these organizations are focused on business. The data set for Cameroon, for instance, lists more than 350 organizations, of which around 50 may be focused on business or the private sector; and, of these, around 12 are estimated to be women focused. The "Voices of Women Entrepreneurs" study for Ghana lists 44 women's business associations and institutions (IFC 2007a).

Some countries present their own challenges to increasing women's membership. Cultural and social imperatives can discourage women from mixing freely with men, especially men from outside their families. In such circumstances, a specialized women's business association makes sense: such networks not only provide women business owners with the support they require, but also help spread new business ideas, facilitate making business contacts, and provide avenues for larger-scale marketing and distribution.

Unclear Benefits of Membership
One problem in increasing women's participation may be that women are ambivalent about business associations that are specifically aimed at women, or believe them to be too small to be worth joining, a self-fulfilling view that can undermine the associations' efforts. An International Labour Organization study reported that women entrepreneurs had mixed views about using business networks and associations as support for business development (Richardson, Howarth, and Finnegan 2004). According to the study, some women entrepreneurs used these organizations extensively as part

of their business development strategies, but many were either unaware of them or felt unable to get into them. Membership seemed low, so the associations struggled for credibility and sustainability. Low membership may also reflect unclear mandates and functions, so businesswomen see little to gain by joining.

Women's low representation in business associations is mirrored in their low representation in business management and corporate decision making, as well policy making. Even in the United States in 2009, women were 13.5 percent of Fortune 500 executive officers and 15.2 percent of board members (Catalyst 2009). And in Europe in 2007, women were only 11 percent of the members of executive committees of listed companies (McKinsey and Co. 2007).

Broadening the Horizons of Women's Business Associations

What do these associations do? They tend to provide direct support to women's businesses, through networking, developing market opportunities, improving business skills, and getting finance—all important. But to tackle the challenges facing women in business, broader policy and legal reforms are needed (as other chapters have shown). Too often women are excluded from formal or informal networks. Gender-based stereotypes and a lack of role models often block women's professional advancement and limit their voices in business communities and policy making.

Women's organizations in Africa are taking part in larger international associations, sharing examples of change. The World Association of Women Entrepreneurs, founded in 1945, has representatives from women's business associations in 10 Sub-Saharan countries.[4]

A recently established regionwide network, the Africa Businesswomen's Network, brings together women's business associations from several African countries; it provides an umbrella to support various national hubs to develop women's business associations, strengthen their capacity to serve members, and lobby for policy changes in the business environment (box 10.2). It explicitly aims to combine business networking with advocacy training.

A case study from Malawi to support a women's business association provides practice pointers, emphasizing bottom-up approaches (box 10.3).

Media events and the Internet expand the opportunities to build capacity (see box 10.4).

The capacity of business associations—particularly women's—to engage in policy dialogue and advocacy also needs to be developed. First, it is crucial to broaden the focus of advocacy to include parliamentarians and others promoting gender-responsive reforms of family and other laws that affect women's economic opportunity. Second, more women need to participate directly in mechanisms influencing policy.

BOX 10.2

The Africa Businesswomen's Network: Amplifying Women's Voices

The Africa Businesswomen's Network is a partnership between local businesswomen's organizations throughout Africa, Vital Voices Global Partnership, and ExxonMobil Foundation. Its goals are

- To build and then support a network of businesswomen's organizations in Africa in order to expand the number of women succeeding as entrepreneurs and leaders in the corporate world
- To raise the profile and credibility of women in business
- To foster global networking opportunities among businesswomen
- To advocate for policies that expand economic opportunities for women

The programs and events of the network provide a forum for peer learning, information exchanges, business development, and access to education, resources, and tools—all expanding economic opportunities and building networks for businesswomen in the region. Members of the network—network hubs—are businesswomen's organizations committed to contributing to economic growth and reform, to supporting the needs of women-led businesses and professional women, and to having a significant social impact. Businesswomen take part in the network through membership in the network hubs being developed in Cameroon, Ghana, Kenya, Nigeria, South Africa, and Uganda.

Network Hub Goals
Network hubs seek to

- Establish a strong network of businesswomen and advance the exchange of best practices and success strategies in business
- Raise the profile and credibility of women in the private sector
- Monitor and highlight the contributions of women to economic growth in the region
- Educate and build the capacity of women for entrepreneurship in small and medium enterprises and beyond
- Promote gender equity in corporate workplace policies and government legislation
- Connect women entrepreneurs to sources of capital and promote women as investors and sources of venture capital

Network Hub Activities
Network activities include

- Outreach programs that empower and inform women to take advantage of entrepreneurial and corporate advancement opportunities

- Special events (training workshops, skills clinics, seminars, conferences, networking events) to provide women with practical learning and information that can be applied immediately in their businesses and, in some cases, in their personal lives
- Advocacy for workplace policies and government legislation that promote gender equity and advance the rights and interests of businesswomen.
- Wide distribution of information to businesswomen through newsletters, websites, webinars, and other means to provide access to public and private resources for business
- Outreach to the media to get broad coverage of businesswomen's success stories and to raise the profile, visibility, and credibility of women leaders in business
- Outreach and education of government officials to improve their awareness of the value of women in business to overall economic development, including the dissemination of high-quality research on women in business
- Outreach to girls and young women, including mentoring and training as well as internship programs for schools, youth groups, or other organizations, to develop the next generation of businesswomen

Source: Vital Voices Global Partnership, http://vitalvoices.org/what-we-do/regions/africa/africa-businesswomens-network.

BOX 10.3

National Association of Business Women in Malawi: Creating a Grassroots Advocacy Program

Thanks to successful advocacy initiated with the help of the Center for International Private Enterprise (CIPE), the National Association of Business Women (NABW) in Malawi has been the driving force behind the growing empowerment of the country's women entrepreneurs. In line with a bottom-up, consensus-building approach, the NABW held regional meetings throughout Malawi to learn about the most pressing needs of women entrepreneurs. Meeting attendance exceeded expectations, with some meetings drawing well over a hundred participants. Just as important, they included a large proportion of women from rural areas, where the majority of Malawi's women-owned businesses are located.

The NABW has complemented the information it obtained at the grassroots level with detailed background studies of its own. The studies contain not only specific data

—Continued

BOX 10.3 *continued*

on the problems businesswomen face in the most important sectors but also specific recommendations on the legal and institutional policies that must change if women-owned businesses are to prosper.

Armed with these data, the NABW invited key government officials and agencies to participate in its membership meetings, where the sectoral development plans and recommendations are discussed and fine-tuned. An impressive array of policy makers participated, including officials from various ministries and other relevant government bodies.

Turning government officials into stakeholders in the reforms that the NABW advocates is paying off handsomely. Several laws and policies that hurt Malawi's businesswomen have been changed. Special government extension services are now available to women running agribusinesses. The Ministry of Finance has increased the funding of several ministries to carry out programs that benefit women entrepreneurs. A new land law policy is up for parliamentary review. One of its key provisions would enable women to obtain property titles, which they could then use as collateral to secure commercial loans.

The NABW is keeping close tabs on the reform process. With financing from CIPE, it has launched a watchdog communications service that reports on its own efforts and those of other stakeholders in implementing the sectoral development programs it has drafted. The service consists of periodic newsletters called "Business Alerts," distributed to NABW members as well as all key government officials and agencies, nongovernmental organizations, and—for good measure—the local media.

The NABW has gained considerable clout in official circles. The government has included association executives in the high-level task force studying changes to the country's small and medium enterprises in a major effort with the United Nations Development Programme. The NABW also has representatives on the boards of para-statal organizations that affect women-owned businesses. And it participates in local and international trade fairs through the Malawi Export Promotion Council.

The main lessons taught by the NABW's experiences are these:

- Advocacy campaigns are more powerful when initiated from the bottom.
- Background studies complement grassroots information.
- Government agencies have to be stakeholders in the advocacy process.
- The campaign has to be accompanied by newsletters and continual communications.
- Donors can bring in their media expertise and reputation vis-à-vis the government.

Source: CIPE Promotion Council, http://www.cipe.org.

BOX 10.4

Resources for Country-Level Advocacy

The International Labour Organization's WEDGE (Women's Entrepreneurship Develop-ment and Gender Equality) program promotes the "Month of the Woman Entrepre-neur" in African countries (so far, Ethiopia, Tanzania, Uganda, and Zambia), organizes events to promote awareness about women's entrepreneurship, shares experience, and designs strategies to assist women entrepreneurs and strengthen the capacities of their associations. The media are central to these events. In Tanzania and Uganda, workshops were held on the role of the media in women's entrepreneurship develop-ment. The media were also active in the events. In Tanzania, newspaper, radio, and television journalists attended the launch of the month's events, and a "road show" toured Dar es Salaam.

The Community of Women Entrepreneurs is a website hosted and moderated by the U.S. Center for International Private Enterprise, a forum for sharing ideas, experi-ences, best practices, and resources to empower women economically and politically. Members of this community are leading entrepreneurs and business advocates who share their knowledge and in return receive ideas from their peers. Discussions in this community focus on supporting a culture of entrepreneurship, expanding the opportu-nities for women in business, and advocating for a better business environment.

Source: Simavi, Manuel, and Blackden 2010.

Bringing Women into Public-Private Dialogue

Given the dialogue between the public and private sectors to improve the busi-ness climate, enabling women to participate more can boost the chances of making their voices heard when government and business leaders articulate and implement investment reform priorities.

Role and Structure of Public-Private Dialogue

The IFC developed its PPD program to facilitate interactions between private and public actors as they identify and address obstacles to an improved business environment (box 10.5). Often anchored at the highest level of government, PPD facilitates the business-environment reform process and the implementa-tion of specific investment-climate reforms. Investors identify and implement reforms and assess the impact of those reforms on the business environment, empowering constituencies and building trust and transparency among key stakeholders. The PPD tool kit shows that PPD programs take different forms, depending on the structure of the private sector, the power of different branches

BOX 10.5

Public-Private Dialogue for Investment-Climate Reform

Governments that listen to the private sector are more likely to promote sensible, workable reforms; and entrepreneurs who understand what the government is trying to achieve in its reforms are more likely to support them.

Talking is thus the best way for the public and the private sectors to set the right priorities—and support common interests. Meeting regularly builds trust and understanding. But a failure to communicate leads to distrust, which leads to inefficiency and waste, inhibiting growth, investment, and poverty reduction.

PPD promotes good public and corporate governance. It sets an example of transparency and dynamism. It also sheds light on the workings and performance of government institutions, and it improves the quality of the advice government receives from the private sector by diversifying sources and promoting more evidence-based advocacy.

Source: Gamser, Kadritzke, and Waddington 2005.

of government, and the degree to which the groups are well organized (Herzberg and Wright 2006). They follow no template.

Thirty countries have adopted the IFC's PPD programs (Toland 2009), and practitioners and academics have a wide array of tools and techniques for conducting them,[5] with annual workshops providing a forum for exchanging global experience.

A common institutional approach, prevalent in most productive PPD programs, involves a dedicated secretariat and working groups that meet often to devise recommendations for periodic plenary sessions. The secretariat organizes meetings, coordinates research efforts and other logistics, sets agendas, rallies members, manages communication and outreach strategies, and is a point of contact for others who want to join.

Through working groups, a range of public and private sector actors define critical issues and reform strategies. The groups are typically organized by industry cluster (for example, agriculture, tourism, or manufacturing), by policy issue (for example, deregulation, taxation, or labor), or by location, enabling them to focus and call on greater technical expertise.

PPD, in regular roundtables or investment council meetings, can take place between central government and private sector organizations representing national and international corporations, and at the local level between local authorities and businesses. Outside these formal structures, government and private sector representatives often network informally.

Figure 10.1 Public-Private Dialogue Enlarges the Reform Space

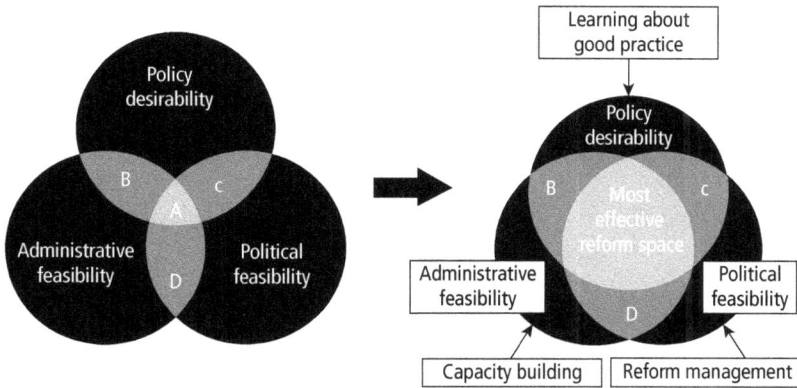

Source: Adapted from World Bank 2004, 68.
Note: The figure represents the difference between the reform space when PPD is absent (left) and when it is present (right). Region A represents the set of potential reforms or actions that demonstrate administrative and political feasibility as well as policy desirability—and hence are most likely to be implemented. Regions B, C, and D represent the sets of policies where at least two of the desirability and feasibility features are present. The aim of PPD is to expand region A—that is, to expand the set of actions that have all three of the desirability and feasibility features.

PPD can enlarge the reform space by ensuring greater inclusion of stakeholders in reform deliberations and facilitating greater local ownership of reform measures (figure 10.1). The potential for PPD to promote gender inclusion among stakeholders, and contribute to enlarging the reform space, is thus considerable.

Unfortunately, women's participation in PPD seems very low—a topic that we now turn to.

Women's Participation in Public-Private Dialogue

It is hard to assess how extensively women are represented in PPD programs, not least because the programs initially had little or no explicit focus on women as participants or on gender issues. In the early years, women's presence appears to have been either negligible or unspecified, and attention to gender differences in investment-climate reform was correspondingly low.

Many of the early case materials and assessments of PPD hardly mentioned women, though some referred to women's groups or women's business associations. The 1998 IFC *Good Practice Manual* on public consultation and disclosure includes a few exhortations about ensuring that the voiceless and powerless (including women) are heard, but provides no specific examples, substantive guidance, or practice pointers (IFC 1998). In 2005, when the World Bank evaluated the presidential investors' advisory councils that it supported in several African countries, women's associations were mentioned only in an appendix on country responses in Uganda (Dewah 2007). Indeed, unless gender was explicitly addressed as a part of the program, the experience of PPD programs suggests very low levels of women's participation in PPD mechanisms, and equally low activity on the part of PPD institutions either to promote gender inclusion or to make space for identifying and tackling business-environment issues of particular interest to women (Gamser, Kadritzke, and Waddington 2005; IFC 2005).[6]

In 2008 the IFC recognized the need to integrate an explicit gender dimension into both the process and content of PPD work. It organized a workshop in April 2008 in Dakar, Senegal, for all PPD practitioners, and it included a session on addressing gender issues in PPD. At the conclusion of the workshop, PPD practitioners were invited to prepare work plans outlining ways in which country PPD programs would address gender issues. Based on these work plans, the workshop proposed that country PPD programs could consider incorporating one or more of the following actions in their work plans:

- Prepare an inventory of women's business associations, women entrepreneurs, and the distribution of men and women in the institutions and organizations involved in PPD, including in the PPD secretariat and in working groups formed to discuss specific issues. This will provide a baseline for outreach to, and dialogue with, women's business groups.

- Invite women entrepreneurs and women's business associations to a dialogue event to discuss the principal issues and constraints in the business environment faced by this constituency, with a view to outlining a program of action, including further dialogue and/or more-detailed analysis and research as required, to address them. This will provide a foundation for addressing gender-focused issues as a PPD task.

- Review, in the context of existing or planned PPD dialogue focus areas, where gender issues are or might be relevant, so as to inform the process. This will provide entry points for gender-focused work within existing PPDs.

This agenda has been pursued in the context of the Liberia Better Business Forum, and its impact has been significant. A similar agenda is being pursued in Rwanda, internationally recognized as a leader in promoting gender equality in the region. Rwanda has made considerable progress in improving the business environment for women (see IFC 2008).

How to Ensure Successful Public-Private Dialogue

A distinction needs to be made between the presence of women in PPD structures and the extent to which women contribute to setting the agenda of the dialogue. The mere presence of women, however important, does not translate into discussion of gender-specific concerns in the business environment. Other proactive steps must be taken to ensure that the gender dimensions of the issues being tackled in PPD are identified—and that gender-responsive measures can be articulated and acted on, as discussed in the rest of this chapter.

Gamser, Kadritzke, and Waddington (2005) provide a useful summary of the key factors that lead to successful PPD (box 10.6). The IFC evaluation of its PPD programs also identifies several factors (some of which overlap with those

---

BOX 10.6

Keys to Effective Public-Private Dialogue

Effective champions drive successful PPD. Active, motivated, and persuasive champions keep processes on course when obstacles are encountered. They keep participants feeling engaged and valued, so that when changes are agreed to, they are implemented. They are focused on results but flexible enough to respond to PPD contributions (as opposed to using these meetings as a vehicle to advance individual agendas). It is difficult to sustain PPD without active work from both a public and a private champion.

Buy-in by both the public and private sector is essential. Both have to commit resources to PPD. The process cannot depend on donor backing; excessive donor support before local buy-in orients PPD to donor agendas instead of to local priorities and discourages local ownership.

Balance between interests and contributions sustains PPD. More participants contribute in successful dialogues, both at the table and in pretable and posttable research and analysis. If one or two participants do most of the work, they tend to have little influence, even if the more active parties are genuinely trying to work on behalf of the whole group.

Planning is vital. There is more to PPD than simply providing space and persuading people to sit together. Agendas should be set well ahead of meetings (and well advertised). Evidence-based materials should be provided to inform and enliven discussions. Timetables should be set for group outputs wherever possible, to support planning and to pressure the group to produce results.

Results drive PPD in the longer term. Dialogue without change cannot be sustained for very long. Careful setting of priorities and sequencing of group activities works better than trying to tackle a large wish list of reforms all at once. The more successful PPD initiatives focus early on low-hanging fruit, where political resistance to change is low and where reforms can be agreed on over short time spans. This strategy builds momentum for tackling tougher, less tractable problems.

Respect keeps groups coming back to the table. In the best PPD processes all parties feel motivated to contribute, and feel that their contributions can make a difference. If groups come to feel that they are brought into a dialogue just to make them change

—Continued

BOX 10.6 *continued*

their minds, they tend not to come back for more—and to harden their contrary positions. Institutions managing the "neutral space" can maintain atmospheres of mutual respect.

Measurement is a key to getting PPD in focus. More-successful dialogues do not just hear complaints and plaudits, they look hard at the costs and benefits of the situation and at possible future scenarios. The mathematics need not be fancy, but there should be some attempt to quantify problems and opportunities in the enabling environment. Regulatory impact assessments are one of many tools that can promote more-effective PPD.

Public relations and communications are vital to change. No matter how carefully PPD participants initially are selected, implementing reform requires bringing more parties to the table. This wider audience should include other parts of government (and parliament), private sector associations, and key civil society groups.

Private sector associations may not be essential to PPD in the short run, but PPD cannot be sustained without capable private sector association participation. In the short run PPD can compensate for association weakness by direct appeals to business. Enlightened entrepreneurs can provide the information and political support to initiate PPD and tackle initial issues. But in the longer run it is too expensive to continue custom-assembling the private sector side of the dialogue as issues evolve. Capable business associations take on this cost in countries with better business environments and more-positive government-business relations.

Source: Gamser, Kadritzke, and Waddington 2005.

---

in Gamser, Kadritzke, and Waddington) that are critical to success, such as having effective champions, having a well-run secretariat, ensuring government commitment to follow-up actions, and using evidence-based analysis, research, and impact evaluation (Toland 2009). Another factor in achieving success is ensuring that PPD addresses sector-specific issues.

Enlarging the Reform Space: Strengthening Gender Inclusion in Public-Private Dialogue

Integrating gender into PPD can occur in several ways. At the policy level, the task is to apply a gender lens to legal and regulatory reforms of the business environment. This approach is complemented by ensuring a gender-friendly PPD process, including appropriate gender representation in, and engagement with, all components of a PPD's structure. The gender lens can also identify sector-specific gender issues, or involve traditional leaders in societies where cultural biases against women may make formal PPD and application of an across-the-board gender approach impractical. None of these approaches has been fully tested yet. But PPD programs are clearly making an

BOX 10.7

Guiding Questions on Gender in Public-Private Dialogue and Business-Environment Reforms

- *Presence of women in the PPD.* How well represented are women/women's businesses in the structures of the PPD—in working groups, secretariat, meetings, and other forums? Are any PPD participants tasked with representing the interests of businesswomen? What (if any) are the links between the PPD and women's business associations? What are the obstacles and opportunities for including women in PPD?

- *Gender dimensions of PPD issues.* To what extent has the PPD process recognized and/or addressed any gender dimensions of the issues with which it is concerned? For example, incentives and opportunities to formalize (register) businesses can be quite different for men and women. What are the obstacles and opportunities for addressing the gender dimensions of PPD issues?

- *Active focus on gender issues in the business environment.* Has there been any real outreach to women in business (and their associations)? Has the PPD provided space to address issues affecting women in business? What has been the experience of the PPD (if any) in addressing issues of particular concern to women? What issues that affect women has the forum discussed in the last six months or year? What success stories are there? What are the obstacles and opportunities for active outreach to women in PPD processes?

- *Distilling the lessons of experience—what works.* Are top-down or bottom-up approaches better? Is it better to mainstream gender concerns into existing PPD approaches, or to have parallel structures focused on gender issues? What does the experience of getting women's voices heard in efforts to improve the business climate tell us about how to do it better?

Source: Based on Simavi, Manuel, and Blackden 2010.

---

effort to address gender gaps much more rigorously than in the past. Actively engaging in and monitoring gender issues and women's leadership in PPD processes—for example, by using guiding questions such as those listed in box 10.7—is now an explicit part of PPD programs (Simavi, Manuel, and Blackden 2010).

Making Sure Women's Voices Are Heard and Acted On

Making women's voices heard and acting on what women say have the potential to transform the business environment. It is important to build on existing initiatives and dialogue where possible. But if these do not exist, are weak, or do not represent the interests of businesswomen, it may be useful to initiate new forums, strengthen an existing forum, or simply provide a mechanism for consultation with women in business. Care should be taken to ensure the process includes very small businesses, which may not be organized into formal associations (Simavi, Manuel, and Blackden 2010).

Uganda shows the importance of not only getting women to the table but also focusing more strategically on the tables that matter. The Uganda Investment Authority Women Entrepreneurs Network, set up in 2000 to create a forum for networking and sharing success stories among women entrepreneurs, has more than 300 female entrepreneurs in varied small, medium, and large enterprises. Its major role is to strengthen women's networking, information sharing, mentoring, and capacity building in business and leadership skills.

The members are women in business, professionals, and corporate chief executives who meet regularly. The network has brought women into the Presidential Investors Round Table, the apex policy dialogue body between the president and the private sector. A total of 22 (11 local and 11 foreign) chief executive officers advise the president on how to improve the investment climate. During the roundtable's first phase in 2004, the Uganda Investment Authority had one domestic and one foreign female entrepreneur. In its third phase, the roundtable has five female members. The goal is to have 11 female entrepreneurs represented—half the roundtable's membership.

These examples show that women's voices in shaping and improving the business environment can be amplified. A combination of bottom-up advocacy work, better networking opportunities among businesswomen, and support at the highest level of government can bring more women to the table and ensure that issues of importance to them—with a specific gender angle or not—are discussed.

This agenda needs continuing support: women's voices will not automatically be included, though the default exclusion of women's voices is shifting in many countries. Examples of success provide role models for others to follow, and the positive track record reinforces the wider benefits of businesspeople's listening to (and acting on) businesswomen's voices.

Notes

1. This work uses "business environment" and "investment climate" interchangeably to refer to conditions external to the firm that affect its performance, for example, infrastructure services, regulations, access to finance, governance, security, and property rights.
2. Similar studies were carried out in Bosnia and Herzegovina (Cutura 2008), Vietnam (IFC 2006a), and Indonesia (IFC–IWAPI 2001).
3. Directory of Development Organizations, http://www.devdir.org.

4. The countries are Benin, Cameroon, Chad, Côte d'Ivoire, Democratic Republic of Congo, Gabon, Guinea, Mali, Mauritius, and Senegal. For more information see the association's website (http://www.fcem.org/www/en/home.asp, accessed February 2011). The association also has six observer/affiliate countries in Africa.

5. These tools and techniques are accessible at the PPD website (http://www .publicprivatedialogue.org).

6. Attention to gender issues was not, for example, initially part of the IFC evaluation of PPDs (Toland 2010).

References

Bowman, C., J. Cutura, A. Ellis, and C. Manuel. 2009. *Women in Vanuatu.* Washington, DC: International Finance Corporation.

Catalyst. 2009. *Statistical Overview of Women in the Workplace.* New York: Catalyst Quick Takes.

Cutura, J. 2008. *Voices of Women Entrepreneurs in Bosnia-Herzegovina.* Washington, DC: International Finance Corporation.

Dewah, E. 2007. *Case Study: Reform in Botswana.* Washington, DC: Center for International Private Enterprise.

Ellis, A., M. Blackden, J. Cutura, F. MacCulloch, and H. Seebens. 2007. *Gender and Economic Growth in Tanzania: Creating Opportunities for Women.* Washington, DC: World Bank.

Ellis, A., J. Cutura, N. Dione, I. Gillson, C. Manuel, and J. Thongori. 2007. *Gender and Economic Growth in Kenya: Unleashing the Power of Women.* Washington, DC: World Bank.

Ellis, A., C. Manuel, and M. Blackden. 2006. *Gender and Economic Growth in Uganda: Unleashing the Power of Women.* Washington, DC: World Bank.

Gamser, M., R. Kadritzke, and R. Waddington. 2005. *Reforming the Business Environment: Mechanisms and Processes for Public Sector Dialogue.* London: Bannock Consulting, U.K. Department for International Development.

Hedditch, S., and C. Manuel. 2010. *Gender and Investment Climate Reform Assessment: Pacific Region.* Washington, DC: International Finance Corporation.

Herzberg, B. 2008. "PPD Product Review." PowerPoint presentation, International Finance Corporation, Washington, DC, November.

Herzberg, B., and A. Wright. 2006. *The PPD Handbook: A Toolkit for Business Environment Reformers.* U.K. Department for International Development, World Bank, International Finance Corporation, and OECD Development Centre. http://www .publicprivatedialogue.org/papers/PPD%20handbook.pdf.

IFC (International Finance Corporation). 1998. *Doing Better Business through Effective Public Consultation and Disclosure: A Good Practice Manual.* Washington, DC: IFC Environment Division.

———. 2005. *Building the Capacity of Business Membership Organizations: Guiding Principles for Project Managers.* Washington, DC: IFC.

———. 2006a. *Voices of Vietnamese Women Entrepreneurs.* Washington, DC: IFC.

————. 2006b. *Voices of Women Entrepreneurs in Kenya.* Washington, DC: IFC.

————. 2007a. *Voices of Women Entrepreneurs in Ghana.* Johannesburg: IFC.

————. 2007b. *Voices of Women Entrepreneurs in Tanzania.* Washington, DC: IFC.

————. 2008. *Voices of Women Entrepreneurs in Rwanda.* Washington, DC: IFC.

IFC–IWAPI (International Finance Corporation–Indonesian Women's Business Association). 2001. *Voices of Women in the Private Sector.* Jakarta: IFC–IWAPI.

McKinsey and Co. 2007. *Women Matter: Gender Diversity, a Corporate Performance Driver.* Paris: McKinsey and Co.

Richardson, P., R. Howarth, and G. Finnegan. 2004. "The Challenges of Growing Small Businesses: Insights from Women Entrepreneurs in Africa." SEED Working Paper 47, International Labour Office, International Labor Organization, Geneva.

Simavi, S., C. Manuel, and M. Blackden. 2010. *Gender Dimensions of Investment Climate Reform: A Guide for Policy Makers and Practitioners.* Washington, DC: World Bank.

te Velde, D. W. 2006. "Measuring State-Business Relations in Sub-Saharan Africa." IPPG Discussion Paper Series 4, Research Programme Consortium for Improving Institutions for Pro-Poor Growth, Manchester, U.K.

Toland, M. 2009. "Independent Evaluation of 30 WBG-Supported Public Private Dialogue and Reform Platforms for Private Sector Development." PowerPoint presentation, International Finance Corporation, Vienna, Austria, April 28–30.

————. 2010. "Gender and Private Public Dialogue." PowerPoint presentation, International Finance Corporation, Vienna, Austria, June 1–3.

World Bank. 2004. *World Development Report 2005: A Better Investment Climate for Everyone.* Washington, DC: World Bank.

————. 2007. *Doing Business 2007.* Washington, DC: World Bank.

Chapter **11**

Toward an Action Agenda

This concluding chapter outlines some areas where policy reforms could improve women's opportunities for entrepreneurship in Sub-Saharan Africa.[1] It focuses on key areas that affect the gender-differentiated patterns. The aim is to enable women to engage in larger, formally registered businesses in higher-value-added lines of business. The emphasis is on reforms of women's legal status and property rights. Gender gaps in rights limit women's business opportunities. As development is not sufficient to close these gaps, they require proactive measures.

The chapter also highlights measures to improve women's access to finance, their financial literacy, and their managerial skills. It discusses broader investment-climate reforms, addressing constraints to growth in areas where women's economic activities are concentrated. And it proposes measures to strengthen women's participation in policy dialogue, which would improve the business environment for everyone.

Reforming the Business Environment

Reforming the business environment expands opportunities for growth, higher productivity, and employment—for all. Broader reforms, such as improving infrastructure, tax administration, and regulations, are likely to benefit both women and men. The extent of the benefits can have indirect gender effects, of course, depending on the types of enterprises that benefit most from reform. For example, lifting constraints on smaller firms and encouraging formalization should help women disproportionately.

Constraints to entrepreneurship that affect women more than men—strongest in areas of property rights, access to finance, and harassment—reduce half the population's potential to participate and compete equally in productive activities, lowering aggregate growth. Particularly if those constraints distort financial markets, so that capital is not allocated to the most productive activities, they have a broader effect on stunting competitive pressures, lowering innovation, and cutting aggregate productivity growth. And they restrict higher-potential women's enterprises the most (Schoar 2010). There is thus an intrinsic and instrumental case for removing gender-based constraints to entrepreneurship.

Increasing Women's Right to Own and Control Assets

The earlier chapters make a strong case for improving the business environment for women through legal reform. Important areas of law, notably family law, place women at a disadvantage in their ability to own property, enter contracts, go to court, and use the justice system more generally. The responsiveness of the justice system to women's concerns can be improved both for substantive law and in procedural and administrative areas.

To ensure women's equal rights, substantive law reforms are needed along several dimensions. As shown in the Women–LEED–Africa database, countries need to bring consistency and coherence to their judicial practice. Governments should be encouraged not only to ratify international treaties and conventions (including the Maputo Protocol, the Convention on the Elimination of All Forms of Discrimination against Women, and key International Labour Organization conventions), but also to "domesticate" and then enforce them. Within a coherent international framework, governments should examine their constitutions to address discriminatory provisions, enhance provisions for gender equality, review how the legal system recognizes customary law and customs, and ensure in particular that constitutional nondiscrimination provisions are applied in family law and property rights in marriage. Contradictory and inconsistent provisions in the law also need to be addressed.

Integral to improving the gender responsiveness and consistency of statutory reforms is the need to tackle discriminatory provisions in family law that reduce women's ability to engage in business. Tackling such provisions applies especially in countries where family law discriminates against married women by assigning the position of "household head" and decision maker exclusively to the man, and where statutory provisions specifically limit married women's legal capacity. Governments need to pay special attention to laws governing marriage, divorce, and succession. Although the framing of business laws and regulations is generally gender neutral, their application is sometimes gender biased, and regulatory reforms can be carried out in a more gender-responsive way.

Key items to address include the following:

- Giving women equal say over the administration and transfer of marital property
- Limiting or removing head-of-household laws that allow husbands to deny permission to their wives to engage in a trade or profession, or to choose the marital home

- Removing provisions requiring a husband's signature to enter contracts or open a bank account
- Enabling married women to testify equally in court
- Recognizing women's rights to marital property on divorce or in inheritance
- Applying constitutional provisions of nondiscrimination in areas of marriage, property, and inheritance
- Building awareness of gender bias, and measures to counteract such bias, among judges and within the broader legal community

Reforms in the administration of law and in the institutions responsible for delivering justice can improve women's access to justice and the capacity of the system to respond to women's concerns. One such reform is facilitating physical access to justice through more, and more appropriately focused, courts, as for family matters and small claims. A second is increasing the participation and representation of women throughout the justice system. And a third is enabling those administering and dispensing justice at all levels to respond to the different constraints and priorities of men and women. Such action requires political will and determination to address the power relations and abusive practices that can undermine the effectiveness of the legal system.[2]

Expanding Women's Access to Finance

A repeated finding in this book is that the line of business, its size, and its formality emerge as more important drivers than gender in entrepreneurs' access to formal finance. However, it is not that gender does not matter. Rather, it comes into play in deeper sources of inequality. Women tend to have less access to collateral, education, and prior work experience—all of which are significant predictors of initial bank loans. Thus with less ability to gain credit, women may be more constrained in their choice of business line, the scale and formality of their business, and even the ability to become an entrepreneur at all. This cycle can then perpetuate itself as the choice of enterprise reduces the likelihood of qualifying for credit in the future. In the longer term, breaking the cycle involves tackling underlying gaps in legal rights and in access to human capital.

Measures to improve women's access to finance include the following:

- Enriching women's human capital. This underlies the agenda of expanding women's access to finance.
- Improving property rights for women. This will strengthen women's control over assets and their capacity to provide collateral for bank loans.
- Building property registries that include movable property. This will also strengthen women's ability to use movable property as collateral.

- Setting up credit registries that capture women's credit history and repayment records in microfinance. This will benefit women disproportionately, given their greater reliance on microfinance.
- Targeting financing mechanisms at women, including microfinance and mobile banking.

Enriching Managerial and Financial Skills

Formal education is important for building women's human capital, but other dimensions also matter, especially in building business-specific skills and capacity. Recent years have seen dramatic declines in education gaps for boys and girls, which is a very promising indicator for the next generation of women entrepreneurs. But more needs to be done. Specifically, today's women have a lower level of financial literacy and use more-limited sets of management skills. Women who do have higher financial literacy and management training benefit from them as much as their male colleagues, so efforts to expand such training for women entrepreneurs should broaden their opportunities. However, as the evaluation literature points out, the method of teaching and content need to be tailored to the initial level of business knowledge. While more training is not sufficient to ensure success, more knowledgeable entrepreneurs are better positioned to grow their business.

Expanding women's human capital can reinforce a virtuous cycle too. Having role models and being part of a network of entrepreneurs are associated with running more profitable enterprises. Currently these connections benefit men more than women, in part as fathers have tended to pass on their connections and practical knowledge to their sons. As more women are successful entrepreneurs and as more fathers apprentice their daughters, more women will be able to take advantage of these connections and skills.

Key activities to build managerial and financial skills include the following:

- Encouraging opportunities for sharing experiences among businesswomen
- Developing a stronger cadre of female role models in business
- Strengthening management training and increasing access to consulting services
- Pairing financial literacy and business skills training with access to finance; tailoring programs to increase women's participation (for example, choice of time, location, provision of child care services)
- Promoting mentoring and other networking opportunities to facilitate business contacts, marketing opportunities, and product development

Strengthening Women's Voices in Business-Environment Reform

Proactively including women business owners and associations in public-private dialogue (PPD) and advocacy efforts can ensure that women's unique constraints are considered in the reform process. PPD is most successful when there are effective champions; a well-run secretariat; government commitment to follow-up actions; and available evidence-based analysis, research, and impact evaluation. To ensure that women's voices are included, it is important both to strengthen the presence of women in PPD institutions and structures, and to build the capacity of women to inform and influence the substantive agenda.

Equally important is engaging a wider set of policy makers in addressing the gender dimensions of business-environment reform, beyond national women's machineries and gender advocates. This approach means engaging with the key economic management ministries and mainstream private sector actors and business associations on the front lines of business-climate reforms. Disseminating the findings of studies such as this one to a wider audience of stakeholders and policy makers is therefore one means of using evidence-based analysis to inform policy dialogue and decision making.

Measures to strengthen women's voices in business-climate reform include the following:

- Encouraging women business owners and associations to join PPD
- Encouraging greater participation of women in business associations
- Building the capacity of business associations to provide better services to members and to contribute more to advocacy for policy reforms
- Carrying out a systematic, gender-informed analysis of business-environment obstacles to highlight issues of concern to businesswomen and then integrating this analysis into dialogue and policy making
- Strengthening the presence of women in PPD institutions and structures, and building the capacity of women to influence the agenda of the PPD itself

Areas for Research

Gaps in the data hamper researchers' ability to undertake gender-disaggregated analyses. Two are particularly relevant. The first relates to the need to know more about how constraints in the investment climate, particularly in access to finance, shape the entry decision. There are scarce data at the individual (as opposed to household) level on constraints facing those who do not decide to become entrepreneurs. One way to acquire more data would be to add relevant questions to household surveys.

The second relates to transitions between entrepreneurship and wage employment. Work in Latin America (for example, Maloney 2004) shows that there can be a fair amount of mobility for men and single women. Much less is known about these transitions in Sub-Saharan Africa. To learn more would require panel surveys of individuals and their labor force decisions.

Notes

1. *The World Development Report 2012: Gender Equality and Development* (World Bank 2011) provides a global perspective on women and addresses additional gender issues such as health, violence, and rural development.
2. Hallward-Driemeier and Hasan (2012) elaborate on this agenda in more detail.

References

Hallward-Driemeier, M., and T. Hasan. 2012. *Empowering Women: Legal Rights and Economic Opportunities in Africa*. Washington, DC: World Bank and Agence Française de Développement.

Maloney, W. 2004. "Informality Revisited." *World Development* 32 (7): 1159–78.

Schoar, A. 2010. "The Divide between Subsistence and Transformational Entrepreneurship." In *Innovation Policy and the Economy*, vol. 10, edited by Josh Lerner and Scott Stern, 57–81. Chicago: University of Chicago Press and National Bureau for Economic Research.

World Bank. 2011. *World Development Report 2012: Gender Equality and Development*. Washington, DC: World Bank.

Appendixes

Appendix A

Sources of Data

Enterprise Data

Enterprise Surveys. Administered by the World Bank to large stratified random samples of registered firms in key industrial centers in a country, Enterprise Surveys cover both manufacturing and services and include information on the owner of the enterprise, enterprise performance measures, and measures of constraints facing the enterprise. As the samples are based in urban centers, it is not possible to make comparisons with formal enterprises in rural areas. The *Enterprise Surveys—microenterprises* also include a parallel survey of microfirms, of which 98 percent have five or fewer employees, for 25 African countries. The survey for this subset is targeted toward informal firms and in the analysis is labeled as informal.

Enterprise Surveys—gender module. For five countries that had completed an Enterprise Survey, the World Bank fielded an additional module to capture more information on the background of the entrepreneur, the motivation for starting a business, the means of starting or acquiring a business, and indicators of management techniques. The modules also refined measures on the gender of both the principal owner and the person running the business. The five countries are Ghana, Mali, Mozambique, Senegal, and Zambia.

Survey of new entrepreneurs. A new survey was fielded by the World Bank covering firms operating in the formal and informal sectors in four countries (Côte d'Ivoire, Kenya, Nigeria, and Senegal). Detailed background information on the entrepreneur was collected, such as the motivation for starting a business, the means of starting or acquiring a business, and indicators of management techniques used. Some additional measures on the constraints faced in setting up a business were also included.

Individual Data

Household surveys and labor force surveys. Thirty-nine Sub-Saharan countries administer their own surveys, which are compiled in the International Income

Distribution Database (I2D2) along with surveys from 62 other countries. While not strictly comparable because countries use different questionnaires (although most adhere to the International Labour Organization definitions of labor) and somewhat different sampling strategies, they have been standardized for a core set of questions to allow cross-country patterns to be examined. These data inform inclusion in different employment categories. More details are available in Montenegro and Hirn (2009).

Household survey—enterprise modules. For those in the households who identify as having an enterprise, additional questions are asked in 20 countries in Sub-Saharan Africa. These data can be used to examine firm performance, particularly for more informal businesses, those operating out of the house, and those with household members working in them. It should be noted that the enterprises covered through the household survey are not necessarily all run out of the home; many indeed are not. Rather, the basis for the sampling of the enterprises is the household, not the enterprise.

FinScope

FinScope surveys are nationally representative samples of individuals that collect information on respondents' perceptions of financial services and issues associated with access to finance. They also collect information on income, education, and location. Administered in both urban and rural areas, they ask respondents to provide information on their use of formal and informal financial services, thus allowing for a more complete analysis of financial markets than would be possible with information on formal services only. Because the surveys sample individuals, the data also allow for comparisons of those who are excluded from financial markets. The surveys are a FinMark Trust initiative, established in 2002 and funded primarily by the United Kingdom's Department for International Development. More information is available at http://www.finscope.co.za.

Table A.1 Microdata Used

Country	Income Level (2011)	Enterprise Survey	Enterprise Survey—gender module	Survey of new entrepreneurs	Household/labor force survey	Household survey—enterprise module	FinScope
Angola	Lower middle income	2006	—	—	—	—	—
Benin	Low income	2009	—	—	2003	—	—
Botswana	Upper middle income	2006	—	—	—	—	2004
Burkina Faso	Low income	2006, 2009	—	—	2003	2003	—
Burundi	Low income	2006	—	—	1998	1998	—
Cameroon	Lower middle income	2006, 2009	—	—	2007	2007	—
Cape Verde	Lower middle income	2006, 2009	—	—	2000	—	—
Central African Republic	Low income	—	—	—	2003	—	—
Chad	Low income	2009	—	—	2002	—	—
Comoros	Low income	—	—	—	2004	2004	—
Congo, Dem. Rep.	Low income	2006, 2009	—	—	—	—	—
Congo, Rep.	Lower middle income	—	—	—	2005	2005	—
Côte d'Ivoire	Lower middle income	2009	—	2010	2002	2002	—
Eritrea	Low income	2009	—	—	—	—	—
Ethiopia	Low income	2006	—	—	2005	—	—
Gabon	Upper middle income	2009	—	—	2005	—	—
Gambia, The	Low income	2006	—	—	1998	1998	—
Ghana	Lower middle income	2007	2009	—	2005	2005	—
Guinea	Low income	2006	—	—	2002	2002	—
Guinea-Bissau	Low income	2006	—	—	—	—	—
Kenya	Low income	2007, 2009	—	2010	2005	—	2009

—Continued

Table A.1 *continued*

Country	Income Level (2011)	Enterprise Survey	Enterprise Survey—gender module	Survey of new entrepreneurs	Household/labor force survey	Household survey—enterprise module	FinScope
Lesotho	Lower middle income	2009	—	—	2002	—	—
Liberia	Low income	2009	—	—	2007	—	—
Madagascar	Low income	2009	—	—	2004	2004	—
Malawi	Low income	2005, 2009	—	—	2005	2005	2008
Mali	Low income	2007	2009	—	2003	—	—
Mauritania	Lower middle income	2006	—	—	2000	—	—
Mauritius	Upper middle income	2009	—	—	—	—	—
Mozambique	Low income	2007	2009	—	2003	—	—
Namibia	Upper middle income	2006	—	—	—	—	2004
Niger	Low income	2005, 2009	—	—	2007	2007	—
Nigeria	Lower middle income	2007	—	2010	2003	2003	—
Rwanda	Low income	2006, 2008	—	—	2005	2005	2008
Senegal	Lower middle income	2007	2009	2010	2001	—	—
Sierra Leone	Low income	2009	—	—	2003	2003	—
South Africa	Upper middle income	2007	2009	—	2005	—	2008
Swaziland	Lower middle income	2006	—	—	2000	2000	—
Tanzania	Low income	2006	—	—	2006	2006	2009
Togo	Low income	2009	—	—	2006	—	—
Uganda	Low income	2006	—	—	2005	2005	2006
Zambia	Lower middle income	2007	—	—	2003	2003	2005

Note: — = not available.

Table A.2 Principal Data Sources, Uses, and Limitations

| | | | | | | Use for gender-disaggregated comparisons and analysis | | | | |
Source	Countries covered (number)	Years covered	Strengths	Limitations	Decision to be an entrepreneur	Enterprise characteristics	Entrepreneur characteristics	Constraints (facing existing entrepreneurs)	Performance
Household surveys	Country statistical offices	39	1998–2008	Representative coverage; allow comparisons of entrepreneurs and nonentrepreneurs	No information on constraints; the surveys do not track the same individuals over time; some variation in questions and sampling across countries	Yes; also include information on those choosing not to be entrepreneurs	No	Yes, including household characteristics	No	No
Enterprise modules of household surveys	Country statistical offices	20	1998–2008	Information on gender and family characteristics; include informal and formal enterprises	The instruments are not standardized, so they do not allow cross-country comparisons on many dimensions; sampling across countries is also not strictly comparable	No	Yes	Yes, including household characteristics	No	Yes

—Continued

Table A.2 *continued*

	Source	Countries covered (number)	Years covered	Strengths	Limitations	Use for gender-disaggregated comparisons and analysis				
						Decision to be an entrepreneur	Enterprise characteristics	Entrepreneur characteristics	Constraints (facing existing entrepreneurs)	Performance
Enterprise Surveys	World Bank	37	2006–10	Standard questionnaire and sampling across countries; stratified random sample; information on constraints (subjective and quantitative) and performance	Focus largely on formal sector, with some microenterprises in informal sector; broad definition of "female participation in ownership" in categorizing female enterprises	No	Yes	Yes	Yes	Yes
Gender modules of Enterprise Surveys	Commissioned for report	5	2009	Separate capture of ownership and decision-making authority, detail on background of entrepreneur, motivation for being entrepreneur; information on managerial techniques	Available for only five countries	No, but some qualitative information on why and how respondent became entrepreneur	Yes	Yes, with more detail on background and "deeper human capital"	Yes	Yes

Survey of new entrepreneurs	Commissioned for report	4	2010	Separate capture of ownership and decision-making authority, detail on background of entrepreneur, motivation for being entrepreneur; information on managerial techniques; capture of new firms; current information on constraints facing new entrants; comparison of formal and informal sector	Available for only four countries	No, but some qualitative information on why and how respondent became entrepreneur	Yes	Yes, with more detail on background and "deeper human capital"	Yes	Yes

Reference

Montenegro, C., and M. Hirn. 2009. "A New Disaggregated Set of Labor Market Indicators Using Standardized Household Surveys from around the World." Background paper, World Bank, Washington, DC.

Appendix **B**

Indexes of Gender Equality across Countries

United Nations Development Programme's Gender Inequality Index

The Gender Inequality Index is a composite measure reflecting inequality in achievements between women and men in three dimensions: reproductive health, empowerment, and the labor market. It varies between 0 (when women and men fare equally) and 1 (when men or women fare poorly compared with the other in all dimensions). The health dimension is measured by two indicators: the maternal mortality ratio and the adolescent fertility rate. The empowerment dimension is also measured by two indicators: the share of parliamentary seats held by each sex, and secondary and higher education attainment levels. The labor dimension is measured by women's participation in the labor force. The index is designed to reveal the extent to which national human development achievements are eroded by gender inequality—and to provide empirical foundations for policy analysis and advocacy efforts.

The index relies on data from major publicly available databases and publications, including the United Nations Children's Fund's *State of the World's Children* (maternal mortality ratio), the United Nations Department of Economic and Social Affairs' World Population Prospects (adolescent fertility), Barro-Lee data sets (educational attainment statistics), the International Parliamentary Union's database on women in parliaments (political representation), and the International Labour Organization's LABORSTA database (labor market participation).

The index is available at United Nations Development Programme, Gender Inequality Index, http://hdr.undp.org/en/statistics/gii/.

World Bank's Country Policy and Institutional Assessments Gender Equality Rating

The World Bank's Country Policy and Institutional Assessments (CPIA) Gender Equality Rating assesses the extent to which a country has institutions and programs to enforce laws and policies that promote equal access for men and women to education, health, the economy, and protection under the law.

These criteria assess the extent to which a country has enacted or put in place laws, institutions, and programs to enforce equal access for men and women to human capital development, productive and economic resources, and equal status and protection under the law.

For human capital development, the focus is on primary school completion and access to secondary education, access to health care during delivery and to family planning, and adolescent fertility. For access to economic and productive resources, the focus is on labor force participation, land tenure, and property and inheritance rights. For status and protection under the law, the focus is on individual and family rights and personal security (violence against women, trafficking, or sexual harassment) and political participation.

Each dimension is rated separately and receives equal weight in the overall rating. The score captures whether gender differences exist in the subject area, whether policies and laws are obstacles, and whether there have been recent efforts to make laws and policies more supportive of gender equality in the subject area.

The Gender Equality Rating ranges from 1 for low equality to 6 for high equality. It is available at World Bank Group, CPIA database, http://www .worldbank.org/ida.

Organisation for Economic Co-operation and Development's Gender-related Development Index (GDI) and Social Institutions and Gender Index (SIGI)

The Organisation for Economic Co-operation and Development (OECD) has two indexes. The first, the Gender-related Development Index (GDI), is a version of the OECD's Human Development Index that not only includes levels of education and health outcomes, but also includes gender gaps in these dimensions.

The second, the Social Institutions and Gender Index (SIGI), measures social institutions reflected by societal practices and legal norms that produce inequalities between women and men. The SIGI is not just an overall measure of these institutions. Instead of measuring gender inequalities in education, health, economic and political participation, and other dimensions, it measures important inputs—social institutions—against such outcome inequalities in non-OECD countries. These social institutions are conceived as long-lasting codes of conduct, norms, traditions, and informal and formal laws. The index and its five subindexes are not therefore intended to reflect fast changes over time.

Each of the subindexes measures a different dimension of social institutions related to gender inequality: family code, civil liberties, physical integrity, son preference, and ownership rights. As the indicators in the SIGI primarily measure social institutions that pose problems in the developing world, the SIGI covers only non-OECD countries.

The SIGI is an unweighted average of a nonlinear function of the subindexes. The nonlinear function arises because it is assumed that inequality related to gender corresponds to deprivation experienced by the women affected, and that deprivation increases more than proportionally when inequality increases. Thus high inequality is penalized in every dimension. The nonlinearity also has the advantage that the SIGI allows for only partial compensation among its components. Partial compensation implies that high inequality in one dimension—that is, a subindex—can be only partially compensated with low inequality in another.

The nonlinearity in the index is achieved by squaring the distance of the respective subindex value from 0, the goal of no inequality. The sum of the resulting squared subindex values divided by the number of subindexes then gives the value of the SIGI. This approach implies a choice of equal weights for the subindexes because there is no obvious reason to value one of the measured dimensions more or less than the others.

The index ranges from 0 for low inequality to 1 for high inequality. It is available at OECD, Social Institutions and Gender Index, http://www.oecd.org/dataoecd/52/33/42289479.pdf.

World Economic Forum's Global Gender Gap Index

With 30 gender-related variables, the Global Gender Gap Index examines the gaps between men and women in four categories: labor force participation and opportunity, educational attainment, political empowerment, and health and survival.

Three concepts underlie the index. First, it focuses on measuring gaps rather than levels. It is designed to measure gender-based gaps in access to resources and opportunities in individual countries rather than actual levels of available resources and opportunities in those countries. Rich countries have more education and health opportunities for all members of society, and measures of levels thus mainly reflect this well-known fact, though it is quite independent of the gender-related issues faced by each country at its own level of income. The global gender gap index, however, rewards countries for smaller gaps in access to these resources, regardless of the overall level of resources. For example, it penalizes or rewards countries based on the size of the gap between male and female enrollment rates, but not for the overall levels of education in the country.

The second concept is that it evaluates countries based on outcome variables rather than input measures. The aim is to provide a snapshot of where men and women stand on some fundamental outcome variables related to basic rights such as health, education, labor force participation, and political empowerment.

The third concept is that it ranks countries according to their proximity to gender equality rather than to women's empowerment. The aim is to focus on whether the gap between women and men in the chosen variables has declined, rather than whether women are "winning the battle of the sexes." Hence the index rewards countries that reach the point where outcomes for women equal those for men, but it neither rewards nor penalizes countries where women are outperforming men in particular variables.

It is available at World Economic Forum, Global Gender Gap Index, http://www.weforum.org/issues/global-gender-gap.

Economist Intelligence Unit's Women's Economic Opportunity Index

Constructed from 26 indicators, the Women's Economic Opportunity Index is a dynamic quantitative and qualitative scoring model that measures specific attributes of the environment for women employees and entrepreneurs in 113 countries.

Five category scores are calculated from both the unweighted and weighted means of underlying indicators and are scaled from 0 to 100, where 100 is most favorable. These categories are labor policy and practice (which comprises two subcategories, labor policy and labor practice); access to finance; education and training; women's legal and social status; and general business environment. Each category features at least four underlying indicators.

The unweighted overall score (0 to 100) is calculated from a simple average of the unweighted category and indicator scores. A weighted overall score (0 to 100) is also included. The weights are generated for the categories, as well as the indicators falling under each of the categories, through the application of principal component analysis. The overall score is a weighted mean of the category scores.

It is available at Economist Intelligence Unit, Women's Economic Opportunity Index, http://www.eiu.com/sponsor/WEO.

Comparing Women–LEED–Africa and Its Peers

Indicator	Women–LEED–Africa (47 countries)	Women, Business, and the Law database, 2010 (28 countries)	Food and Agriculture Organization of the United Nations Gender and Land Rights Database (28 countries)
Sources of law	Constitutions, international conventions, statutes—each reported separately	Constitutions, international conventions, statutes—but no differentiation in the indicators of the source of law determining the indicator	Constitutions, international conventions, statutes—each reported separately
Treatment of customary law	Whether customary law is recognized in constitution and/or statutes; extent of limitations on gender-based nondiscrimination protections	Not included	Whether customary law is formally recognized
Property and land rights	Property rights in marriage, on divorce, and inheritance; land rights	Gender equality in movable and immovable property	Land rights
Legal capacity	Indicator addresses statutes and recognition of customary and religious law; equality in separate transactions (for example, opening a bank account or working outside the home)	Indicator shows whether "equal" or "unequal," but without showing which transactions trip the indicator (details may be provided in future editions)	Not included
Labor	International Labour Organization Conventions, constitutions, and statutes—separately	Provisions (based on combination of International Labour Organization Conventions, constitutions, and statutes); includes parental leave	Not included
Database of laws	Yes	Yes	Yes
Additional material	Examples from case law where conflicting and/or overlapping sources of law apply (to illustrate how women's economic rights are interpreted in practice)	Information on credit bureaus and small claims courts	Statistics on land ownership

Index

Boxes, figures, notes, and tables are indicated by b, f, n, and t following page numbers.

ECO-AUDIT
Environmental Benefits Statement

The World Bank is committed to preserving endangered forests and natural resources. The Office of the Publisher has chosen to print *Enterprising Women: Expanding Economic Opportunities in Africa* on recycled paper with 50 percent post-consumer fiber, in accordance with the recommended standards for paper usage set by the Green Press Initiative, a nonprofit program supporting publishers in using fiber that is not sourced from endangered forests. For more information, visit www.greenpressinitiative.org.

Saved:
• 5 trees
• 2 million British thermal units of total energy
• 372 pounds of net greenhouse gases (CO_2 equivalent)
• 2,019 gallons of waste water
• 135 pounds of solid waste

green
press
INITIATIVE